The 53

The 53

Rituals, Grief, and a Titan II Missile Disaster

Jason S. Ulsperger

Foreword by J. David Knottnerus

LEXINGTON BOOKS
Lanham • Boulder • New York • London

Rowman & Littlefield
Bloomsbury Publishing Inc, 1359 Broadway, New York, NY 10018, USA
Bloomsbury Publishing Plc, 50 Bedford Square, London, WC1B 3DP, UK
Bloomsbury Publishing Ireland, 29 Earlsfort Terrace, Dublin 2, D02 AY28, Ireland
www.bloomsbury.com

Published by Lexington Books
An imprint of The Rowman & Littlefield Publishing Group, Inc.
4501 Forbes Boulevard, Suite 200, Lanham, Maryland 20706
www.rowman.com

86-90 Paul Street, London EC2A 4NE

British Library Cataloguing in Publication Information available

Library of Congress Cataloging-in-Publication Data

Names: Ulsperger, Jason S., author.
Title: The 53 : rituals, grief, and a Titan II missile disaster / Jason Ulsperger ;
    foreword by J. David Knottnerus.
Other titles: Fifty-three
Description: Lanham : Lexington Books, 2022. | Includes bibliographical references and index.
Identifiers: LCCN 2021053794 (print) | LCCN 2021053795 (ebook) |
    ISBN 9781793609748 (cloth ; alk. paper) | ISBN 9781793609755 (epub)
Subjects: LCSH: Ritual—Social aspects—United States. | Ritualization. |
    Death—Social aspects—United States. | Nuclear accidents—Arkansas. |
    Titan (Missile)—History.
Classification: LCC HM1033 .U47 2022 (print) | LCC HM1033 (ebook) |
    DDC 203/.8—dc23/eng/20211123
LC record available at https://lccn.loc.gov/2021053794
LC ebook record available at https://lccn.loc.gov/2021053795

♾™ The paper used in this publication meets the minimum requirements of American
National Standard for Information Sciences—Permanence of Paper for Printed Library
Materials, ANSI/NISO Z39.48-1992.

For those still grieving

Contents

Foreword

J. David Knottnerus

It was early in my development of structural ritualization theory (SRT) that Jason S. Ulsperger entered the Sociology graduate program at Oklahoma State University. He took a number of my seminars and became interested in SRT. Like me, he wanted to know more about social processes involving rituals. I ultimately chaired his doctoral dissertation committee, and we went on to publish a number of studies dealing with rituals.

SRT, a perspective that informs the analysis of disaster and sorrow in this book, focuses on the role rituals play in society (see Knottnerus 1997, 1999, 2005, 2010, 2016, and forthcoming). It grounds itself on the assumption that numerous social and personal rituals define everyday life. These often taken-for-granted rituals have many consequences, some of which are unanticipated. They occur in many social settings, for example, face-to-face interaction, small groups, formal organizations of all sizes, society as a whole, and even globally.

In the original presentation of SRT (Knottnerus 1997), I emphasized how rituals rest upon cognitive schemas and express symbolic meanings or themes. Rituals are "ritualized symbolic practices (RSPs)." I formally defined ritualization and presented a set of four factors that influence the importance of rituals in a social setting and explain structural reproduction and transformation. The four factors, which influence the rank (dominance or importance) of RSPs, are salience, repetitiveness, homologousness, and resources. The original formulation emphasizes the importance of embedded groups or groups nested within a more encompassing collectivity. As thoroughly explained in this book's chapter on sociology and rituals, a plethora of findings on SRT research exist. They include studies of ancient Sparta, youth in nineteenth-century French elite educational institutions, slave societies in America, and contemporary experimental task groups (see Knottnerus 2016).

Dr. Ulsperger is well versed in SRT. Separate from me, he has published SRT studies on volunteer work and farmers' markets, and he also has an ongoing line of research examining child vision problems and parental adjustment rituals (Ulsperger, McElroy, Robertson, and Ulsperger 2015; Ulsperger and Ulsperger 2017; Ulsperger, Ulsperger, and Partin 2015). Our research deals with the enactment (i.e., activation and mobilization) or failure to enact ritualized practices in organizations, communities, and by way of individuals.

One line of our work concerns ritualized maltreatment and neglect in nursing homes. It looks at how bureaucratic structures facilitate certain kinds of ritualized behaviors in the daily lives of people who work in elder care organizations (Ulsperger and Knottnerus 2016). We argue that bureaucratic work rituals are an important part of social life for nursing home employees and these behaviors can lead to unanticipated, negative consequences involving neglect. Our research indicates that certain ritualized symbolic practices such as staff separation, rules, documentation, and efficiency lead to rituals of physical neglect, medical dereliction, personal negligence, and bodily harm in both for-profit and nonprofit nursing homes. We moved beyond theory in this area and developed a culture change alternative discussed as the Centralized Alternative Ritual Enactment (CARE) model. It advocates for the cultivation of non-bureaucratic rituals.

Another one of our research areas reveals how corporate actors sometimes engage in RSPs involving risk, personal gratification, pride, and fantasy imagery (Knottnerus, Ulsperger, Cummins, and Osteen 2006; Ulsperger and Knottnerus 2010). We focused on Enron and found that the organizational culture set the stage for the corporation's eventual implosion. Rather than a few key people at the top making decisions to push the business over the edge, employees throughout the corporation regularly engaged in certain practices leading to an eventual catastrophic demise. We have also produced compelling research on ritualized strain and mass homicide (Ulsperger, Knottnerus, and Ulsperger 2017). That work argues that psychological resources certainly have an influence on people who murder multiple people at once. With a sociological emphasis, it also points out that taken-for-granted ritualized symbolic events (SREs) with stressful characteristics produce homicidal acts.

I have developed several different categories of SRT research. They all build upon and involve an extension of the previously described original formulation of SRT dealing with embedded groups and reproduction. One area of interest directly relevant to this book involves disruption, deritualization, and reritualization (DDR), that is, interruptions of social and personal rituals, their effects, and the ways people may cope with such experiences by reconstituting old or new ritualized symbolic practices (Knottnerus 2016). Research laying a foundation focused on internment in concentrations camps, displacement during revolution, earthquakes, tornadoes, ecological degradation, regime change, and polar expeditions (for elaboration, see Knottnerus 2016). These ideas and related research are, I believe, highly relevant for the study of grief and sorrow. Major events can interrupt, if not terminate, the ritualized behaviors people engage in, including the rituals they shared with the victims of catastrophic events. In other words, technological disasters are an extremely disruptive experience. They create deritualization. So too, rituals can be extremely important if individuals reconstitute old or create new RSPs after these grief-producing experiences. Stated somewhat differently, I believe reritualization is an essential and crucially important dynamic that helps people cope with their sorrow, sense of loss, trauma or emotional angst, and possible social isolation or at least diminished social interaction and relations with others. That is why this study of a missile disaster involving the loss of life is so significant. By examining the symbolic (cognitive) and emotional dynamics of rituals surrounding the event, we gain a new understanding of how such an experience can affect individuals, and what might be done to help people cope with and adjust, both immediately after the event and in the long-term. I believe this study will contribute to the growing body of literature on technological disasters and be a major force in death studies. This is very important because of a lack of focus on catastrophic occurrences and long-term consequences in this literature and, at best, a limited amount of attention to the ritual processes that influence the anguish people feel when tragic events occur.

In summation, this book is very relevant and extremely valuable for a number of reasons. It provides a clear account of sociohistoric issues leading to the Titan II missile disaster of 1965. It contributes to the study of death, dying, and the sociology of sorrow with innovative attention to grief lasting days, months, or even years. It breaks new ground in the sociological (and psychological) study of disaster and trauma. It extends SRT research by considering grief as related to DDR. It represents the first time anyone has used multiple methods, including autoethnography, to study SRT. I strongly encourage everyone, whether they are academics, members of a wider audience, scholars, or those with a personal interest in this topic to read this excellent book.

J. David Knottnerus
Emeritus Regents Professor
Department of Sociology
Oklahoma State University

Preface

Chapter 1 allows you to meet the Titans. Traditionally evoked as mythological Greek gods, you will see that the word "titan" involves more. Chapter 2 provides sociohistorical background on the Titan II and details one of the deadliest missile disasters in American history. Chapter 3 reviews an essential sociological framework applicable to this project— structural ritualization theory (Knottnerus 1997). Chapter 4 supplies an understanding of disaster research, while providing additional information on the Launch Complex (LC) 373-4 incident. Chapter 5 reviews literature on the sociology of sorrow (see Jacobsen and Petersen 2020a) and death rituals. Chapter 6 briefly reviews my research approach. Chapter 7 highlights the disruption for families of the 53 men lost. Chapter 8 looks at deritualization in their lives. Chapter 9 concerns reritualization. Chapter 10 summarizes findings and recalls the elimination of the Titan II.

Previous projects briefly look into the LC 373-4 disaster. They hold up some parts of this book. Stumpf's (2000) work gives technical details. Schlosser (2013) provides us with an understanding of how the nation came to accept the dangers associated with the missiles. His book focuses on the 1980 Damascus incident, so I view this book as a prequel of some sorts. Anthony's (2018) research fills us in on what communities experienced when Titan II mishaps occurred. Focusing specifically on the lives of families who lost loved ones in a Titan II disaster, I believe I have complimented their work and given a more complete picture of the event.

Finally, I want to note that I wrote a majority of this book during the COVID-19 pandemic. To frame this work, I use examples related to it. Maybe some will trigger future research or enhance pandemic studies already underway. Nevertheless, I hope that a majority of the devastation from this novel coronavirus is well behind us by the time this book is in print.

Acknowledgments

I deeply appreciate people from the 53 families for displaying courage and openness during our discussions. I truly believe your information will help so many others better understand technological disaster research and long-term sorrow. A majority of you are engaged in a fierce battle to keep memories of loved ones alive. You inspired me to clear the hurdles I faced during this project.

I want to express my gratitude to Arkansas Tech University for the needed sabbatical. Thank you to Josh Lockyer and Stan Hodges for all the recommendations and support, scholarly and otherwise. I also want to express an abundance of appreciation to Sahara Collins, JoElla Kloss, and Kristen Ulsperger for helping locate interviewees and reading drafts. Kristen, you stand by my side in the darkest times and deserve a majority of credit in the brightest. Many thanks go to Sherry Organ, Gary Wekkin, Michael Kelly, Mary Donaghy, and J. David Knottnerus. The first four planted the seeds for my career, Dr. Knottnerus made it blossom. Thank you to Ella, my go-to for insight and inspiration. I commend the Titan Missile Museum for helping me fill important gaps. Chuck Penson deserves appreciation too. He took a break from dodging bison and bears in Yellowstone to modify existing illustrations for me.

If it were not for Courtney Morales, this book would not exist. Lexington Books is fortunate to have her. I am also forever indebted to the anonymous reviewer with expertise in disaster studies. Finally, I want to thank Chris for asking how the book was going, and let Sarah, Tyler, Elizabeth, and Philana know they are always in my thoughts.

Chapter 1

Meet the Titans

Every day, I have been hearing about something called COVID-19. It is early 2020 and a new coronavirus is here. It can be deadly, especially for older people and those with preexisting conditions. Death is on my mind (Rabin 2020). My aunt Linda is too. "I'm ready . . . I'm ready" were some of the last words she spoke not too long ago from her hospital deathbed. A few minutes before she died, her daughter said, "You'll be in heaven soon. You're going to get to see your daddy again." She was referring to Delphard Owens, my mother's father, my grandfather. I saw a few pictures of him before, and I have one of his old fedoras from Powell Clothing Store. Adults did not talk about him much when I was growing up, but I heard stories. My mom says he affectionately called her "Kitten." All I have to hold on to from his life are memories, memories of other people's memories.

The day my aunt died, I was in a unique position. Women wailed and moaned along while beeps from medical equipment rang in everyone's ears. Men in the room stoically stooped their heads, avoiding eye contact and holding back tears. I found myself on an emotional roller coaster. Though I was managing my own grief-based responses, I was also feeling the need to absorb the reactions of others. As a sociologist, I have spent years teaching classes that explore some of my favorite topics, including organizational deviance. I have also taught a course on death and dying for 15 years. The classroom provides me with distance from the realities of dying. My aunt's death is one of the few times I actually found myself in the presence of someone exiting life. Just a few years before, I was with my father's mother, Annie Lucille, when she was dying. Some call her Annie. She was always Grandma Lucille to me, sometimes simply "Granny Indiana."

Standard in these times, I was in a hospital when Lucille died. A few years before, my father and I transported her "back home" to Arkansas. Her health was failing. I walked through the door to her house in Indiana expecting a hint of gratitude for supplying transportation. I simply received the comment, "Why are you wearing sandals? I hope you don't dress like that all the time." The connection was never there for us. I rarely saw her, so being there when she was dying was substantially different from what I experienced with my aunt. It was also dissimilar because I was alone with my grandmother just before she died. It was less social, though I did have a serious conversation with her though she was motionless on her hospital bed. I focused on what we meant to each other. Regardless, I would soon find my aunt and grandmother's lives connected in a strange way. Linda lost her father in a missile silo disaster. Lucille lost a former lover in the same event.

When my aunt died, Delphard Owens was not in the room, was he? Many there heard the same stories I had, and they valued their own memories of memories. He was inside of us all. Let me give you a better idea of who he was. He was born on June 10, 1912, near the small, rural town of El Paso, Arkansas. He never knew who his father was. He had one brother. He married a local girl, Odean Blasingame. The Blasingame name is prominent in El Paso. Records indicate that in 1848, a handful of people met at the house of a "Mr. Blasingame" for worship services. The congregation grew and members established a formal church. At one point, it was the largest Baptist church in White County. The town flourished until April of 1880 when a tornado ripped through the area causing colossal damage. Several people died. Defined by disaster, El Paso never thrived again (Hazel 1999).

A journeyman, Delphard moved from job to job. He always had his family with him. He found himself in Iowa at one point, engaged in factory labor while Odean made ends meet with a job at a bakery. He was back in El Paso by the late 1950s. He sporadically farmed with migrant workers then became a field boss in southern Michigan when blueberries were ready for harvest. Kitten remembers him playfully scolding her for eating berries before the workers counted them. He later convinced Odean to help him run a small restaurant close to Beebe in Ward, Arkansas. Lucille was probably in school there at the same time. He fitted the restaurant with a jukebox and pool tables. It did not last. Door-to-door mattress sales came next. Then, in the mid-1960s, he sought work through the Laborers' International Union of North America. A Nebraska-based company needed workers to upgrade an underground military site in White County. It contained something called a "Titan II" missile (Christ 2016).

Soon after Aunt Linda's death, I became preoccupied with my grandfather's story. I can envision him hearing about that union job with his felt fedora atop his head. If I try hard, I can hear him in anticipation excitedly whispering, "I'm ready . . . I'm ready." I felt compelled to learn about Titans, so I began to keep a journal.

I will integrate information from that journal throughout this book.

BANISHED TO THE UNDERWORLD

I started seeing the word "titan" everywhere. Was my grandfather's ghost sending me messages? I think not. This happened because of what psychologists refer to as "salience bias." When emotional intensity surrounds an experience, you are more likely to recognize things around you relating to that experience (Tsakanikos 2004). If you are in a group of people and can see some of them more clearly than others, it has an impact. If someone asks you later on who instigated a particular activity within the group, you are likely to point the finger at someone who stood out the most. A better example might be this. When you hear about a lot of crime on the news, you may start seeing people you think look like criminals. This certainly has implications on grief. We find connections with the dead when looking for connections. It does not matter if it is with Ouija boards or spirit mediums (Scott 2017).

My research journal is flooded with examples of "Titans." I forgot one of my favorite films from childhood was *Clash of the Titans*. I thought I remembered a Titan missile bursting through a teenage house party in another favorite movie, *Weird Science*. It turns out that it was a Pershing II. Thrift stores I frequented all seemed to have copies of the sports film *Remember the Titans*. Looking for a used truck, I could only find Nissan Titans. *Teen Titans Go* became one of my daughter's favorite cartoons. I kept seeing National Football League headlines for the Tennessee Titans. I watched a show on the solar system highlighting the largest moon of Saturn—"Titan." I soon found myself digging into the history of the word "titan."

It now notes great size and strength, but the word "titan" originated in Greek mythology. Before Zeus sat atop his Mount Olympus throne, the Titans ruled. Their mother, Gaia, was the goddess of the earth. She emerged from the abyss of chaos and was the mother of the Titans' father—Uranus, god of the sky. Scholars say Gaia created Uranus to be her equal. He ruled the universe, and they had children. Twelve were Titans. The others were Cyclopes and giants known as "the Hundred-handed," each having 50 heads and 100 arms (Rose 2015).

Cronus was the youngest Titan. Threatened by his children's power, Uranus trapped them in their mother's womb. Angered, Gaia and Cronus developed a plan to dethrone Uranus. One night Gaia called for Uranus, and Cronus emerged from the shadows and castrated his father. Cronus then married his sister, Titaness Rhea. They bore Zeus. As his own father was, Cronus was paranoid his children would take power from him, so he swallowed them all. Zeus disguised himself as a servant and slipped his dad a drink made to trigger vomiting. Cronus regurgitated his children one by one. A war called the Titanomachy followed. Cronus led Titans on one side, and Zeus led his fellow Olympians on the other. With the help of the Cyclopes and the

Hundred-handed, Zeus won. He banished the Titans to a deep abyss in the underworld (Rose 2015).

Echoing Judeo-Christian tales related to the casting of angels from heaven, Cornelis van Haarlem's sixteenth-century oil painting *The Fall of the Titans* powerfully depicts the event. You can see it at the National Gallery of Denmark in Copenhagen, but it is on the cover of this book too. To avoid controversy due to subject matter, including the display of unclothed figures, curators hid the painting away for years. Most forgot about it. However, the memory of it was significant to an employee who later championed its importance. The museum restored it, and put the piece on display again in 1988 (Peterson 2020).

Enclosed by a tunnel of darkened smoky clouds, gods in the form of men appear en masse. Ghosts of their former selves, they are visible in a variety of ages. Some are falling from high above, frantically reaching out to help others. Many have already hit the surface below, creating an accumulation of bodies. One man situated close to the middle of the image is holding a long, cylindrical device with flames rocketing from the top. His expression does not reflect the same state of panic and self-preserving desperation on the face of others. Perhaps we should pity him, but his disposition also makes you believe he is in some way to blame for violent brush strokes on the canvas. Welding the darkness around with illuminated horror, the device he grasps appears to be a torch. To the lower left, the oldest person in the painting has haunting eyes, a furrowed brow, and a silver mane of wisdom. So many of the others are looking up through the heavy air blanketing them toward a trace of light, but this man knows there is no hope.

Knowing the details of my grandfather's death, the painting made a heavy impression on me. Just as disaster defined Delphard Owens' hometown of El Paso, Arkansas, another disaster defined him and my family. Salience bias I am sure, but I wondered how things I had seen through my life related to my grandfather and his end.

THE WHITE SANDS OF TRINITY

I was on a road trip with my wife in the summer of 2001. We traveled from Oklahoma toward the sunset. The American West remains a favorite. There is an unparalleled visual bearing on your emotions when staring into the Grand Canyon or at walls of rose-colored Navajo Sandstone in Zion. In southern New Mexico, between Las Cruces and Alamogordo, a place of great splendor exists—White Sands National Park. If you are there at the right time, you can see ultramarine blue skies offset by smooth, white sand. Over 100 million years ago, rainwater dissolved sulfate minerals from the Sacramento and San

Andreas mountains. It formed a lake in the Tularosa Basin, the water evapo-rated, and miles of dunes made of powdery, crystallized gypsum remained (Schneider-Hector 1993).

It is spectacular to drive through the park's mounds of snowy sand. Tourists sled on circular saucers down them (Eidenbach 2010). After my wife and I visited the first time, the park called us back—first with my younger brother and then with my daughter. I have pictures of both beaming with joy gliding down dunes with crystallized gypsum spraying through the air. They appear full of life, hope, and promise. Neither realizing how close they are to the birthplace of the most damaging instrument of mass destruc-tion known, something that would ultimately have a place in the death of their grandfather.

The first nuclear explosion occurred just north of the park (Atomic Heritage Foundation 2019). With it, the term "anti-mimesis" comes to mind. The root "mimesis" has a variety of meanings, including one that relates to illusions people create when constructing impressions for others to consume (see Goffman 1959). Most notably, it refers to the construction of reality through mimicking of others. As the oft-forgotten sociologist Gabriel Tarde (2013) proposed, life imitates life. Therefore, with anti-mimesis, life imitates something else. Oscar Wilde (2016) notes that there is an imitative instinct built into the human condition, but it sometimes flows from creativity unin-hibited by boundaries of existence. In other words, life imitates art. Consider the atomic bomb and maybe COVID-19 too—see the film *Contagion* (Burns 2011). In the novel *The World Set Free*, H. G. Wells (1913) writes about a radioactive weapon of mass destruction. An arms race emerges around the device. After reading the book, Hungarian physicist Leo Szilard became obsessed with nuclear technology.

Szilard obtained his PhD in 1922 and ended up at the Kaiser Wilhelm Institute. There, he befriended Albert Einstein. Interestingly, he met with Wells in the late 1920s. He wanted to obtain rights to his novels, but he also wanted to use them to help develop cutting-edge ideas. He knew Hitler's scientists were on the verge of creating atomic weapons. He wanted to beat them to it. In 1933, Szilard followed Einstein's lead and fled Germany. He became an American citizen and taught at Columbia University. There, he built one of the world's first nuclear reactors (Atomic Heritage Foundation 2019). He produced radical research on chemical chain reactions, and his academic life was moving along splendidly. However, he could not get his mind off Germany. Nazi scientists were publishing research on uranium-based nuclear reactions. Just before Hitler's invasion of Poland, which would trigger the beginning of World War II, Szilard met with Einstein. They wrote a letter expressing concerns about German weapon development and delivered it to President Franklin D. Roosevelt on the morning of October

11, 1939. After the president reviewed it, action occurred quickly (Sherwin 2003; Gainor 2018).

The U.S. government shifted attention to the atom bomb in 1939. Two fronts emerged. On one, preventative measures existed. Starting in September, Germans actively attempted to secure uranium. Preventing that was critical. On the other, the United States focused on its own nuclear capabilities (Barlow 2020). Lyman Briggs received thousands of dollars to lead the effort. He was the director of the National Bureau of Standards, the government's official science laboratory. He would develop and chair a group called the Advisory Committee on Uranium (ACU). Perhaps due to health issues, or maybe the typical lethargy of bureaucracy, things were not moving fast enough. Intelligence reports indicated that the Germans were close to establishing a serious nuclear arsenal. Briggs was out, and Vannevar Bush took control (Sherwin 2020).

Holding patents for inventions and previously residing as president of the Carnegie Institute of Science, Bush made his opinions on "hard science" known. He would have hated this book. Discussing his abhorrence for the social sciences, he once noted, "I have a great reservation about these studies where somebody goes out and interviews a bunch of people and reads a lot of stuff and writes a book" (Zachary 1997:94). He pushed for the short-lived National Defense Research Committee (NDRC), which expired in 1941. It attempted to bridge the divide between civilian scientists and government atomic energy employees. Bush transformed the NDRC to the Office of Scientific Research and Development. Reporting directly to Roosevelt, he promptly took over the ACU and made the Army the main military branch in charge of nuclear weapon development. The Army named their work the "Manhattan Project." Its home was initially New York City, with headquarters across from City Hall. The location was ideal because of local piers for importing supplies, including uranium. Facilities in Tennessee and Washington existed. Of course, the most known location was in New Mexico, surrounded by white sand (Kelly 2007).

In March 1942, Bush notified Roosevelt of Robert Oppenheimer's research. The United States had entered the war after the bombing of Pearl Harbor by the Japanese. James Conant, an NDRC committee member and one of Oppenheimer's professors at Harvard years before, brought Oppenheimer to Bush's attention. A former U.S. National Research Fellow, Oppenheimer was working as a physics professor at the University of California-Berkley. Before he started that job, he fought tuberculosis. Believing the climate had a positive impact on his condition, he ironically spent a great deal of time at his brother's ranch in New Mexico. The Land of Enchantment called him back, but for different reasons. He became a member of the Manhattan Project and directed the Los Alamos Laboratory (Monk 2014).

The White Sands National Park calls the White Sands Missile Range its "next-door neighbor." This is definitely polite, innocuous terminology considering the area's past. Established on July 9, 1942, as the White Sands Proving Ground, at the northern boundary, you can find the Trinity site. Oppenheimer based its name off some poetry he liked written by John Donne. Speaking of Donne, the bell tolled for President Roosevelt on April 12, 1945, and Harry Truman was soon in charge of nuclear decisions. With his dedication to "unconditional surrender" on the part of the U.S. enemies, he approved the first detonation of a nuclear device at the Trinity site. It happened on July 16, 1945, at 5:29 a.m. (Maddox 2004).

Nicknamed "the Gadget," the first atomic bomb detonated weighed over 5,000 pounds and resembled a giant soccer ball (Schlosser 2013; Gainor 2018). It had a plutonium core surrounded by smaller explosives. Held together by gold foil, washers, and screws, Manhattan Project scientists assembled it in an old ranch house. They then drove it to a 100-foot tower and lifted it to the top. After detonation, the team watched as extreme bright light cut through the sky for just over 2 seconds. Heat shot out into the surrounding area. Civilians felt the shock wave over 100 miles away. Hues of purple and green filled the air, and the resulting mushroom cloud stretched out over 7 miles. Oppenheimer was ecstatic, but that faded. Realizing the potential to destroy humanity, someone beside him said, "Now we are all sons of bitches." His thoughts turned to a verse of Hindu scripture. The father of the atomic bomb introspectively commented, "Now I am become death, destroyer of worlds" (Hijiya 2000:123).

Twenty-eight days after "the Gadget" exploded, a Boeing B-29 with the moniker *Enola Gay* dropped a uranium-based atomic bomb code-named "Little Man" over Hiroshima, Japan. Three days later plutonium-based "Fat Man" rocked Nagasaki. Related deaths neared a quarter of a million. With European fighting finished for months, and Japan already preparing to surrender, was such an action necessary? Perhaps that question is better suited for history scholars (see, for example, Alperovitz 2010). Regardless, what we know is that U.S.-Soviet tension was mounting. Disagreements about what to do with Europe after World War II existed. Roosevelt worked well with Stalin, but Truman despised him (Maddox 2004:36). Some imply Truman used atomic bombs against Japan to gain the upper hand in the negotiations on Europe (Conine 2015).

The Soviets soon tested their own atomic bomb. The U.S. intelligence called it "Joe-1." Calling it "Stalin" seemed too direct, so the Soviets called it RDS-1 or "First Lightning." On August 29, 1949, in Kazakhstan, unaware caged animals waited. Situated among buildings, roads, and bridges built to simulate an actual city, they waited for devastation. Along with measuring infrastructure damage, the Russians planned to study the biological impact of radiation on the animals after the explosion. However, there was nothing left (Sherwin 2020). The stage for the Cold War was set. He died three years earlier, but I bet H. G. Wells saw it coming. It would not have shocked him to hear world leaders say they needed a faster way to deliver nuclear destruction.

GIANTS SLEEPING BELOW

Four years before the Soviets detonated Joe-1, the U.S. Joint Intelligence Objectives Agency (IOA) emerged to organize Operation Paperclip. Truman approved the IOA to secure as many German scientists as possible. German scientists already in America were skeptical, including Einstein. He drafted a letter to Truman telling him that Nazi scientists had deep religious and racial hatred. The Federation of American Scientists agreed. Unfazed, Truman allowed the program to continue. To him, Nazi knowledge was essential. Germans accused of war crimes would not hang after the war if they had intellectual capital. By the fall of 1946, 233 Nazi scientists were in the United States. One was Wernher von Braun (Crim 2018).

Von Braun was born in 1912 in Wirsitz, Poland. Gifted a telescope when he was young, he developed a passion for the skies and anything in them. Rocket power consumed him, even after an arrest at the age of 12 for setting off fireworks attached to a toy car. He obtained a mechanical engineering degree. Continuing his academic studies, he received a doctoral degree in physics in 1934. Though he became obsessed with space travel, contributing significantly to the growth of NASA, he would start his career with missile development. Of note is his work on the V-2 rocket (Ward 2005).

Von Braun was working on his doctorate when the Nazis overtook Germany. Aware of his landmark progress on missiles, they approached him. Violating the Treaty of Versailles concerned the Nazis. However, they knew provisions did not include rocket-guided weaponry. This is an interesting example of culture lag, technology outpacing social rules. In October 1942, the first successful V-2 launch happened. Spearheaded by an igniter tip atop a warhead, the 47-foot-tall cylindrical weapon stood large with stabilizing fins at the base. Its altitude limit soon expanded, and it was ready for combat. Two years later France and Britain felt its wrath. By World War II's end, over 1,000 V-2s shook the Western Front. A predecessor with the capability to hit New York City never materialized, and Allies obtained remnants of V-2s and started their own missile development. In 1957, with considerable help from Operation Paperclip scientists, the United States had its first successful Intercontinental Ballistic Missile (ICBM) test. It was the same year the Soviets launched the first Earth-orbiting satellite. After Sputnik, the terms "space race" and "missile gap" became common (Ward 2005).

The question was how to develop a missile that could travel long distances and deliver a nuclear warhead. The answer was the Atlas. Do you remember the Titanomachy? Atlas was a Titan sentenced by Zeus to hold up the heavens. Atlas was also the name for the parent company working with the U.S. government to develop a new missile. The original model used up to seven engines and stood 160 feet tall (Penson 2019). It had a 10-foot diameter, weighing around 130 tons. A radio signal guided early versions. Later ones used motion sensors and computers. The 2-ton warhead was 1,000 times more powerful than the "Fat Man" bomb. It launched 24 times, with only a 50 percent success rate. It clearly had problems. In Nosferatu-like fashion, the Atlas would lay horizontally in an above-ground bunker. They actually called it a coffin. For launching, personnel partially raised it above the earth, fueled it, and then lifted it to maximum vertical height. It could hit a target up to 8,000 miles away. As grand as it was, the missile took too long to prepare for an enemy attack. These missiles found another function, helping to propel the first American astronauts into orbit. After 1965, the Atlas was no longer viable (Gainor 2018).

The Titan I supplemented the Atlas. It used liquid oxygen and refined petroleum for propulsion. Development existed during the same time as the Atlas. The Martin Company produced many of the 102-foot-tall, 115-ton missiles at a plant in Colorado. With a range of 6,000 miles, it could not go as far as the Atlas, but its aerodynamics and lighter weight made it faster. It launched faster too. California's Vandenberg Air Force Base was the initial operational hub. Soon after the first successful launch, Titan I missiles were on alert at five different locations. It was the first ICBM with underground storage ability. The government immediately built silos to hide and house them. In the early 1960s, 163 non-mythological Titans, banished to the underworld—giants sleeping below, were ready to attack (Anthony 2018; Penson 2019).

Chapter 2

The Titan II

Like the Atlas, the Titan I had issues. It consistently hit within 3 miles of targets but had fuel storage problems. For an intercontinental ballistic missile (ICBM) like the Titan I to have adequate launch capabilities, it needed liquid oxygen, an unstable fuel source. Engineers made it a requirement to fuel just before launch, but that took up to 20 minutes. Moreover, though you could put a Titan I underground, you still had to raise it to the surface for launch. Another new missile was vital. Early in his presidency, John F. Kennedy was already deep into the Cold War. Weapon innovations under his predecessor, Dwight Eisenhower, kept long-range missile development going. However, during "Ike's" administration, there was also a concentration on intermediate-range missiles. This included Thor missiles with a 1.4-megaton warhead, ready to launch from Great Britain to Eastern Europe. Jupiter missiles could also launch from Italy and Turkey and hit Soviet targets. In addition, the Minuteman missile was well into development. It was small and cheap (Karlsson and Acosta 2020).

Kennedy found out the Soviets were planning for their own strategic missile placements. In January 1961, there were only 12 Atlas missiles on strategic alert. The Russians planned to set up warheads in Cuba. They could reach America with ease, and Cuban missiles would triple Soviet strike capabilities. With shipments of missiles looming in October 1962, Kennedy ordered a naval blockade around Cuba. A U.S. invasion was simmering, but Kennedy backed off. In exchange, Soviet leader Nikita Khrushchev halted missile delivery. JFK avoided a crisis. He also managed to save face by withholding details of the deal. Most were not aware of the real reason Khrushchev pulled back. Kennedy agreed to remove all Jupiter missiles from Turkey. Regardless, the event motivated Kennedy to revamp his strategy. He wanted more ICBMs, and he wanted them ready fast. In November 1963, a surge for more nuclear capabilities occurred again. An assassin killed Kennedy in Dallas. Lyndon Johnson took his place, and Secretary of Defense Robert McNamara pushed for assured destruction. He wanted the United States to have enough missile muscle to obliterate 30 percent of the Russian population (Schlosser 2013; Conine 2015). It was an unprecedented time.

WE HAVE LIFTOFF

The Martin Company and Los Alamos Laboratory had a Titan I replacement ready in early 1962. It was the Titan II. It could hold a W-53 warhead and produce 9 megatons of power. It had a range of nearly 10,000 miles, was accurate within a mile, and could reach nearly any location on earth within 30 minutes. Out of all launches, it only failed 6 percent of the time. Of utmost importance, its more advanced design allowed it to store permanent fuel, aerozine-50. Coming into contact with dinitrogen tetroxide, also inside the missile, would trigger propulsion. At most, launch time was just under 60 seconds, and the Titan II could take off from underground (Penson 2019; Sherwin 2020).

Envision a test launch. Two soldiers, the site Missile Crew Commander (MCC) and Deputy Commander, snap safety seals off launch commit covers and simultaneously turn keys to wake the Titan II. With the low hum of fans in the site control center, the MCC states "Crew, we have a launch enable lighted and the missile batteries are activated" (Womack 1997:68). A door over the silo opens and reveals the launch duct, otherwise known as the "gun barrel." Looking at the launch control console, the MCC sees lights reading "Guidance Go" and "Fire in the Engine" glowing bright red. Seconds later, nearly all lights on the console fade out and an electric horn screams. The "Fire in the Engine" light starts flashing, appearing to mimic the rapidly escalating heartbeat of the two people standing near. The MCC kills the horn with a punch, it sounds off again to signal the presence of oxidizer vapor in the gun barrel. The warning horn stops again, and the MCC glances toward the upper right corner of the launch console. There, a white light glows to confirm a completed sequence. The MCC announces, "Crew, we have liftoff" (Womack 1997:69). The world seemingly stops for a split second until the rocket engines shoot the missile into the atmosphere with a loud "whoosh." It mimics the voice of air escaping from a highly pressurized tire, and 430,000 pounds of thrust builds into a wall of sound impersonating a freight train. Just as the auditory assault begins, it ends. The ground rumbles for miles. With nothing but a faint thunder left behind, close to 50 miles in the air, a sensor recognizes that the fuel tank was empty from the first stage of the launch. Then, the missile's main engine shuts down and the unit drops, now unnecessary, launch components. A second-stage engine kicks into gear. A few minutes later, just over 200 miles into travel, the onboard 8-pound computer shuts the additional engine off and activates a miniature explosive to separate the nose cone from the unit. Fifteen minutes later, the warhead peaks at 800 miles. It starts falling toward the target at speeds up to 20 times that of a bullet (Conine 2015; Penson 2019).

Testing for the underground silo concept started by way of Space Technology Laboratories and Aerojet-General with a small-scale Titan II. They built the model and sample silo in just two months. Though the actual silos would be below ground, the model was all above ground to ensure access to all components of the facility. By the end of 1962, funding for over 50 underground facilities existed and construction began. Early Titan II testing started at Cape Canaveral. This was beneficial since plans to use the Titan II for space exploration launches were underway. However, the focus shifted to Vandenberg Air Force Base, where the first test of a Titan II launching from underground occurred. There were not accompanying celebrations. The missile cleared the gun barrel opening, but only after the silo doors malfunctioned, electrical cords failed to detach, and the missile began an irregular rotation resulting from the aforementioned cords. With those problems corrected, Titan IIs were on their way to each Launch Complex (LC) around the country (Stumpf 2000).

If there was a Soviet nuclear attack, policymakers believed missiles could come from the East or the West, so the military built many silos in the middle of the country. Kansas and Arkansas were the primary locations. Then, Arizona and California came into play. As opposed to Kansas and Arkansas, the two western states held Titan IIs for offensive purposes. California had the fewest facilities among the four. Arizona, Kansas, and Arkansas had 18 each. By the mid-1960s, the United States was ready to launch over 1,000 ICBMs, including Titan IIs (Stumpf 2000; Christ 2016).

STRATEGIC AIR COMMAND

After driving Lucille to Arkansas, my dad asked me to go back with him to Indiana a few weeks later. My grandmother left a staggering amount of items behind. My daughter was not a year old yet, and I hesitated to leave my wife alone. Regardless, my dad needed me. An auctioneer was to sell off everything in Lucille's house. Frantically organizing the night before the auction, I came across items my dad told me to keep. I decided to let the auctioneer sell them, but do some bidding to help my grandmother out financially. One item I "won" was a long-sleeved U.S. Air Force (USAF) shirt. Over the right pocket, a royal blue rectangle boxed in the name "Ulsperger." Harold

Ulsperger was my grandmother's husband. He adopted my father, who Lucille coincidentally named Harold some time before she met her husband-to-be. The family affectionately referred to my dad as "Harold Wayne" to avoid confusion. Dad never knew for sure who his biological father was. His adoptive father served in the Korean and Vietnam wars. Over the left pocket of his shirt, there was a patch resembling a shield with yellow lining. Inside of it, a powder blue background with clouds creeping in on opposite corners provided the backdrop for a fist cloaked in silver armor. The fist held contrasting images of power and concord, red lightning bolts, and an olive branch. It was the Strategic Air Command (SAC) insignia, their motto—"Peace Is Our Profession" (Conine 2015:400).

After World War II, Truman reorganized the military. With the National Security Act of 1947, the USAF became an autonomous branch under the umbrella of the Department of Defense. The year before, the U.S. Army Air Force created SAC to consolidate bombing missions and aerial reconnaissance. SAC would fall under USAF control. Bombers were the face of deterrence, and strategic currents led the government to put nuclear weapons under the purview of SAC. In 1948, they turned to "Iron Ass"—Lieutenant General Curtis LeMay (Conine 2015:44). Previously, he was the point man for Operation Paperclip. He led SAC for nearly 10 years. He was also a national celebrity. In 1955, a movie called *Strategic Air Command* glorified SAC and had a fictionalized character based on LeMay. Media stories touted the general as "The Toughest Cop of the Western World" (Schlosser 2013:148).

LeMay once noted, "If we maintain our faith in God, love of freedom, and superior global air power, the future looks good" (Conine 2015:113). Under his lead, SAC soon controlled much of the USAF budget. They started the 1950s with 13 bases in the United States. Within a decade, numbers surpassed 60. Bases existed in places like Arkansas and Nebraska, but would eventually stretch overseas as far as Japan. Lucille's husband Harold served in all those locations. As SAC absorbed responsibilities on ICBM development, LeMay shifted his headquarters to Offutt Air Force Base (AFB). He built an underground bunker with walls 2 feet thick, and filled it with enough supplies for 800 inhabitants (Weitez 1999).

SILO CONSTRUCTION

SAC Titan II silo construction was underway before the missiles were ready. With "missile gap" fears, the United States felt it essential to move quickly lest they fall behind the Soviets (Conine 2015). Everyone would just have to address problems as they emerged. Penson (2019:12) argues this process saved time, but was "expensive because all the bugs" got "worked out with a jackhammer instead of an eraser." It took approximately 3 years to complete all 54 sites, which SAC supervised via Monthan AFB in Tucson, Arizona, McConnell AFB in Wichita, Kansas, and Little Rock AFB just outside of Jacksonville, Arkansas. Building the $12.6 million facilities occurred in three phases (Stumpf 2000).

In the first phase, civilian workers did the bulk of construction. Various military personnel, including soldiers assigned to missile maintenance, were present. Digging a hole in the ground was the inaugural move. The early oblong cut into the earth carried the name "bathtub" (see figure 2.1). It provided the starting point for silo excavation down to 155 feet. Metal beams spaced a few feet apart gave an outline for walls and electromagnetic shielding. The floor was a thick, steel radiation-resistant plate. An internal wood shell provided spacing from the wall where workers poured thick concrete reinforced with rebar. Sites could withstand a 10-megaton bomb explosion from a mile away. To support the heavy doors that exposed the missile to the world, the top 30 feet of the silo hole had 8-foot-thick walls. The door opened and closed on wheels placed on accompanying tracks. There was a focus on technical components after digging. Consider the emergency generator.

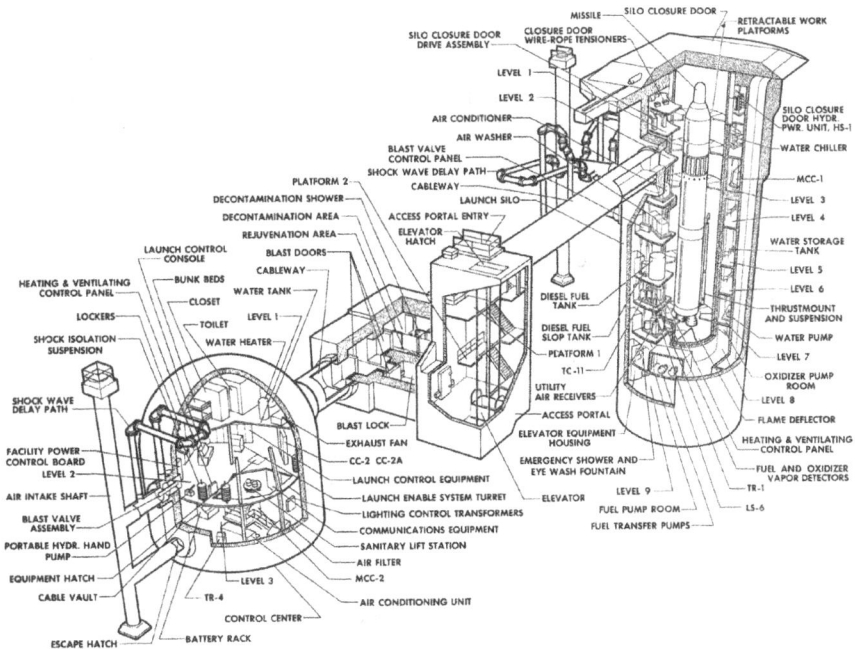

Figure 2.1 Titan II Facility Diagram. *Source:* Image provided for use by Chuck Penson via Titan Missile Museum archives.

Workers lowered it into the silo hole with a crane, because fitting it in the shell later would be impossible (Penson 2019; Stumpf 2000).

Two hundred and fifty feet from the silo hole, workers dug another hole. It was for the Launch Control Center (LCC). Nine feet below the ground and stretching downward another 42 feet, the domed structure was 37 feet in diameter. It had three concrete floors setting on springs and walls gapped 3 feet from the side of the surrounding earth. If it experienced a shockwave, it could bounce and swing in its suspended shell providing a functioning environment for the soldiers inside. This included a crew commander, deputy crew commander, a ballistic missile analyst/technician, and a missile facilities technician, all brandishing .38 caliber sidearms (Conine 2015).

Two of the crew always remained on "alert," living somewhere "between boredom and exhaustion" (Womack 1997:21). The other two needed a place to eat, sleep, and relax. That was LCC Level 1. However, the crew spent a majority of time on LCC Level 2. Systems there allowed monitoring of the entire site and the ability to order a launch. LCC Level 3 held the main power distribution center, backup batteries, decoding equipment, and a wastewater ejection pump to carry sewage to a septic tank. An escape hatch with a ladder to the surface existed on the side of the LCC farthest from the silo. You could reach it from LCC Level 3. The first part of construction took up to 14 months (Stumpf 2000).

During the second phase, contracted workers put the final additions on internal structures. They situated the 700-ton doors over the silo opening. They installed launch duct platforms and blast valves. They finished the "blast lock" shaft stretching 250 feet between the silo and LCC. It had a floor and ceiling 5-feet thick and walls 4-feet thick. Along with an elevator for bulky items, an entrance door above ground opened to a staircase leading to the entrapment area in the blast lock, 50 yards from the silo. No high-security device protected the door, only an electromagnetic lock. Interestingly, someone could open it within 15 minutes with a crowbar. Near the top of the stairs, after passing through a pair of steel blast doors 5-feet wide and 6,000 pounds, you got to the silo. If you wanted to reach the LCC, you would go down 55 steps and pass through a different set of blast doors with the same dimensions leading you away from the silo. Practically impenetrable when locked, the doors opened easily, balanced perfectly on hinges. The steel door sets would never be open simultaneously, always protecting the blast crew from the missile in the silo. Shafts allowed for underground air circulation. Two provided fresh air intake, with one bored out near the LCC and the other close to the southwest corner of the silo. Workers created another shaft for air exhaust on the northwest corner. A voice signaling system connected all areas with speakers underground and above. Emergency phones existed at five different locations, including in the short cableway on the silo side of the first set of blast doors. During this construction wave, laborers also installed electrical wiring for power, hydraulics, plumbing, a heating system, and air conditioning units. This phase could take up to 13 months (Stumpf 2000; Schlosser 2013; Penson 2019).

With the third phase, the USAF took over a majority of labor. This limited civilian knowledge on the finer, classified aspects of a site. They would install the launch control console and a backup launch officer's console. They hooked up the emergency war orders clock, which kept official time for the site. It operated on Greenwich Mean Time, which was the same for all facilities. The universal time removed the possibility of confusion when bases and personnel communicated across time zones. Other clocks in the facility matched the ones at the missile support base. Military personnel hooked up communication systems providing radio transmissions from other military stations and specific units allowing the launch team to talk to helicopters bringing supplies and VIPs to the launch site. At this point, soldiers also connected necessary components to the missile for operational capacity. This included linking the power control board to emergency systems to control propellant release, setting up the butterfly valve lock control to prevent accidental launches, and installing breakers with the ability to cut power to explosive components (Schlosser 2013; Conine 2015; Penson 2019).

TITAN IIS IN ARKANSAS

The 308th Strategic Missile Wing's (SMW) SAC soldiers supervised Titan IIs in Arkansas. Their motto was *Non sibi sed aliis*—"Not for self but others" (Schlosser 2013:8). It was a two-prong wing, made of the 373rd and the 374th Strategic Missile Squadrons (SMS). Each wing was responsible for nine missile locations, and both coordinated efforts through the Little Rock AFB. Missile sites had nicknames, sometimes designated by words. Arizona's LC 571-7 was "Copper Penny." A mine was in the vicinity. Most sites had designations with the last two digits of their name. For example, soldiers sometimes referenced LC 373-1 the "three one" (Womack 1997; Penson 2019).

The two SMSs in the 308th were born in 1942. They were B-24 bombardment squadrons based out of Utah and Arizona. They ended up in China by 1943 and Japan in 1945. During World War II, both participated in air raids and propaganda leaflet drops. In 1947, they engaged in weather reconnaissance from Alaska. Following a period of abeyance, in 1961 SAC repurposed both squadrons to supervise Titan II launch sites. Home would be Arkansas. The construction of sites in the Natural State was not an easy task. Hard bedrock and earth slides during digging called for special excavation (Stumpf 2000).

The geographic strategy led to launch sites in Arkansas, but politics and money did too. Elected officials craved financial possibilities. In each state, it took 5,000 workers to complete all the sites. It cost millions of dollars annually to maintain them, with a sturdy amount of money from the USAF flowing into the local economy (Russell 1987; Penson 2019). It was no coincidence a political Titan of the time, the highly influential Wilbur D. Mills was the chair of the House Ways and Means Committee during silo site selection (Schlosser 2013). He was born in White County, Arkansas. His hometown was Kensett. Many of the silos in Arkansas ended up close to it. Mills always stood at the edge of a Supreme Court nomination. He did not wait for presidents to meet with him. It was the other way around. His name still echoed through the wooded hills, farmlands, dirt roads, and impoverished towns of North Central Arkansas when I was growing up. For years, my mother-in-law worked at an educational cooperative carrying his name. A congressional colleague once told a reporter, "I never vote against God, motherhood, or Wilbur Mills" (Smith 2017). Detailed in *The Stripper and Congressman* (Foxe 1975), as with other charismatic men who make politics their business, Mills's only weakness appeared to be monkey business.

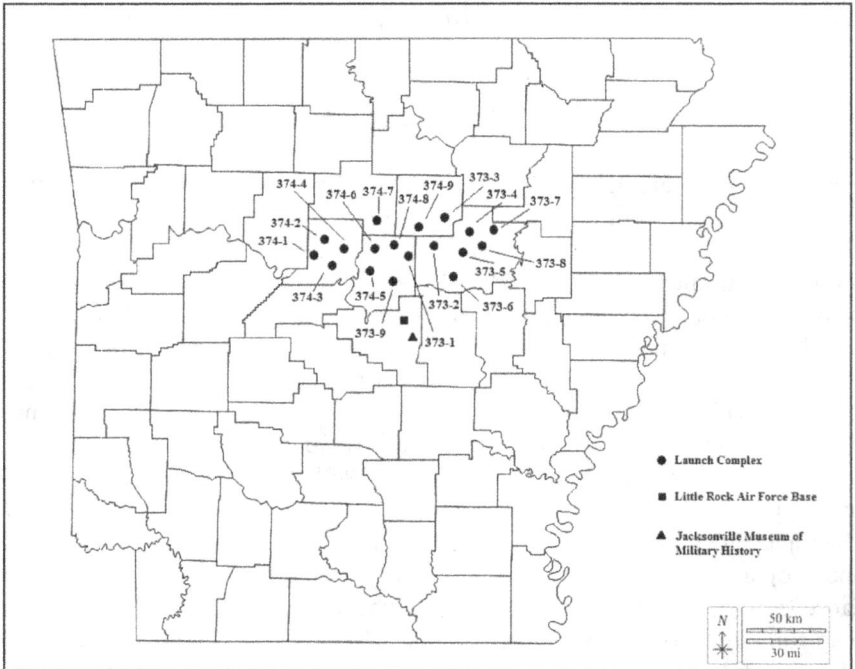

Figure 2.2   Arkansas Titan II Silo Locations. *Source:* Designed by author using d-maps. com (2007–2021) free resources.

For the SMS 374, Arkansas sites included areas close to Blackwell, Plummerville, Hattieville, Springfield, Wooster, Guy, Qutiman, Pearson, and Damascus (see figure 2.2). More relevant to this work, the SMS 373 focused on compounds near Mount Vernon, Rose Bud, Heber Springs, Center Hill, Russell, Judsonia, and Holland. One of the launch sites existed near the current community of Antioch. This was the closest to my hometown of Beebe. When my wife and I were dating in high school, we would frequent the area for teenage clarity. We admired the seclusion, but it did not always smell pleasant because cattle populated the land then. The proud members of the 308th called it the "three six," but we called it "Cow Shit Road." There is another site not yet listed—LC 373-4, located in White County outside of Searcy. It was to receive the first Titan II in the state on February 6, 1963. However, after it was unloaded, an inspector found a thrust chamber leak in the Stage 1 engine and seal failures in the oxidizer pump. That first missile averted disaster, but the second one would be in the launch duct surrounded by death soon enough (Stumpf 2000; Anthony 2018).

PROJECT YARD FENCE

NBA great Scotty Pippen was born in Hamburg, Arkansas, in 1965. That same year, Yell County's Arthur Lee Hunnicutt starred as an elderly Butch Cassidy in the hit movie *Cat Ballou*. Pharaoh Sanders, Little Rock's own jazz genius, joined John Coltrane's band. Blytheville-born Junior Walker had a dance hit with his song "Shotgun" (Welky and Keckhaver 2013). Women across America let fabric edge 4 inches above the knee. The miniskirt became the en-vogue sexual symbol of the time. Cesar Chavez held mass demonstrations with the support of activist college students to boycott unethical labor practices. The Voting Rights Act banned discriminatory practices such as manipulating literacy tests, but disenfranchised minorities in areas such as Los Angeles rioted in the streets, pushing against racial injustice. Young men in their muscle cars roared down streets blaring "Ticket to Ride," "King of the Road," "I Got You Babe," "My Girl," "(I Can't Get No) Satisfaction," and "Mr. Tambourine Man" from eight-track decks. At the year's end, over 180,000 U.S. troops were in Vietnam (Glennon 1999). Back home, mothers stood at their stoves cooking fried chicken and okra, and children like "Kitten" waited by the door for fathers like Delphard to return from work.

Only two years after securing 54 missiles in their underground dens, SAC initiated Project Yard Fence. Confidence in the Titan II was high. On March 23, America's two-man Gemini-Titan spacecraft launched Gus Grissom and John Young into orbit. It was not Grissom's first space trip. Four years earlier, a Redstone missile launched him nearly 120 miles above the earth.

The smaller, less powerful rocket was not in the same league as the Titan II. Reflecting on his first glimpse of a Titan II, Grissom remembered thinking the "big beast" was "beautiful" (Chappell 1968:52). He would only live for two more years. Lost forever, he was aboard the Apollo 1 in February 1967, when a cabin fire during launch rehearsal killed him. Safety crews could not rescue Grissom and his fellow astronauts because the plug door hatch would not open. Launch personnel reported afterward that they failed to focus on safety measures since the launch missile did not have fuel in it during the rehearsal (Furniss 1989).

Yard Fence equated to design upgrades. The goal was to enhance the complex's ability to survive enemy nuclear attacks. Updates included two concrete neutron shields positioned on the north and south sides of the silo door (Strang 1967). This gave additional protection to exhaust ducts when the door closed. It increased the weight of the silo doors to 758 tons. The improvements also involved modification of hydraulic systems, blast doors, and emergency lighting. The estimated cost was $13 million (Stumpf 2000; Schlosser 2013).

Titan II complexes looked the same. The launch duct of each silo had nine levels. Level 1 was just under the silo door. There you would find the 40-horsepower motors used to open and close the door and expose the missile. It also held the motor for the silo elevator and the accumulators, the trigger to initiate a launch. Level 2 contained pumps, fans, filters, dehumidifiers, and a collection of other materials used for air control—see Level 2 Layout at the beginning of the book. This area also held a device that looked like an old slide projector—the azimuth alignment set. It projected a beam toward the missile that would reflect back to the device in order to maintain appropriate directional calibration. On Level 3, an emergency generator pushed by a 510-horsepower diesel engine existed. Cooled by water, it let off steam that would blow out of an exhaust air shaft leading to the surface. There was also an electric cabinet used to start backup power and an access hatch. The hatch led to a large water tank attached to the side of the silo. The water fed into a sound suppression mechanism and was also for putting out fires. Level 4 included the core parts of an evaporator cooling system, which engineers decided to replace early on with a conventional air conditioner due to humidity issues. On Level 5, there was a large fan for air recirculation and a fuel tank for the aforementioned diesel engine on the third level. Level 6 had monitors for missile fuel and oxidizer vapors. A self-contained lab constantly analyzed air samples for safety. According to a former crewmember, Vapor Detection Malfunction lights stayed on 25 percent of the time (Womack 1997; Schlosser 2013).

Beside the lab was a manual-override panel for the ventilation system. Oddly, there was also a tank with oxblood. That is not a nickname for a secret substance. It is my understanding that it was actually blood from oxen. Workers could mix it with water to create foam for fire suppression if one of the many detectors in the facility deemed it requisite. Water pumps used to pressurize the domestic water for the crew and the industrialized water for operations were on Level 7. Adjacent to them, you found an air compression system used to start the diesel generator and operate locking pins for work platforms. Level 8 contained the fuel and oxidizer pump rooms. On Level 9, a concrete wedge existed to deflect missile exhaust up two shafts leading straight up the silo past defecting cascade vanes to the outside world. There were also sump pumps to remove accumulated water from the bottom of the launch duct (Penson 2019).

Project Yard Fence called for the removal of the warhead while civilians worked up and down the levels of the silo. It was back in Jacksonville at the Little Rock AFB (Hicks 2000). The actual missile stayed since it could take up to two weeks to remove one and two more to install it back. However, the fuel and oxidizer tanks remained filled and other systems remained in place. The launch crew stayed in the LCC. In the summer of 1965, a group of laborers, mostly from Arkansas, was working via a union out of Little Rock for Peter Kiewit Sons Incorporated to upgrade LC 373-4 (Chicago Tribune 1965; McCoy 2019). They had a long history of working with the U.S. military. Taking advantage of FDR's New Deal, the Nebraska-based outfit signed on for several projects through the Public Works Administration. Eventually, they were using civilian labor to complete projects in eight states. By the end of World War II, the company collected close to $500 million for defense-related construction. In 1952, Kiewit signed a $1.2 billion contract with the Atomic Energy Commission to build a uranium plant in Ohio. At the time, it was the largest contract the federal government ever signed with one company. Projects for the U.S. Corps of Engineers followed, including Alaska's first nuclear facility, radar stations in Greenland, and half a billion dollars for helping to construct federal highways. Sources indicate F.E. Newbery Company had contract labor at LC 373-4 as well (LaGrossa 1980; Hicks 2000).

DISASTER AT LC 373-4

Just after lunch on August 9, 1965, at LC 373-4, civilian men were hard at it on all levels of the silo. Some painted hatches, a few flushed out hydraulic systems, and others installed perforated steel covers on acoustic modules. Without notice, a sound echoed through the launch duct resembling the ignition of a gas stove. A wave of hot air followed. Workers on Level 1 looked at the level just below (Orval Eugene Faubus Papers 1965). Bright yellow flames marched toward everyone above. The complex alarms sounded and the men yelled out in panic. Three times on the public address system, crew commander Captain David Yount ordered everyone to evacuate after seeing the Fire Diesel Area indicator light demanding attention (Stumpf 2000).

There was auditory confusion, but most of the men could at least see where they were going, until the lights went out seconds later. Emergency lights clicked on, but they were not bright enough to cut through the murky air. Moreover, hydraulic fluid on the floors caused some to lose footing while trying to flee in the midst of burning electrical cables and melting equipment. Smoke from the fire filled the silo. All of the power shut down (USAF 1965). Topside workers saw revolving red lights on a warning pole and witnessed menacing clouds of air seep through vents on the main silo door. Waves of the sinister smoke grew into a dense wall, reducing the possibility of successful rescue attempts. Two of the launch crew grabbed fire extinguishers and headed down the shaft connecting the LCC and the launch duct. They attempted to fight their way through the shadowy air, but it mercilessly forced them back down the corridor and away from the silo. They said they never saw flames but decided to turn back anyway, but not before grabbing a passed-out worker, later throwing him in a contamination shower. On the other side of locked blast doors, one person made it to the elevator. He was stuck once the power went out. A majority of others, confused without light, packed the exit ladder running parallel to the missile. Deprived of oxygen, suffocating bodies could not fight anymore. The 308th commander, Colonel Charles Sullivan, probably seated in the executive boardroom at the Little Rock AFB, demanded a physical count of everyone at the site (Schlosser 2013; McCoy 2019).

He got it, but was also told over 50 were missing. Firefighters from the base flew in on helicopters, as did the Missile Potential Hazard Team (MPHT). Believing there was no safe entry to the launch bay; neither group provided much help. Some rescuers, donning asbestos suits, tried to enter a small ventilation shaft but could not make it through due to intense fumes. Moreover, the breathing equipment used would only hold 30 minutes of air. That was simply not enough of a supply to work through the launch duct even if rescuers made it past initial waves of smoke (Searcy Daily Citizen 1965a; Orval Eugene Faubus Papers 1966; Stumpf 2000). With no power in the compound, the temperature in the silo was rising fast and it would soon trigger an explosion in the oxidizer tank. Through the night, with the Arkansas National Guard, White County Chapter of the American Red Cross, and some family members of the missing workers on hand, portable generators pushed energy to industrial air conditioners to lower heat levels in the gun barrel. Responders tried to douse lingering flames. At 10:40 p.m., the SAC Disaster Control Center officially reported fatalities (Searcy Daily Citizen 1965b;

USAF 1965). My mother's father was one of them. My dad's father was too. He did not know it yet, but one of Lucille's former lovers from nearly 20 years earlier died that day as well.

It remains the worst American industrial accident at a nuclear silo (Anthony 2018). Flags in the state flew at half-staff. Representative Mills said, "Heartfelt sympathy goes out to those who have suffered this loss" (Arkansas Gazette 1965a:1). Arkansas Governor Orval Faubus stated that the 53 lost had "given their lives to work which is necessary to insure the defense of the nation and the preservation of its freedom" (Arkansas Gazette 1965b:9A). It was evident the men tragically lost were titans themselves. They were men working to improve the safety of their country against the enemy. No doubt highly important to them, they were working to support their families. However, just like the Titan II missile beside them, they found themselves banished to the underworld. Just like Cronus and his siblings in *The Fall of the Titans*, they found themselves enclosed by darkening clouds with nothing but flames illuminating their surroundings. They had no hope and were ghosts of their former selves. The 53 all died in less than 5 minutes. On Level 2, MPHT found 12 of the deceased and 24 on Level 3, with the remains of 8 on Level 4, 1 on Level 5, and finally 4 on Levels 6 and 7. They either failed to match names with locations or did not release that information (USAF 1965). Perishing just over a few hills from his El Paso birthplace, someone would have to tell "Kitten" and Linda daddy was not coming home.

CONFRONTING GHOSTS

Two workers made it out of the launch duct. One worked at the complex for the shortest period, and the other may have worked there the longest. Gary Lay graduated from high school a few months earlier. He was earning college money, with ambitions to attend the University of Arkansas. His father worked for Local 155 out of Little Rock, had men at LC 373-4, and got his son the job. Excited to be around a "rocket," it was one of his first days on site that summer, but he had worked there the summer before. In the 68-degree temperature regulated "hole," he was mostly cleaning up after others. He remembers seeing a sign that said, "206 days without an accident" outside of the "underground city" (Hicks 2000; McCoy 2019). Earlier in the day, he was at the bottom of the silo wiping down wall panels. He was about to go back down but could not help but stop to chat with 12 other employees before his descent when the fire started (Roberts 2015; McCoy 2019).

The yellow-flamed blaze sprang up behind him near the shock isolation platform for a water chiller. As everyone fled, Lay followed, headed toward the ladder. After only moving a few feet, fleeing workers created a logjam at the ladder. He realized he would never have a chance to escape (Strang 1967; Hicks 2000). He made his way toward the fire hearing someone yell, "Help me, God, help me!" as he exited (Arkansas Gazette 1965c:9A). He found an opening to the cableway leading to the LCC. Hubert Saunders was painting on Level 1. He had several years of experience working at Titan II facilities. He smelled smoke and knew insidious dark air would follow. He held his breath and headed toward the shaft like Lay. They somehow made it to the LCC, gasping for clean air along the way and getting help from the soldiers who briefly headed down the cableway before turning back. Depending on the source you consider, Saunders crawled most of the way on his hands and knees or ran down the tunnel connecting the LCC and silo. He told one reporter, "This old Irishman can move when he has to" (Arkansas Gazette 1965a:9A). Once Lay and Saunders reached LCC, Lay had burns on his face and hands, while Saunders suffered from extreme smoke inhalation. Lay kept telling himself, "God, don't let me die" (Stumpf 2000; Roberts 2015; McCoy 2019).

The emergency room at a hospital in Searcy knew about the accident after Lay and Saunders arrived freshly decontaminated from the shower at the site. Medical staff rushed to assemble supplies and waited for a surge of injured. After several hours it was apparent, no one was coming (Schlosser 2013). Lay and Saunders escaped one of the deadliest industrial accidents in the history of the United States. It remains the most catastrophic disaster associated with an American nuclear facility. At the time, it was considered a fire that killed more people than any other in Arkansas history (Arkansas Gazette 1965d; Anthony 2018). Lay remained in the hospital for 21 days and SAC suspended Project Yard Fence temporarily to investigate (LaGrossa 1980; Hicks 2000).

Some reports indicate a welder on Level 2 unintentionally hit a hydraulic line with the electrode of his tool. That weakened the stainless steel braiding on the line and produced a pin-sized hole in the Teflon. Once that happened, hydraulic fluid hit residual heat from the weld or the welding electrode. Then, flames came. Soon, 90 gallons of oil would be in the launch duct. The fire burned through a set of cutting-torch tank lines close by and intensified the blaze. A personnel location board maintained by one of the contractors showed someone was welding on Level 3. However, some investigators believed the person could only reach what he needed by kneeling on the floor on Level 2, leaning through guardrails, and reaching around a web of hydraulic lines. It is possible the welder died, not from asphyxiation, but from drowning in hydraulic fluid. I assume that is only if he removed his mask after the hydraulic leak started, if he was even welding at all. Also, note that personnel were purging some of the lines around Level 2. It is possible not all of the lines even had fluid in them (Stumpf 2000; Roberts 2015; Penson 2020).

The day after the disaster, an information officer at SAC headquarters in Nebraska reported body recovery was complete, but water filled the bottom of the silo and the rescue team was still probing it. As they pulled bodies out, personnel took them to a tool shed, identified them by their employee badge numbers, placed them in bags, and drove them to nine local funeral homes in trucks (Arkansas Gazette 1965a; Searcy Daily Citizen 1965a). According to obituaries, the dead included people from outside of Arkansas, such as Oklahomans Joseph C. Cloud Sr. and Freddie Philo Conway, along with Texans Marion A. Sewell, James R. Stuckey, and William Henry Stuckey. Men were from nearby states, such as Jim S. Best of Shreveport, Louisiana, James Terry Wallace from Columbus, Mississippi, and William D. Merchant from St. Louis, Missouri. Some were even farther away from home, like J. Dee Headley of Denver, Colorado, Herbert O. Wahrmund of Michigan City, Indiana, Lewis Mack Phillips of Chesterton, Indiana, and Aubrey E. Reynolds from Chicago, Illinois. Most were from areas all around Arkansas, including Odra M. Vaught from Fort Smith, Archie A. Martin of Texarkana, John Paul Elkins from Pine Bluff, George W. Richmond of Pine Bluff, Kendall H. Belote of Enola, Harry E. Fisher of Harrison, Pressly Harrod Sanson from Vilonia, and Bobby Gene Scott of Booneville. There was Charles H. Shaw of Quitman, J. B. "Junior" Mobbs of Greenbrier, William Rayburn Keel of Hot Springs, Charles P. McMahon from Ozark, and Hershell Ray Linn of Damascus. Several were from the Little Rock-North Little Rock area, including Herbert E. Melton, Yonley A. Williams, Samuel Charles Hicks, Thomas L. Hoggard, Lowell H. Cook, Willis "Bill" Briley, Thurman D. "Jack" Milam, Bill E. Bennett, Lucian Jack Adams, Mervan H. Wood, Kenneth W. Squires, Donald Alvin Dean, Foster G. Pemberton, Raymond Helton, James C. Harvey, and Gillis Ray Patterson. It seemed some smaller towns disproportionately suffered after the event. Conway mourned for Cecil F. Taylor, John Francis Evans, and Archie Hamilton. The community of Beebe experienced great heartache with the passing of Harold Shelton, Delphard H. Owens, William C. Holden, Charles H. Fulson, and Echol Thurman. Ward lost Sidney S. Phillips, Wilburn Q. Bailey, Henry Hampton Hegi, and Charles Lee Dove (Stumpf 2000).

Ben Scallorn, a site maintenance officer for the 308th SMW, supervised activities for at least six sites and helped to retrieve the 53. In one source (Schlosser 2013:227), he states:

It was a sobering experience. Thick black soot covered almost everything. But handprints could still be seen on the rungs of the ladders, and the bodies of fallen workers had left clear outlines on the floor. [You could] make out the shapes of their arms and legs, the positions of their bodies as they died, surrounded by black soot. All that remained of them were these pale, ghostly silhouettes.

Post-disaster, SAC put the silo back in operation within days. It was on alert status 13 months later. Crewmembers saw strange things in a launch bay with still charred walls. At what soldiers would eventually label the "ghost site," manually operated pumps came on without human intervention, lights sporadically powered up, and the bell for the elevator that traveled from Level 8 to Level 2 would ring on its own. Concerned with an incursion, crew would radio the LCC and receive confirmation that no one else was in the silo (Schlosser 2013:22). The *Dictionary of Superstitions* defines a ghost as "the spirit of someone who is dead . . . seeing to some unfinished business" (Pickering 1995:116). Ghosts are more than that. They are things we know to be true, but we never seek out evidence to confirm. They are memories we have of loved ones, but they are also fabricated memories of those we have never known.

I do not believe my father's stepdad Harold Ulsperger had anything to do with SAC in Arkansas at the time of the tragedy. That he had anything to do with SAC at all seems an odd coincidence. What I do know is that when going through Lucille's belongings before the auction in Indiana, I found a frayed, discolored envelope with my grandmother's handwriting. It said, "Harold Wayne." I heard whispers when I was growing up about my dad's biological father. There was a rumor that he died at LC 373-4 like my mother's father Delphard. In my mind, rumor moved a bit closer to fact when I looked inside of the envelope. There was a newspaper article from August 1965 about the 53. I went downstairs and showed my father. He said it was true. Both of my grandfathers died in the disaster. A DNA test he recently took backs up his perspective. He also told me that not long after his mother died, he visited one of his aunts. She was distant and hesitant to talk. He took that as his cue to leave. As he was reaching for the door, she handed him an old clipping. You know what it detailed. Over 50 years after the catastrophe at LC 373-4, I simultaneously experienced the joy of knowing and the pain of loss.

THE DESIRE TO KNOW MORE

Complex geopolitical forces paved the way for the advancement of the Titan II missile program. Just as complex were the bureaucratic procedures and technological dynamics associated with launch complexes built in states such as Arizona, California, Kansas, and Arkansas. Great effort went toward silo construction. Financially, the government via taxpayers paid the price. Unfortunately, some citizens paid with their lives. Project Yard Fence, designed to improve silos, led to the death of 53 men. Two were my grandfathers, and I was striving to come to terms with it. Were other surviving family members doing the same years later? Site personnel claimed that ghosts roamed LC 373-4. Was it possible that thoughts of the 53 still haunted family? Astronauts like Grissom strapped themselves to high-powered projectiles like Titan IIs in search of the unknown. I knew conflicting reports about the disaster existed, and I knew no records about experiences of the children of the 53 existed. With that in mind, I decided I was going to use my sociological knowledge to explore the unknown too.

The next three chapters focus on theoretical issues in order to establish formal research questions. You will read about sociology and its relevance to rituals. You will come to understand the study of disasters, how some of it is applicable to the 53, and that a void is present when it comes to researching technological disasters, survivors, and loss. You will also learn about aspects of grief, referenced as the sociology of sorrow.

Chapter 3

Sociology of Ritual

Lately, my eyes hurt. It is probably time for a visit to the ophthalmologist. I think the problem relates to me staring at my iPad too much. What I am experiencing goes beyond typical conspicuous consumption via Amazon.com or creeping on Facebook. One billion others in the spring of 2020 are doing what I am, spending too much time staring at the Johns Hopkins Coronavirus Dashboard (Raymond 2020). I am in the "pandemic is real" camp. My mind is drifting to my Aunt Linda again. She had cancer. I am glad COVID-19 did not compound it. Some coronavirus patients get acute respiratory distress syndrome. My wife's father died of it years ago, and his decline due to oxygen deprivation was heartbreaking.

As a sociologist concerned with death, I am fascinated with the number of those lost to the pandemic. I watched as numbers in Italy climbed over 20,000. Analysts implied those numbers were horrific, perhaps insurmountable for other nations. It is nearing the end of April, and New York City alone might reach a similar number of deaths. We turn our heads away from death on so many levels, but we certainly do not have that luxury now (Tampone 2020). Just as the incident at Launch Complex (LC) 373-4 affected the lives of people connected to it, this new virus is clearly affecting our reality. Using some pandemic-related examples, this chapter gives us sociological insight into how daily reality comes into existence, specifically in terms of ritual.

SOCIOLOGY AND RITUALS

Sociologists study human behavior. In uncomplicated form, the discipline concerns the way people act. Inherited factors play a part, including biology and psychology. For sociologists, to understand the behavior you must consider social context (Henslin 2019). The era, the culture people are born into, and the influence of others are crucial. On a deeper level, there are taken-for-granted rules humans create through interaction that define behavior. People with power have a significant impact on that process. Variables like dependence on others or impressions others have of us, actual or perceived, modify our actions. I am simplifying the discipline, but I hope the point is clear. As pointed out by Emile Durkheim, social dynamics are essential when studying humans.

A sociological pioneer, Durkheim was born in 1858 in France. He came from a religious family and drifted into academia. Religion clearly influenced his scholarship. With the industrial revolution, he argued that moral decay was rising due in part to the breakdown of social bonds and the growth of individualism (see Durkheim [1893] 1965a; [1915] 1965b). Durkheim thought the only thing that would keep industrialized societies functioning was a deep dependence on each other. Durkheim ([1897] 1966) also studied suicide. He argued it is the result of sociological factors. His point was revolutionary. He narrowed in on social bonds and the regulation of everyday life, contrasting a variety of social factors, such as religious orientation and marriage. He found people with low social bonds and disruptions in everyday life are more susceptible to suicide. Even those in fields such as psychology still have a hard time denying the significance of this (see Joiner 2007). His work on rituals is relevant to this book.

A ritual is a set or a series of actions. Recognizing the importance of religion, Durkheim ([1915] 1965b) studied the rituals of the Australian Aborigines with a focus on the structure and the functions of religion. With totems, like a Christian cross, Menorah, or star accompanying a crescent, he contended that values are intangible social facts. In collections of people, they manifest as sacred, tangible items via rituals. Shared cognitive reverence for sacred objects leads to social bonds. This pulls people together and creates social order. Several scholars enhanced this groundbreaking work (see, for example, Douglas 1970; Bell 1992; Rappaport 1999).

Academicians argue rituals exist beyond religion. Civic Crossman rituals include anything from voting to displaying flags (Gusfield and Michalowicz 1984; Mitchell and Allagui 2019). You might throw activities related to mask-wearing in the mix these days. Regardless, Warner (1959) looked at the U.S. holidays and revealed that Memorial Day involves sacred beliefs and dramatic rituals. Putting flowers on a grave on a designated date is notable. We also create national bonds through shared remembrance (see also Warner 1962; Etzioni 2000). Court decisions verify social order, while trials degrade offenders and support government authority (Frank 1936; Garfinkel 1956). At the same time, they probably follow suit with other civic rituals by allowing the powerless an outlet of expression and the ability to create personal connections (for example, see Kertzer 1988; Guttmann 2004; Matthews 2020). As Arnold van Gennep's ([1909]1960) classic scholarship indicates, nonreligious rituals also include "rites of passage" throughout the life course that reflect our transition into new roles, applicable from childhood to retirement (see also Van den Bogaard 2017).

RITUAL AND EVERYDAY LIFE

Sociologist Georg Simmel focused his writings on secret societies. He found rituals within them often reflect rituals pulled from the surrounding social world (Simmel 1906). Think of a university with flags emblazoned with specific colors. It has a president, vice president, senate, and voting procedures modeling government. Wider cultural themes such as bureaucracy and consumerism also influence university culture (Chan and Fisher 2014). Half a century after Simmel, Erving Goffman's (1959) research emerged. It promoted understanding of how people ritualistically present themselves to others. Goffman proposed that in the routines of everyday life, people (actors) attempt to generate favorable impressions for others (audiences). This takes place with the use of dramaturgical tools. We prepare for performances in the backstage, scripts dictate what we say, and costumes shape perceptions (see Edgley 2013). However, people do not always control performances. From a structural perspective, the proper way to act is sometimes predetermined. If a child is riding a merry-go-round, the display of childlike joy is acceptable. The same is not true for an adult. In such an instance, actors separate themselves from roles—also known as role-distancing (Goffman 1961, 1967).

While Goffman was writing on rituals, Peter Berger and Thomas Luckmann (1966) produced a groundbreaking book—*The Social Construction of Reality*. It reflects phenomenology, a field concentrating on human experience and internal awareness. It argues that social reality grounds itself in subjective understandings, and our conception of everyday life is dependent on a three-stage process. First, humans create something. Second, we separate ourselves from what we create. Finally, we come to believe what we created is a thing in and of itself. A constructionist would make the case that time is not an objective reality. It is something created to organize daily life. Mull over leap year or the ritual of moving clocks forward and then back on specific dates. To explain behavior, these two sociologists combined agency and structure. In other words, they believed individual exertion of power and macro-level factors simultaneously carry relevance for the human condition.

Anthony Giddens (1984, 1989) indicates that structure hampers and enables us. Additionally, people are not the only ones with agency. We act, but organizations, social classes, and macro-level entities such as governments do as well. Moreover, individual action represents structure. Norms are an important component of this, but how powerful people influence norms is too. With a current example, people in my town are wearing protective masks more to help fight the increase in COVID-19. This happened after the governor issued an executive order. The order requires mask use when social distancing is not possible (Higgs 2020). However, maybe he felt comfortable issuing the order when more people started wearing masks.

French sociologist Pierre Bourdieu's (1977, 1993) constructionism focuses on habitus and field. These concepts reflect the impact of daily rituals on our thoughts and actions. Habitus concerns taken-for-granted cognitive frameworks, essentially internalized social structure. It develops through ritualized experiences in an interaction area, a field. Every field has implicit and explicit rules. If a person knows the rules and follows them, interaction within a field can occur. Therefore, knowledge of rules is a resource. It is "cultural capital." If a person does not have the cultural capital to fit into a field, others will confront the person with symbolic violence. I experienced a light form of this yesterday. My department had a Webex meeting. I have been having Internet problems. During the meeting, my video feed cut out and the sound became choppy. I could still hear my colleagues, though they thought my connection dropped. It was not fun hearing them laugh about my poor connection and imply I "must still be on dial-up." Let us call this a new postmodern ritual—"tech shaming." Other more serious examples relating to age, gender, race, and social class exist (Leander 2010; Bourdieu 2020). When you do not have the tools to fit into a particular field, you experience hysteresis. This is a mental and social crisis. You can either alter your cultural capital or leave the field. Bourdieu does argue people have the ability to change ritualized characteristics of a field, but he fails to conceptualize how to do it. Therefore, his work more favors the power of structure on the individual, than the back and forth between individual and structure.

Randall Collins created ideas on "interaction ritual chains." These are linked experiences and the essence of human action (Collins 1975, 1981). People do things. Social classes, organizations, institutions, and other larger groups of people do not. Consider Twitter. If only one person used it, would it exist? It takes more than the mere presence of intercommunicative infrastructure for Twitter to keep going, so "macrostructure consists of nothing more than large numbers of micro encounters" (Collins 1987:196). Collins (2014) actually advances Durkheim ([1915] 1965b), who pointed out that something called "collective effervescence" exists when ritualized actions are present. This is tantamount to an emotional buzz emerging in a group where shared routines with deep symbolic meaning reside. Think of "feelings" linked to certain religious practices associated with salvation in Christianity. Is it the Holy Spirit or collective effervescence? I will leave that existential question for you to ponder, but plainly point out that ritual interaction chains involving rhythmic movement and mutual focus produce shared "emotional energy" (Collins 2014; Soeffner [1996] 2018).

To be direct, sociological studies tell us a lot about why it is worthwhile to consider the force of rituals on human behavior. Rituals shape our religious perspectives. However, they also configure our everyday lives. They tell others, and ourselves, who we are or want to be. They create bonds between us, even stimulating emotional connections. They facilitate divisions and keep those in power in control. They provide structure and social order. They let us know when we, and others, are transitioning from one stage of life to another. These predominantly taken-for-granted practices come from a variety of places. Smaller arenas of interaction pull from the rituals that characterize larger cultures. Sometimes micro interaction creates new rituals on its own. Sometimes wider culture and the interaction of a few create rituals simultaneously. With all this in mind, previous work on rituals is lacking. It does not provide a systematic definition of rituals for us to thoroughly break down regularly engaged in symbolic actions. Despite that, one contemporary model of rituals provides promise.

STRUCTURAL RITUALIZATION THEORY

David Knottnerus' (1997; 2016) structural ritualization theory (SRT) underscores the role and explanatory nature of rituals. It is interrelated to other theories and complements previous efforts on rituals too. It maintains that taken-for-granted rituals typify life. This includes the sacred and secular. It also includes socially shared and individual rituals. Given this, the theory argues ritual dynamics occur at different levels. Connected to Giddens' (1984) interplay between the micro and macro, it contends small-scale, day-to-day rituals sway larger social structures. Meanwhile, higher planes of interaction simultaneously affect small-scale, daily rituals. The theory upholds that rituals provide us with cognitive stability. As Goffman (1959) insinuated, SRT says ritual behaviors designate who we are and determine how we symbolically express ourselves. New to the study of rituals, this line of theorizing clearly defines what a ritual is. It also offers us a way to standardize and measure ritualized behavior in a variety of settings and on multiple social levels. It helps us understand exactly how rituals generate social structure and reproduce it. Overall, rituals are "like an engine that drives much social life" (Knottnerus 2016:11).

The theory focuses on *embedded groups* and *ritualized symbolic practices* (RSPs) in its original form. Similar to Bourdieu's (1993) "field" concept, embedded groups are collectives of individuals situated in a larger environment. Domains of interaction characterize encounters for embedded groups. A *domain of interaction* is a "bounded social arena which contains two or more actors" engaged in "face-to-face interaction" (Knottnerus 1997:261). This concept allows us to distinguish multiple regions of social activity. It also provides recognition of multiple domains of interaction, known as a *domain set*. A socially standardized action driven by a person's thought structure is a RSP. This clarifies that rituals involve actions and cognition. This component of the theory involves repetitive forms of behavior with symbolic significance and specific measurable components. When routinely performed, RSPs within a group reflect those of the wider context. In other words, they are part of a cognitive script with the capacity to dictate behavior. Members of embedded groups do not just copy the practices. They express them in ways that may confirm patterns of behavior in the larger environment and then feedback into it. From Berger and Luckmann's (1966) standpoint, reproducing rituals and creating variations that support wider webs of interaction "reifies" social reality. The theory discusses this as *reproductive structural ritualization*. This may or may not be of benefit to a person or group helping to bolster social dynamics characterizing surroundings. For example, research indicates in slave societies, slaves themselves will mirror behaviors supporting status distinctions (see Knottnerus 1999; Knottnerus, Monk, and Jones 1999). Keep in mind, SRT downplays assumptions on human rationality. It asserts that the rituals people engage in can relate to conscious action, but a majority of the time we give little conscious attention to our regular behavior (Knottnerus 1997, 2016; see also Mills 1940).

Reflect on some of the theory's examples as applied to organizations. People in groups with lower levels of status often replicate RSPs from the top-down. This produces and recreates existing structure from the bottom-up. I dropped my nine-year-old daughter off at school this morning after six months of quarantine. She and I have anxiety relating to what will characterize patterns of interaction in pandemic-era public schools. Teachers and administrators all had masks on and appeared to be wearing them appropriately outside of the building during drop-off (domain of interaction). Social distancing existed with employees helping buses unload and directing students into the building after hand sanitizing. I wonder if RSPs will be similar inside of classrooms, in the cafeteria, and on the playground (domain set). Interaction in schools in another country years ago imparts insight.

Administrators in early nineteenth-century France ritually dealt with students forcefully. Children resented this. However, the embedded social world of students showed signs of normalized aggressive relations too. This included informal domains exclusively involving students. In other words, the ritual actions of administrators shaped the relationships in domain sets with students. However, aggressive behavior between students simultaneously reinforced the wider structure (Knottnerus and Van de Poel-Knottnerus 1999; Van de Poel-Knottnerus and Knottnerus 2002). Of course, there are many differences between nineteenth-century French elite schools and the U.S. public schools now. Regardless, SRT suggests the general rule of RSP reproduction will ring true when considering the "new normal" for COVID-19-related protocols.

COMPONENTS OF SRT

Striving for clarity in the study of rituals, there are four components to a RSP—salience, repetitiveness, homologousness, and resources (Knottnerus 1997, 2016). Each plays an essential role in the theory, especially in terms of rituals and interaction dynamics. *Salience* involves the "degree to which a RSP is perceived to be central to an act, action sequence, or bundle of interrelated acts" (Knottnerus 1997:262). This involves the prominence of a specific ritual. Is it noticeable? In the elite school systems previously discussed, staff always exercised strict discipline. They stoically required pupils to defer to their commands. In most circumstances, they did not show any form of sympathy. These ritualized, formal ways of behaving were visible in all domains of interaction. They guided actions in academic and nonacademic settings (Knottnerus and Van de Poel-Knottnerus 1999; Van de Poel-Knottnerus and Knottnerus 2002). With public schools and pandemic-related RSPs, if teachers inflexibly emphasize the importance of cleaning hands, it sets a tone for impressionable children. This line of theorizing leads us to believe that kids will then gear their cognitive structures toward the serious nature of hygiene. In turn, the importance of cleaning your hands becomes paramount for many (see McCabe 2020).

Repetitiveness entails the "relative frequency with which a RSP is performed" (Knottnerus 1997:262). Ritual repetition varies. In a domain of interaction, the presence of an RSP might be rare. In other domains, actors may repeat the RSP often. RSPs may happen several times a day in certain contexts. Again, think of secondary schools in nineteenth-century France. Interaction involving teachers and students happened hundreds of times per day (Knottnerus and Van de Poel-Knottnerus 1999; Van de Poel-Knottnerus and Knottnerus 2002). Since students witnessed a majority of these rigid exchanges, the likelihood of social reproduction related to stern RSPs increased (Knottnerus 1997). Shift to contemporary public schools in the United States and the COVID-19 pandemic. When students see teachers cleaning their hands repetitively, both in and out of the classroom, modeling this behavior is more likely (for more information, see Armstrong 1993).

Homologousness implies a "degree of perceived similarity among different RSPs" (Knottnerus 1997:263). It is possible that multiple rituals exist in a domain set which have a degree of similarity. Greater correspondence with a large number of rituals leads to a greater chance of reproduced behavior. In other words, similar rituals reinforce each other, and this enhances their impact. For example, in nineteenth-century French schools, teachers addressed students in a rigid, coercive manner in the classroom. Throughout the campus, staff members were also distant and formal with students. Administrators such as the principal and vice principal were authoritarian as well. Therefore, classroom rituals and those from the outside represent a domain set with homologousness (Knottnerus and Van de Poel-Knottnerus 1999; Van de Poel-Knottnerus and Knottnerus 2002). It is possible for a person to experience similar rituals outside of a domain set. This increases the power of RSPs (Knottnerus 2016). Therefore, it is a bonus if all of these related rituals take place consistently across several domains of interaction. With the pandemic and public schools, kids may engage in RSPs related to the importance of hygiene when their teachers tell them it is important. Some may be more likely to buy in if they have already been practicing hand cleaning at home or elsewhere. As with vaccinations, they will no doubt resist if their parents and other important people in a variety of domains in their life fail to find value in what experts identify as health-conscious behavior. Implied earlier, if teachers within the school do not require them to follow health precautions in multiple domains, including the classroom, cafeteria, recreation rooms, hallways, and so on, inconsistency may lead to a decrease in students following mandates (see Bart 2020).

Resources are "materials needed to engage in RSPs which are available to actors" (Knottnerus 1997:264). The greater the availability of resources, the more likely an actor will engage in a ritual. Resources might include nonhuman materials such as money, supplies, equipment, clothing, food, time, and proximity to a domain of interaction. Resources also pertain to human traits. Interaction skills, physical strength, and intellect are vital here. Teachers ridiculed students to establish their authority in French nineteenth-century schools (Knottnerus and Van de Poel-Knottnerus 1999; Van de Poel-Knottnerus and Knottnerus 2002). They were able to do so because they had more expertise. As such, resources empower, but also limit, a person's ability to engage in specific rituals (Knottnerus 1997). With the U.S. public schools during the COVID-19 pandemic, the students wearing masks and cleaning their hands may be the ones who have the capacity to understand the importance of hygiene. They may also be students who are used to wearing masks and applying hand sanitizer because parents provided both early in the pandemic (for research reflecting similar themes with American plantations, Spartan youth, and lab settings, see Knottnerus 1999; Knottnerus et al. 1999, Sell et al. 2000; Knottnerus and Berry 2002).

You measure the four components of a RSP with *rank*. This involves "the relative standing of a RSP in terms of its dominance" (Knottnerus 1997:266). A RSP has a high rank if repetitiveness, salience, homologousness, and resources are all present. Moreover, the sum of rank is important. That is to say, a RSP ranks high if repeated often, very visible, has considerable ritual similarity, and people have plenty of resources to take part in it. The original formulation of the theory weighted all four factors equally. It is possible that the value of factors can vary in a modified version of this line of theorizing. Regardless, in general, the higher the rank of a ritual, the more likely the reproduction of it happens. Great equivalency of RSPs in embedded groups and the larger environment represents *structural isomorphism* (Knottnerus 1997, 2016). Let us assume you buy into Centers for Disease Control (CDC) recommendations with the COVID-19 scenarios that this chapter discusses. Schools that find health precautions important have kids who regularly engage in related rituals, have kids that take part in related rituals in all domains of interaction in the schools, and have plenty of sanitizer and masks for kids to use will be more likely to engage in activities safeguarding well-being. Moreover, the kids will probably reproduce rituals related to health precautions in their own informal groups.

RITUAL TRANSMISSION AND TRANSFORMATION

There are social conditions that aid or hinder the transmission of rituals. They include social structure arrangements, power dynamics, form of communication, nature of interaction, and purpose of interaction. Social structure arrangements entail people existing in a wider context. Simply put, you need others to engage in RSPs. If there are no kids in school, there are no new COVID-19 rituals in that physical domain. Social, political, and organizational power relate to people or groups deliberately encouraging certain rituals. Consider the importance of a leader's experience or training. Would a school board comprised of people with medical backgrounds make the same COVID-19 decisions as ones with previous jobs exclusively in coaching (see McCarthy and Zald 2002)? We will return to this idea in a moment. Form of communication includes, but is not limited to, verbal, written, face-to-face, and electronic interaction patterns. It also involves social currents concerning personal and artistic expression, mass media, interaction between institutional figureheads, and legal regulations. Consider it in conjunction with nature of contact, which involves forced interaction—intentional or unintentional. In-person and online classes may have different levels of influence on students during the pandemic. The purpose of interaction involves collective ritual events. Festivals, political rallies, and religious gatherings are especially potent in setting the stage for RSPs, as are ethnic, political, and religious protests (Knottnerus 2016).

Transformation of rituals is important to this form of theorizing too. In line with Durkheim ([1915] 1965b), people use rituals to create new social forms and move away from old ones. This is *transformative structural ritualization* (Knottnerus 2016). Ritual transformation occurs when people experience a range of RSPs. This can happen in one or more domains of interaction. When alternative rituals possess a high rank, people will integrate them into their behaviors. New rituals conflict with old, disrupting structural isomorphism. Then, a synthesis of old and new rituals leads to different behavior (see Dorrien 2020). Old and new rituals could subsist together. Conversely, new rituals might increase their salience, frequency, and similarity. People could start using novel resources to support new rituals. Subsequently, cognitive maps will shift and a new everyday reality will emerge, perhaps in terms of COVID-19 we should say a "new normal" (Knottnerus forthcoming; also see work on personal transformations for drug offenders from Liang, Knottnerus, and Long 2016; Lanier and DeVall 2017).

OTHER DETERMINATIONS OF SRT

Supporting Durkheim ([1915] 1965b) and Collins (2014), this line of theorizing confirms that engaging in rituals with others triggers emotions. This is applicable whether at political-military rallies, in musical events, in online gaming environments, within Internet-based domains of commerce, or on virtual social networks (see Knottnerus 2010, 2014; Meij et al. 2013, Ulsperger and Ulsperger 2017; Simpson, Knottnerus, and Stern 2018; Bartholomew and Mason 2020). This may also apply to health-care precautions in schools. My 4th grader is a strong believer in wearing her mask at school. As the infection rates are reducing, she still insists on wearing it though the norm of mask-wearing at her school has waned. In her case, she tells me that in certain domains, such as the playground, mask-wearing kids are coming together and friendships based on their pandemic-related proclivities. This line of logic strengthens traditional sociological arguments that rituals shape our identities when we engage in specific behaviors with others, but concurrently those same rituals can produce social division (see Guan and Knottnerus 1999; Van de Poel-Knottnerus 2005; Minton and Knottnerus 2008; Mitra and Knottnerus 2004, 2008; Varner and Knottnerus 2010; Sen and Knottnerus 2016).

Suggested previously, aspects of SRT also support the idea the wider context molds smaller forms of interaction. This is true of normative and deviant behavior. For example, work on corporate deviance shows organizations ritualistically use fantasy imagery from popular fictional stories to suspend reality associated with misdeeds (Knottnerus et al. 2006; Ulsperger and Knottnerus 2010). However, the active promotion of alternative forms of RSPs has the possibility of alerting people to dysfunctional rituals and changing abhorrent behavior (see Ulsperger and Knottnerus 2007, 2008, 2009a, 2009b, 2016, 2020; Ulsperger, Knottnerus, and Ulsperger 2014; Carlin and Lokanan 2018).

Focusing on personal rituals, this line of theorizing reveals that stress-based ritualized symbolic events (RSEs) lead to problems. People with certain psychological resources, such as a disposition toward self-blame, may be less prone to act out against others when experiencing stress. Yet others may gear themselves toward blaming others first and subsequently act out violently against them (see Ricciardelli and Memarpour 2016; Ulsperger, Knottnerus, and Ulsperger 2017).

For individuals and groups, SRT divulges four roles that allow for the manipulation of rituals to achieve goals—ritual sponsors, legitimators, entrepreneurs, and enforcers. Sponsors develop and promote rituals within a particular collectivity. This has the ability to create cohesion in environments where individuals come from different backgrounds (Lin, Guan, and Knottnerus 2011; see also Ojo and Nwankwo 2020). For example, a principal might advocate following health precautions to streamline a collective of students with diverse backgrounds and divergent ideas on safe/dangerous behavior. Legitimators validate specific rituals. A school nurse might meet with each class to discuss certain protocols. Entrepreneurs intentionally stimulate certain rituals for their own gain. A coach might dispel the importance of certain safety precautions such as social distancing in order to get his or her athletes active sooner. Enforcers use rituals and their position of power to dominate others (see Knottnerus and LoConto 2003; Guan and Knottnerus 2006; Knottnerus, Van Delinder, and Edwards 2011; Ulsperger et al. 2015; Knottnerus 2016; Delano and Knottnerus 2018; Lewis 2018). Back to schools and COVID-19, will it matter if teachers or students want to take strict health precautions if a school board drops mandates rejecting the recommendations of health professionals?

RECENT ADVANCES

Recent advances of SRT not mentioned yet that closely relate to this book entail disruption, deritualization, and reritualization (DDR). It is appropriate to introduce basic ideas on this classification. The book will elaborate on them later when focusing on the words of family members of the 53, while also applying some other SRT concepts just reviewed.

Disruption is an event or development that interrupts the rituals of people or groups. A variety of things can break down ritualized behaviors at the individual, group, and larger social levels. This includes, but is not limited to, the death of loved ones, marital problems, injury, employment issues, financial problems, retirement, medical problems, and shifts in living conditions. These events, along with others occurring at the macro level, can differ in their strength and deeply influence our everyday lives (Knottnerus 2005, 2016, forthcoming). If you want a more basic example, consider the inability to use a public restroom during the pandemic.

Disruption leads to *deritualization*. It involves the breakdown or loss of previously engaged in RSPs. Remember that thoughts and actions comprise RSPs. Both dissolve with disruption. This happens separately or at the same time. In short, disruption leads to the collapse of life meaning and associated behaviors. Let us go back to public restrooms. If they are not open, what happens to our ability to urinate in communal areas outside of the home? In the early days of the pandemic, my family started venturing out for short road trips. My mother-in-law would sometimes go with us on such trips pre-pandemic. She did not want to go this time noting, "Where will I pee? I'm not going to just do it beside the car!" With disruption, remember that SRT pays attention to resources and their impact on ritualized actions (Knottnerus 2005, 2016, forthcoming). It is possible that people and groups with superior resources experience deritualization quite differently. This in no way is applicable to my mother-in-law, but perhaps an older person during the pandemic opts to stay home instead of going for a drive because he or she has incontinence issues. Consider a different example. Children with divorced parents who have access to emotional support fair better (Kourlis et al. 2013).

It is also likely that people void of certain resources adjust to deritualization better than those with an abundance of them. For example, rituals involving family visits are imperative in elder care. When you ritualistically visit an aged loved one in a facility, it sends a message to staff. They may think, "People outside of the facility care about this person, so I better make sure I provide quality care" (Ulsperger and Knottnerus 2016). During the pandemic, many nursing homes and assisted living complexes followed CDC (2020) advice. They stopped family and friends from visiting. At this point, millions of the aged have not seen people dear to their hearts for close to half a year (Bradfield 2020). For those who had several family members visit regularly, this deritualization is certainly taking a toll. It is diminishing not only social contact and mental health but perhaps treatment some people are receiving too. Counter that with residents who did not have many friends and family visit in the first place.

Reritualization is the recreation of RSPs after disruption and deritualization. You reritualize by engaging in old RSPs or by creating new ones. New rituals have the potential to soften the blow of deritualization. As you reconstitute old rituals, new ones act as a bridge. They create cognitive clarity and lead to plans of action related to the disruption of rituals. This facilitates reassurance and stability. With public restroom closures in the middle of the pandemic, some people turned to a "free urination lifestyle." They bought containers allowing them to urinate on the go, including silicone devices that allow women to pee standing up (Blum 2020). Regardless, new rituals, including transformative ones, help us make it through tough situations while we attempt to restore a sense of normalcy (Knottnerus 2016, forthcoming). For example, elderly people like to shop. As a ritual, shopping on a regular basis at the same stores provides continuity and increases the quality of life. The elderly are a COVID-19 high-risk population. Fortunately, early in the pandemic, many stores decided to give an extra layer of help, offering exclusive shopping times for the aged. Elderly people may be frustrated with the disruption of their regular shopping hours, but at least the health-conscious ones can shop with a higher sense of safety until old shopping rituals continue (Ho and Shirahada 2019; Lowe 2020).

RITUALS AND THE 53 FAMILIES

As you would suspect, all of these sociological ideas on rituals swirling in my head made me want to know more about what happened with LC 373-4. As you may have after reading this book so far, I had many questions. What could a sociological exploration of the event reveal? Could talking to surviving family members yield new insight? Would they be able to give us details on rituals related to their losses? Did certain rituals help them adjust post-disaster? Did certain rituals impede their adjustment? Did family dynamics shape responses? Did surviving family members put on different emotional masks while navigating their situations? Do some people still engage in rituals associated with the absence of their loved one over 50 years later? Have they taken part in those rituals individually, with other family members, or perhaps with people from other families of the 53? With SRT in mind, how often did survivors engage in RSPs associated with the event or the loved ones taken from them? Has the repetitiveness of those rituals decreased? Does the importance of those rituals vary? Is there homologousness, or similarity, with certain rituals? Did certain resources help surviving families move forward? Did a lack of resources play a part in post-disaster adjustment? Did powerful entities facilitate or impede traditional, ritualized outlets of expression for survivors as they progressed through life?

Children of the 53 who have already left us, daughters like my Aunt Linda, never knew the answer to some of these questions. Soon you will, but now

I want to revisit the events leading to the incident. Keeping in mind our knowledge of rituals, let us look at an area of study called the "sociology of disaster." It is going to enhance later discussions on DDR related to surviving family members. It will also give us a fresh perspective on the constructed realities used to explain what happened at LC 373-4 on August 9, 1965.

Chapter 4

Sociology of Disaster

April 3, 2006, marked a first for *Time* magazine. They ran a cover titled "Be Worried, Be Very Worried." They urged us to think about environmental changes, implying it is hard to deny ecological changes via weather shifts (Running 2006). Contemplate hurricanes. Numbers are increasing. Reflect on wildfires. We are seeing more of those too. Perhaps this is due to lightning and temperature increases. However, sources also indicate people cause up to 85 percent of wildfires (Concha-Holmes and Oliver-Smith 2019; Mietkiewicz et al. 2020). Blame for a recent wildfire in California fell on a pyrotechnic device used at a gender reveal party. It led to the annihilation of over 7,000 acres of property (Mansoor 2020).

Wildfires on the West Coast are nothing new. My mother-in-law always dreamed of driving down the Pacific Coast Highway. My family flew into Portland with her in 2017. We rented a car, drove to Cannon Beach, and headed to San Francisco. For outsiders, it was bizarre. Road signs flashed warnings. Blazing grass and forest closed Multnomah Falls. We drove south through California wine country encompassed by burnt land and inciner-ated homes. Several years before, I toured Prince William Sound in Alaska with my wife. We saw whales, otters, and glaciers, but also saw the damage inflicted by the Exxon Valdez oil spill. As a teen, I was an Oakland A's fan and will never forget watching Game 3 of the 1989 World Series when Al Michael's panicked voice said, "I'll tell you what, we're having an earth" fol-lowed by a blank TV screen. An earthquake was shocking to me. Tornadoes, I was familiar with them. I lived in Arkansas and Oklahoma most of my life. A twister ripped through my hometown in January 1999. I recollect looking out Odean's front window and seeing the path the tornado cut through her neighborhood and my old school.

This chapter marks a strong return to our discussion of Launch Complex (LC) 373-4. It helps us make better sense of what a disaster is. It distinguishes natural and technological disasters, and areas in-between. It reviews sociological-related studies, introducing fundamental findings related to technological disasters. It also discusses previously existing literature on structural ritualization theory (SRT) and disasters.

RESEARCH AND DEFINITIONS OF DISASTER

Disaster research began in the late 1940s, at the same time the U.S. military cogitated the social effects of dropping an A-bomb. The government wanted information on what survivors would do. The closest "real-world" scenario mirroring atomic aftermath was a natural disaster. Scholars obtained government funding and started to concentrate on disasters (see Quarantelli 1954, 1960; Fritz 1961; Dynes 1970). A research group emerged through the National Academy of Sciences. By 1963, the Disaster Research Center (DRC) at the Ohio State University appeared, now housed at the University of Delaware. With affiliated offices around the country, it remains a leading entity for disaster studies (Webb 2007).

Analysts define disasters as dramatic events resulting in physical damage, social disruption, and unexpected loss of life (Webb 2018). A single disaster can kill a few dozen or millions and cause millions of dollars in damage (Tierney 2019). Besides hurricanes, natural disasters include fires, storms, droughts, and tsunamis. Prior to the emergence of the DRC, natural disasters were the only kind researchers discussed. They gave some attention to political unrest and issues involving war, but early work narrowed on sudden on-set events, known as "acts of God." Findings, related to casualties, infrastructure damage, and financial loss, demonstrated that communities often emerge stronger economically and socially after natural disasters. Individuals undergo short-lived psychological stress, with levels dependent on the intensity of the incident and pre-event mental health status. One of the important things to emerge from this early research was the establishment of disaster phases, including preparedness, response, recovery, and mitigation (Drabek 1986; Gill and Ritchie 2018).

Some disasters are human-made. Note the Great Chicago Fire, the sinking of the Titanic, and space exploration tragedies (Guiberson, 2010). I live a couple of miles from a nuclear power plant. A few years ago, a temporary crane was removing a "component" weighing 525 tons when the crane collapsed. The load dropped through the floor of the turbine building (Lockbaum 2018). Vibrations disconnected one reactor from the power grid. Backup generators lost functionality because of split cables. The irradiated fuel in the reactor core lost cooling function and vibrations damaged fire suppression systems. The shaking also broke a water pipe that flooded the facility, prompting an electrical explosion. Water from a nearby lake prevented a meltdown. One person died, and others had injuries (Sanchez 2013). This event does not qualify as a disaster, but reveals that human behavior is critical to think about with risky laden technology (Lockbaum 2018), something disaster analysts came to realize several decades ago.

In the 1970s, significant events involving human cause caught the eye of disaster researchers. This includes the Buffalo Creek flood that ravaged 16 communities and killed 125 people, the discovery of toxic contamination of land near the Hooker Chemical company in Niagara Falls, New York, and the Three Mile Island nuclear reactor meltdown in Middletown, Pennsylvania (Gill and Ritchie 2018). In the 1980s and into the early 1990s, these technological-related events triggered a scholarly reorientation toward technological disaster. Researchers targeted the occasions just mentioned, but also looked into the long-lasting underground coalmine fires in Pennsylvania (Couch and Kroll-Smith 1985), a chemical release in India that killed an estimated 15,000 (Shrivastava 1987), and toxic contamination in the state of New Jersey (Edelstein 2002, 2004). Studies started on the Chernobyl Nuclear Power Plant core reactor explosion (Giddens 1990, 1991), a train derailment and toxic spill in Louisiana (Gill and Picou 1991), and the notorious Exxon Valdez oil spill in Alaska (Gill 1994).

Scholars established that different forms of disasters exist, but there was still ambiguity. They soon asked questions like, "Human behavior leads to technological disaster, but can it lead to natural disaster too?" Sociologist Robert Brym (2009) goes so far as to say there is a "myth of natural disasters," with many being caused by, if not broadened due to, complex human factors, including environmental shifts. In a recent issue of the journal *Natural Disaster*, Adam Straub's (2021) article starts with the title, "Natural Disasters Don't Kill People, Governments Kill People." Moreover, natural disasters can escalate due to technological breakdown and human behavior combined. Showalter and Myers (1994) frame these situations as natural-technological disasters, using the term "natech." Incidents such as the Fukushima Daiichi nuclear meltdown of 2011 fit here. With it, an earthquake off the coast of Japan led to a tsunami, which subsequently led to the power plant's problems. Hurricane Katrina is noteworthy too (Gill and Ritchie 2018).

Katrina raged through the Gulf of Mexico hitting New Orleans on August 29, 2005. It reduced its ferocity, moving from a Category 5 to a Category 3, after hitting the tip of Florida. Still, Katrina caused nearly 2,000 deaths and over $125 billion in damage. Poorly designed levees were void of refurbishing. Thousands found themselves trapped. New Orleans mayor Ray Nagan failed to issue a mandatory evacuation. The Secretary of the Department of

Homeland Security flew to a conference in Atlanta. New Orleans was not a pressing priority. Louisiana's transportation secretary did not have plans to secure safety for nursing home residents and people in hospitals. The New Orleans Police Department only had three small boats with no extra fuel. Layers of bureaucracy prevented people in charge from making a difference and natural, technological, and social factors led to the hurricane's devastation (Brym 2009; Freudenburg et al. 2009; Pardee 2014; Tierney 2019). Keeping technological dynamics in mind, consider some research on vulnerable populations, normal accidents and recreancy, the darkside of organizations, secondary trauma, and some other cultural components of disasters. Some of it overlaps, but I will do my best to distinguish it.

VULNERABLE POPULATIONS

Communities with few resources have a harder time with disaster response (see Couch and Kroll-Smith 1985, 1992; Blaikie and Brookfield 1987; Cuny 1994). Social capital is important. People with quality bonds and reciprocal relationships show more resilience with disaster recovery (Ritchie and Gill 2007; Aldrich 2012). People with less status, power, and wealth can be more vulnerable. Some disaster research argues marginalized people receive fewer benefits compared to people who already have resources. This can include children, older adults, and people with disabilities, and minorities, who have significant problems recovering from disasters (Bolin and Stanford 1998; Fothergill, Maestas, and Darlington 1999; Bolin and Kurtz 2018; Kroll-Smith 2018; Jerolleman 2019). Poor women are in the worst position (Enarson and Morrow 1998; Fothergill and Peek 2004; Pardee 2014; Mamun et al. 2019).

With the LC 373-4 disaster, think of the 53 families left behind, especially the women. One crew commander describes driving through the places widows called home stating, "The houses are run down, many abandoned and some gutted. Through El Paso, past Romance, and in Rose Bud, behind a white clapboard church a possum lies dead near the road" (Womack 1997:111-112). Thinking about that marsupial and an outside force taking his life out of nowhere, I think about the 53 and their families. Like roadkill, did the government and politicians callously push the families of the dead out of the way with ease? The silos their loved ones worked in provided so much to their communities. They stimulated economic development for local businesses. They helped raise the state's influence, being an intricate part of the Little Rock Air Force Base's (AFB) functioning. They reinforced power for local politicians. They helped the U.S. citizens feel safe and secure. One year after the disaster, attorneys for some families reached a $4 million settlement. They asked for $38.4 million. Math tells us, without considering attorney fees and other legal expenses, each family did not receive much. On top of that, the private companies involved only paid 5 percent of the settlement, around $200,000 (LaGrossa 1980). That is an interesting figure considering a rep said post-disaster "the civilian outfit" controlled "the entire area from the access portal through the silo" (Arkansas Gazette 1965a:9A). There is more on this point to come.

NORMAL ACCIDENTS AND RECREANCY

Perrow (1984) believes we live in a world progressively characterized by organizations and "normal accidents." He studied the Three Mile Island reactor meltdown, problems with design, equipment, procedures, and supplies. He contends operator error was central, and up to 80 percent of all accidents occur because of it. The human mind is not a computer, so blunders are inevitable. People can only process so much information in certain organizational contexts. Some may process it better, or perhaps they just process it differently. Dealing with system irregularity, humans have to do their best when making spontaneous judgments to flip a switch or warn others of danger in risky, chaotic situations. With the Three Mile Island nuclear meltdown, Nuclear Regulatory Commission representatives initially told only pregnant women and pre-school children close to the facility to evacuate. Contradictory information released later led to over 140,000 people hurriedly leaving the area under a veil of confusion (Baum, Fleming, and Singer 1982). With COVID-19, think, "You don't need a mask," "You need a mask," or "You only need a mask in certain situations." It might be worth commenting that in such situations, there is always an instinct for organizational leaders to blame others (Schlosser 2013; Mahaffey 2014). This relates to recreancy.

Freudenburg (2000:116) defines recreancy as "the failure of experts or specialized organizations to execute properly responsibilities to the broader collectivity with which they have been implicitly or explicitly entrusted." Using classic Durkheim and Weber's (1946) ideas on unintended consequences of bureaucracy, the basic point is that we live in a world of interdependence and put great confidence in organizations to look out for us. This includes the government and business sectors. Reflecting the existence of "corrosive communities," the growing objectification of citizens and the actions of powerful entities have increased public distrust, uncertainty, and fear (Freudenburg and Jones 1991). To reduce concern, organizations ritualistically create impressions of ethical actions, controllability, and safety as related to economic, social, and environmental consequences (Giddens 1991; Beck 1992; Kroll-Smith and Couch 1993; Ritchie, Gill, and Farnham 2013). With the normality of accidents in a highly complex, technological world managed by fallible humans, recreancy is apparent (for a specific example see Baum et al. 1982). With the case of the 53, it is glaring on many levels. Contractors and the government expected high levels of public trust ahead of the incident but shamefully took minimal responsibility afterward, even with clear missteps attributed to them.

Families certainly expected their sons, husbands, and fathers would receive superior training when going into a military facility to complete upgrades. With LC 373-4 safety training, civilian workers only had to watch a video titled *You and the Titan II*. Supervisors gave the men a mask to use as an air filter if needed, masks that did not offer protection from fire fumes. They also told them to take the supply elevator to get out of the silo quickly if there was an emergency (Stumpf 2000; Schlosser 2013). After the incident, the government claimed a welder started a fire, sometimes described as an explosion, leading to the 53 deaths. Did he have adequate training related to safety protocols in such a risky situation? Regardless, one man who escaped the disaster disputes the claim that a welder triggered an explosion, or that one even occurred at all. In one source, his counter-claim reveals, "I have heard and read accounts that said the fire was caused when a flame from a welder's torch touched a nearby hose and ignited hydraulic fluid. There was no one welding down there. There was no explosion." He also contends that security at the facility was "lax" on the day of the mishap, with guards playing gin (Hicks 2000).

The U.S. Air Force (USAF) pictures shown after the accident show a welding machine at ground level with lines dropping to Level 3 and then looping up to Level 2. They also show a welding rod in the area, along with a welding mask and helmet (Strang 1967). The survivor contends wires shorted out and started a fire. The military previously reported that hydraulic fluid used at missile sites was not flammable (Conine 2015:423). Post-disaster, one USAF report implied the military erroneously used National Fire Protection Association standards and should have realized "under certain conditions" the hydraulic oil used was flammable (Strang 1967:305). Retired USAF Col. Jimmie Gray, a former curator for the Jacksonville Museum of Military History, disagrees. He says the USAF report was definitively conclusive that the welder was at fault. In one source, he says, "The hydraulic fluid went into his lungs and killed him" (Roberts 2015:10A). Interestingly, the other worker who made it out said there was no noise before he evacuated. He just knew to get out because of the smoke (LaGrossa 1980). Reflecting "normal accident" foundations, Conine (2015:424) contends, "Incompatible safety conditions created by scheduling multiple, simultaneous tasks" and "several different teams and the individuals scattered throughout the silo" were culprits investigators did not focus on enough.

In terms of normal accidents, contemplate engaging in the same task repeatedly. You become cognitively satiated, and what you are doing loses meaning. In terms of SRT, we might say meaningful RSPs like safety checks can become routine and insignificant. Technological disasters, whether marine accidents, air traffic catastrophes, or nuclear meltdowns, result from a series of errors, not just one person. Moreover, "tight coupling" exists. One mistake influences other processes in an interaction chain. This is especially true if lines of action are complex and not linear (Perrow 1984).

Related to Titan II sites, Missile Commander John Womack (1997) provides insight on how disorganized launch complexes were while citizens nearby assumed they were finely tuned military compounds. He kept diaries on his service when working at sites in Arkansas. He fondly remembers camping not far from my current house on Petit Jean Mountain. Some of his memories about Titan II facilities are not so warm. People cycled in and out of all launch complexes, especially in the beginning of the program. He sometimes "felt out of place" and without control having so many "civilians running around" (Womack 1997:11). He wondered if they even knew enough about the facilities to be inside of them. SRT is relevant. Lack of environmental knowledge is a resource void that can adversely influence behavior (Knottnerus 2016). As Kearl (1989) contends, contracted workers' deaths often occur around risk-based technology when people are "attempting to deal with abnormal tasks," especially when rushed.

With LC 373-4, when recovering the bodies, rescuers found cigarettes and lighters in worker pockets, a violation of policy. Workers failed to have hand tools tied to their bodies or surrounding support beams, something that would prove detrimental at the Damascus facility years later (Anthony 2018; Guerrieri 2020). Even if workers knew the purpose of everything in the launch bay, previous issues created an inadequate work environment. One report shows that heavy pipes containing hydraulic lines on Level 2 did not have the proper support with "unusual bending," leaving lines hanging "lower than the desired position" (Group Report 1965:1). In terms of the hydraulic line that helped spark the fire on Level 2, Penson (2020) points out that the USAF reports have so much conflicting information that it is hard to tell which lines workers were purging when the disaster started. Workers left deadbolts extended on blast doors so they could freely move through them. They propped one of the heavy doors open with a bungee cord. Knowing some climbed down the emergency ladder toward the bottom of the silo when the disaster started, had anyone ever cemented in their minds the facility layout and location of exits? One person who escaped explained that the civilians working in the silo "knew it was dangerous business" and "had masks and emergency equipment," but he also detailed that no one ever cared to wear them (Arkansas Gazette 1965a; 1965c:9A; Group Report 1965).

Just three years before, Edward Robles (1962), Lead Systems Engineer for the USAF, told an audience that worker safety around ballistic missiles ranked low on lists of concern, if it even ranked at all. Unfortunately, for the 53, the trend sustained itself. As a crew commander, Womack (1997) also had worried it was too hard to tell who the boss was with so many construction workers, carpenters, painters, electricians, and pipefitters around. Once when at site LC 374-1, he showed up to a "swarm" of people fighting about who could give orders. He gained control after some serious arguing and decided to suggest that headquarters remove the crew commander he relieved from duty. With the LC 373-4 disaster, a post-incident report shows the military failed to interview all civilian workers. Apparently, it was "difficult to identify which personnel were present when the accident occurred" (Group Report 1965:1).

Besides chain of command confusion, there was a constant focus on warnings. Maintenance lights set off alarms for no reason. At some facilities, snakes crawled across transformers and shorted them out. In Arkansas, during some stretches, vapor-detection warning lights remained on 25 percent of the time. Often, warning alarms went off for no apparent reason. Womack remembers opening a silo door for maintenance and oxidizer pressure warnings occurring for nearly 10 hours. He kept calling Little Rock AFB to tell them. They had his crew leave the door open. They continued to work. The term "alert" still bothers him. He notes, "Other than the fact that you are always ready to launch the missile, the term 'alert' seems a fantastic misnomer. The missile is on alert, but the crew members are usually somewhere between boredom and exhaustion" (Womack 1997:21). Was this the case on August 9, 1965?

THE DARK SIDE OF ORGANIZATIONS

Diane Vaughan (2016) says focusing solely on human error is the easy way out. Her work details "the darkside of organizations." It describes mistakes due to organizational divisions, characterized by departmental secrecy and complex relationships. It details misconduct, which happens when cognitive frameworks promote rule violations to gain an advantage over competing organizations. It explains that disasters occur with an overabundance of complex regulations. Simply put, organizations drift away from formal, required lines of action toward practical behaviors that produce better results (for a discussion of how disasters push organizational members toward informal coalitions, see Vollmer 2013). There is often pressure to complete tasks too quickly. People feel pressure to remain silent when evidence shows imminent danger (see also Janis 1972). NASA is relevant.

Vaughan (1992, 2016) tells us the Challenger space shuttle did not explode in January 1986 because of human error. Human "processes" were at play. Cognitive frames of acceptable risk emerged within NASA. The O-ring, which seals a different valve point off during ignition, was a safety issue. In fact, it had been since the late 1970s. Administrators ritualistically let launches occur while suppressing troubling signs. Some employees even stigmatized others who brought up O-rings. O-rings had not caused a major shuttle disaster before, so the logic was they would probably not ever cause one (for subculture responses to complacency and risk, see Drabek 2013). Besides that, the Challenger launch was highly publicized due to public school teacher Christa McAuliffe's involvement. She was going to teach from space, and NASA was eager to launch because they had delayed so many times, especially on the verge of President Reagan's State of the Union.

Back to the 53, Conine (2015) says the gun barrel in Titan II launch complexes only had a single emergency ladder. Escaping during a disaster was impossible for more than a few. Maybe it was a design flaw or something personnel felt uncomfortable questioning. Regardless, many of the 53 were stuck trying to climb the ladder in August 1965. Post-disaster, USAF regulations limited the number of people allowed in the silo area. The final USAF report clearly indicates the lighting system should have been stronger. Then, it would have penetrated smoke and allowed workers a better chance at escape. As with the classic studies on flooding, design flaws were an issue. For example, research shows the dam preventing water flow in the Buffalo Creek incident was improperly constructed (Erikson 1976).

With the silo, the collimator room was located on one side of the silo on Level 2 (see figure 4.1). Its purpose was to provide cooling to part of the guidance system. On other levels, workers could freely move around in a complete circle when navigating platforms. Think of walking around a track with nothing in your way. You end where you started. Now, reference the Level 2 layout at the beginning of this book. When the fire broke out in Quadrant III, it trapped workers in Quadrant I and IV. They could not move clockwise to the cableway. The only choice was to go through the fire or try the escape ladder. The wall to the collimator room was impenetrable. After the disaster, the USAF installed kick-out panels on the collimator wall to guarantee two exit paths if a situation similar to LC 373-4 occurred. Later, engineers decided to remove collimator rooms completely (Strang 1967; Stumpf 2000; Morris 2020). Like the blast doors, there was confusion over the missile door above the launch bay. Officials told reporters post-disaster that cutting the electrical power prevented the door from opening. They also told them that the lid was undergoing modifications preventing operators from lifting it. Later one captain reported, "All facts considered" the crew simply "did not wish to open it" (Arkansas Gazette 1965a:9A).

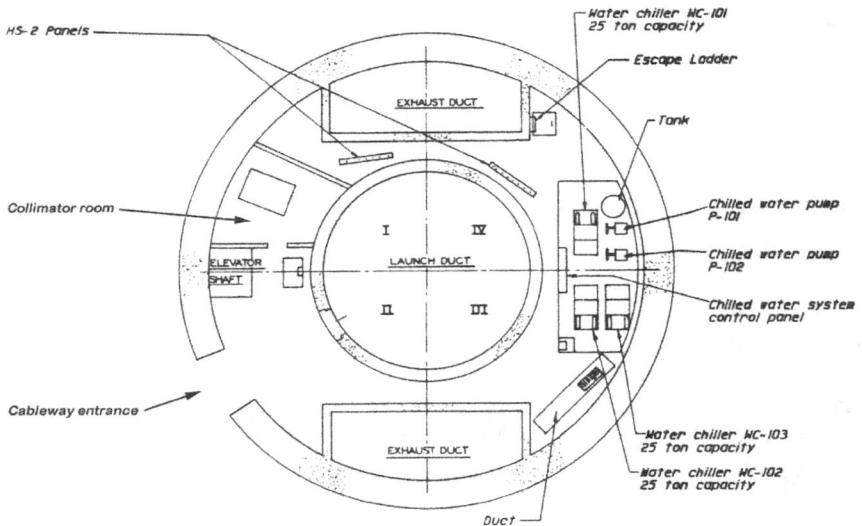

Figure 4.1 Level 2 Layout. *Source:* Illustration modified, provided, and approved for use by Chuck Penson.

With NASA, Lee Clarke (1999) says that organizations know disaster is inevitable and a lot of preparation done is for outsiders needing reassurance. Providing scary details on potential disasters breaks the safety facade. Related to recreancy and the need to build public trust, he calls written procedures for response and informational brochures for the public "fantasy documents." Goffman (1959) would be proud (see also Easthope 2018). As stated earlier, personnel at launch complexes took safety manuals and launch procedures seriously. Conine (2015:387) indicates, "In that setting, the weapon system's readiness, and the performance of its ground crews were pushed to an extreme in an environment that was demanding, stressful and sometimes hazardous." The public knew this but still demanded more safety measures. Note that some theorize that fantasy documents are less likely to exist in high-reliability organizations dealing with nuclear power (Roberts and Bea 2001).

Fantasy documents sometimes became fantasy rhetoric. In January of 1978, Van Buren County LC 374-7 had a problem. The USAF evacuated 20 local families and 400 students from a nearby school. No human deaths occurred, but several farm animals met their fate (LaGrossa 1980). The community thought the worst might be behind them. However, in October, oil-based hydraulic fluid was all over the missile. Water would not clean it, so the workers used Freon to scrub it. They let their dirty towels fall to the silo floor and began feeling dizzy after the rags piled up below. A sergeant volunteered to retrieve them while holding his breath. He could not resist inhaling after reaching the bottom, breathed in the Freon, and immediately vomited. Another sergeant made his way toward the towels, also got sick, and headed for the control center. He never made it. He collapsed in the equipment room and died at the Little Rock AFB medical center a short time later. A subsequent report blamed the men, but also showed that the air circulation system was not cycling enough fresh oxygen into the silo (Anthony 2018).

The resulting investigation also indicated several site deficiencies at the Damascus facility. People in the area were on edge, especially with memories of what happened to the 53 just a short distance away. A movement demanding a warning system to notify civilians of leaks emerged. Representatives from Little Rock AFB had a meeting in Bee Branch. They told everyone the leaks from launch complexes were unlikely and facilities were safe. Arkansas senator Dale Bumpers concurred. In October of 1979, Bumpers said that proposed Armed Services Committee hearings on the safety of Titan II facilities were unnecessary. Though he did push for warning sirens at Titan II complexes, he was disappointed that Senator Bob Dole of Kansas supported the hearings. According to Bumpers, Dole "had gone too far on this thing" (LaGrossa 1980:1B). Dole disagreed. He later cosponsored a bill with Arkansas senator David Pryor asking for warning sirens so the public would have knowledge of site issues. Constituents were frustrated that the USAF had done nothing and a slew of calls hit senator offices. Pryor reached out to the military. The then commander of the 308th Strategic Missile Wing told Pryor that at least nine propellant leaks occurred at Titan II sites in Arkansas the previous year. Dole was concerned with a string of nuclear capable B-52 bomber fires. He also found what happened at LC 533-7 near Rock, Kansas, in August of 1978 troubling (Schlosser 2013).

A new missile was coming to LC 533-7 and a Propellant Transfer System team was filling oxidizer tanks. They embraced fellow soldiers who called them a special "category of crazy" for wanting to work with explosives. They lived up to their "bad boy" moniker in this case. However, it was because something bad happened. The quick disconnect failed when they pulled the transfer line away from the oxidizer tank. You will never guess what was jamming it—a loose O-ring left in the valve. Red vapor filled the facility. Two technicians disregarded orders to climb the emergency ladder and evacuate topside. Instead, they opened a blast door and headed down the cableway to the control center. The team chief rushed to the lead and tried to seal it off with his hand. His safety suit had a design flaw and the fumes rushed inside of it leading to his death. Another team member died a week later in the hospital. Do you have any clue as to where the blame laid in the investigation report that followed? It said the accident was the fault of the transfer team because they failed to follow procedures (Conine 2015).

One year later in Arkansas, LC 373-3 had a problem. The crew commander was checking the emergency lights when a rod fell and initiated a fire in a wire panel. The temperature increase in the launch bay had the missile moments from exploding. Personnel extinguished it in time. No one told anyone in nearby Heber Springs. Pryor pushed Strategic Air Command (SAC) harder than ever. They did not want warning systems. This solidified that facilities were dangerous. They put him off with promises of an extensive study. Then, they used him for good press. He toured facilities to calm voters, only later admitting he had no idea what he was seeing. While this farce took place, the USAF hid that over 70 percent of launch complexes in the state had faulty oxidizer gas sensors. In late 1979, Pryor issued a statement asserting that he trusted workers at each site 100 percent. He had to know he was blowing just as much smoke as some of the missiles in his state. On one tour, a technician told him it was hard to get engineers to solve new problems because they did not have enough time to fix old ones (Anthony 2018). Near Damascus, LC 374-7 was not finished wreaking havoc. The USAF put a new missile in the silo. The serial number was 62-0006, the same missile in LC 373-4 when the 53 died (Dillard 2019). This is eerie since missile matches with launch complexes were random. Secretary of State Henry Kissinger wanted to retire Titan IIs in the previous decade. Funding to maintain them reduced. Perhaps this related to the recycling of structures previously witnessing misfortune. Regardless, leaks were common from 1975 onward (Womack 1997; Anthony 2018).

In mid-September of 1980, workers were using a new substance to seal a manhole at 374-7. They removed an oxidizer tank during the process and reloaded it with fluid after putting it back in place. Pressure dropped in the tank a few times over the next couple of days and the workers returned to top it off on September 18. Removing the vent pressure cap, a socket weighing nearly 6 pounds fell between the missile and a work platform. It hit a thrust mount ring 80 feet below and shot toward a fuel tank. The tank was punctured and liquid shot out immediately turning into toxic gas. Contaminants within the gun barrel caught fire, warning lights flashed, and an electric horn screamed into the flames (Guerrieri 2020).

The fuel tank was leaking 10 gallons of propellant per minute. Soldiers communicated with superiors at Little Rock AFB and requested to evacuate. Request denied. After an hour, the water supply to put out fires ran out. The crew commander could have ordered the activation of purge fans to alleviate the heat buildup in the launch duct. A recent safety upgrade prevented the fans from working if the system showed a fire. Approximately 30 minutes later, the Wing Commander ordered an evacuation. No one was sure what to do (Schlosser 2013). Around 6½ hours later, SAC personnel decided technicians should put on the special gear and make their way to the launch center to flip the purge fan switch after disabling the installed safeguard. As they made their way underground, their portable hazardous vapor detector was off the charts. They turned back. When they made it topside, the voices of 53 souls echoed through the edge of the Ozarks as the missile exploded. One of the technicians who made it out just in time died in the hospital from inhaling toxic fumes. Some believe the warhead caught up with the silo and the door bounced off. Supposedly uncompromised, it landed nearby (Conine 2015; McCoy 2019).

SECONDARY TRAUMA

In examining the Buffalo Creek flood, Erickson (1976) found that with technological disasters "secondary trauma" emerges. Part of this concerns a lost sense of communality. Levin's (1982) work on chemical exposure of citizens of Niagara Falls clarifies that survivors will often have conflict with each other, sometimes publicly, about whether the event caused great harm (a maximalist position) or no harm at all (a minimalist position). Moreover, note that survivors of natural disasters experience "lifestyle" changes. This means disruptions influence their everyday taken-for-granted lives temporarily, on more of a perfunctory level. Survivors of technological disaster experience "lifescape" change (Edelstein 2002, 2004). In other words, domains of interaction shift as preexisting ritualized behavior changes. Five dimensions of lifescape change exist. Risk-based behavior replaces typical actions. Local environments, or external domains of interaction, represent uncertainty. As with recreancy, trust in institutions diminishes. Everyday feelings of powerlessness and isolation become significant. Finally, home transitions from a safe environment to a place of danger.

Backing up other research looking at the mental health implications of disaster (Norris, Friedman, and Watson 2002), research on the Exxon Valdez event shows technological disaster survivors have chronic psychological turmoil by way of feelings of stress, guilt, isolation, and loss of control. It also reveals survivors have elevated feelings of helplessness, levels of avoidance as a coping mechanism, illicit drug abuse, alcohol use, and domestic violence. Children specifically experience regressive behavior, panic attacks related to fear of exclusion, exaggerated startle reactions, nightmares, delinquency, poor academic performance, social withdrawal, depression, and aggressive defiance coupled with justifications based on traumatic experiences. Research also notes risk-based sexual behaviors along with hesitance to engage in new experiences and go new places. Children who traumatically lose a parent in a disaster are also more likely to have an early shattered image of surviving parents. Normally people realize their parents' limits incrementally through life, but with disasters they see them break to extreme levels of stress (see Impact Assessment Inc. 1990, 1998; Roden et al. 1992; Weisaeth 1994; Endter-Wada 1993; Lubit and Eth 2003; Picou and Martin 2007; Ritchie 2012).

A follow-up study on Buffalo Creek shows that nearly 15 years after the flooding, some people still had major depression, anxiety disorders, and symptoms of posttraumatic stress disorder (Green et al. 1990). As with the Livingston, Louisiana, train derailment, survivors sometimes want to move from the community where the event took place but feel strain because of the economic support and social networks they will leave behind (Gill and Picou 1991; Gill, Ritchie, and Picou 2016). For those who stay, they integrate the disaster they experienced into their sense of self. Consider people from New Orleans who, sometimes with a sense of pride, identify with hurricanes and Alaskans who do the same with the Valdez oil spill (see Wenger and Weller 1973; Kroll-Smith, Baxter, and Jenkins 2015; Gill, Ritchie, and Picou 2016). Knowing Arkansans as "tornado people," I can relate.

Some secondary trauma comes from survivors managing insufficient government responses and ensuing litigation (Couch and Kroll-Smith 1992; Erikson 1994). This book discusses insufficient government responses in other places, in addition to legal issues. However, here it is worth introducing the litigious aspects of LC 373-4. They directly relate to the previously mentioned idea of recreancy, especially in terms of legal representation, trust, financial rectitude, and organizational responsibility.

With the 53, local attorneys definitely gave it a go trying to build client lists with families from White County and surrounding areas. Some of their names sound like they came from a John Grisham novel or someone emblazoned them on a liquor bottle. Consider "Red Morgan" and "Mutt Jones." Others from more populated areas had more tame monikers, such as "Eugene Matthews." However, as just mentioned, powerful, well-known attorneys took control of several families and their decisions. Ignoring any conflicts of interest, men with previous high-level positions in government, military connections, and relationships with pro-missile presidents discussed early in this book decided it was best for them to represent the less fortunate who lost their loved ones at LC 373-4. Of note, consider Sid McMath. He was a man Arkansas senator David Pryor (2003) once said challenged "private interests" and fought for the "little guy." McMath's firm represented nearly half of the surviving families (McMath 2003).

For the case, McMath utilized his law partner and longtime friend Henry Woods, who was a former FBI agent, McMath's former campaign manager, and eventual U.S. District Court judge. Sid was the 34th Governor of Arkansas, ending his term around a decade before the silo disaster. Born near Magnolia, a town I once lived in, the charismatic former marine and prosecutor turned to practicing law after a failed third run for governor (Lester

1976). With roots in the Old South, economic depression, and hard times, he championed himself as an advocate for the people. He represented litigants fighting big named companies like General Motors and ALCOA. I bought a copy of his self-authored book and reading through it found a card with his autograph. I had mixed feelings when finding it. He appeared to be an advocate for equality and justice, but my research on the aftermath of the disaster did not leave me with the same high opinion McMath had of himself. His autobiography has a section on "cases that made a difference." There is one page focusing on LC 373-4, right at the end of the book in Appendix XV. There, I start to question his dedication to the case and details surrounding it. He erroneously identifies one of the contractors, Peter Kiewit and Sons, as "Peter Klewit and Company." Providing little to no details, he goes on to explain that the trial was called off right before it started, though he prepared extensively. Then, as if knowing someone would question his actions related to the lawsuit someday, he states, "Recovery of compensation for a client does not necessarily resolve the client's economic woes" (McMath 2003:460). In an odd way to wrap up his life story, he dedicates the rest of his book to blaming families for how they spend their settlement money. He says, even though widows are "particularly vulnerable to con men, charlatans, and sometimes relatives" looking out for their self-interest, someone's "lawyer does not, cannot, must not, handle the client's money or advise the client as to how the money should be spent" (see McMath 2003:461). Perhaps he was retroactively addressing complaints received from families, individually and collectively, experiencing some form of secondary trauma.

CULTURAL COMPONENTS

Wisner (2019) recently called for more attention to individuals living around high-risk technology. Considering cultural components, he points out vulnerable populations have little control when power players determine to control their spaces and resources (see also Castree et al. 2014). How do people living in risky landscapes manage fear? We know people push against risky technology in their own backyards, but once it is there, how do they manage their perceptions of it? In terms of recreancy, powerful entities use fantasy documents to help craft narratives of safety, but what else happens? Do vulnerable citizens collaborate in the development of response procedures before or after disasters? With natural disasters, it seems like they are more prone to, but with technological disasters, the standardized steps of preparedness, response, recovery, and mitigation do not apply the same (Gill and Ritchie 2018). Why do public officials and private businesses with stakes in local spaces not follow the natural disaster model? Perhaps, as Green (1996) implies, powerful entities directing risky technology engage in actions along a "continuum of deliberateness," somewhere close to purposeful acts of harm directed toward others for personal and organizational gain. They do not want to get too close to the public, so they distance from them. They objectify them. It makes dealing with recreancy factors much easier to handle. With Titan IIs in Arkansas and Kansas, one study deals with this.

Anthony's (2018) work is on Titan II hazards and disclosure of safety issues. It also gives a nod to environmental consequences. It tells us previous scholars present excellent examinations of engineering. However, they dismiss cultural factors. For example, Stumpf (2000:215) seemingly brags to us, "human error was the cause" of Titan II fatalities because "missiles, subsystems, and launch complexes" did not have "hidden flaws." Once more, the position of this chapter is that it is not just a single person making one mistake that culminates in disaster. It is everything that humans touch in the process of creating, managing, and operating technologically driven devices. Anthony (2018) argues that the government knowingly put people at risk, blindly assuring them a high level of protection. They also provided false evidence of safety and a false sense of security. Supporting Vaughan's (2016) conclusion on pressure to complete projects, he says the arms race related to a "missile gap" that led to the rushed production of Titan IIs. Surprisingly, the USAF did not heed warnings from earlier incidents. They could have improved safety based on them. On May 24, 1962, a blocked vent at the Chico, California, complex caused an explosion damaging the inner silo. No workers were inside, so apparently, the military did not believe an adequate follow-up investigation was relevant. Modification based on that accident might have saved the 53.

Again reflecting earlier points on recreancy, Anthony (2018:19) contends putting everything on the welder in the LC 373-4 disaster kept "public opinion unchanged." If it was just an issue with one person, intercontinental ballistic missiles (ICBMs) could stay near civilians. Even if the welder was at fault, before civilians started working in the facility, hydraulic lines haphazardly draped over piping. Emergency fire extinguishers were missing. Was that the welder's fault? The military glossed over the accident report of 26 other factors contributing to the event. They included previously mentioned ventilation issues but also improperly designed silo roofs, an absence of elevators that could transport more than six people, poorly positioned exits, and first responders with little knowledge of silo layouts. An investigative report given to the Department of Defense did not even include these details (John McClellan Papers 1965). In 1965, McDonald's was 10 years into its existence with over 100 million hamburgers sold. The military was modeling their processes. This was a fast-food report (see Ritzer 2011). Like the building of silos, the goal was speed rather than quality. Anthony (2018:20) says,

"By not bringing to the public eye the 26 changes which needed to occur to make the facilities safer, they were able to fix the problems without answering public criticism about the shoddy development of silos in the first place." He also believes if the USAF addressed safety omissions, the welder would have been the only decedent.

People pushed back hard when the military set up Minuteman missile facilities in states throughout the Midwest (Heefner 2012). People complained some about warning systems in Arkansas, but why did they not complain more? Anthony (2018) disagrees with my belief that they valued financial benefits related to the presence of silos and the Little Rock AFB. He instead argues that they lacked a key resource—knowledge. Arkansans did not truly understand what having ICBMs in their backyards entailed. Ralph Parish sold his land to the government in 1961 so the USAF could use it for LC 374-7. He said the missiles sounded like something "out of a movie instead of real life" and assumed the launch complex was safe. The USAF did not tell him otherwise. He would find out on his own after experiencing five evacuations with no information on why he had to leave. Following incidents fueling distrust, people protesting against subsequent missile systems had the benefit of knowing what happened in Arkansas and Kansas (Handberg 2002).

SRT AND DISASTERS

Studies of disruption, deritualization, and reritualization (DDR) are important. They improve our grasp on the personal realities of disaster experiences. Remember with SRT, disruptions involve the interruption of RSPs, a breach of everyday life. As Vollmer (2013:11) notes, disruptions "are defined by events challenging or intercepting the continuation of structures and processes by which a given configuration of social order has previously been specified by analysts." They involve abrupt and gradual changes but also individual and social disorganization. With Titan II facilities, this could involve immediate confusion over a loved one's safety and forced evacuations. It might relate to a person's cognitive disarray from vapor exposure, physical reactions to toxic air, and the death of animals. At the same time, it could include shifts in family dynamics related to frustration of loss, varied personal reactions, and maintaining familial bonds. It might concern familial conflicts and skirmishes with those believed to be responsible for the disruption. Either of these could take place over months, even years, as people seek to define a new life context (Vollmer 2013; Knottnerus 2016).

Deritualization involves the loss of previously engaged in rituals, or, in terms of disaster literature, lifescape changes. For citizens associated with Titan IIs, this could link to a lack of time with loved ones lost, disappeared income, and the physical process of decontamination. It could also tie into restructuring your life for grief management and even locating new sources of income. After the 1980 Damascus incident, cows died. Farmers had trouble making money off the ones left. People did not want to buy livestock that grazed near the silo (Anthony 2018; see also Johnson, Knottnerus, and Gill in progress).

Reritualization refers to the re-creation of RSPs. Technological disasters such as silo mishaps relate to memorializing the dead while carrying out old activities. Also, consider seeking out new partners, using surviving relatives as proxy parents, returning to church, attending school again, going back to an old job, working somewhere new, engaging in daily tasks after an evacuation, buying a new house, or finding new ways to use old sources of income. After Arkansas silo incidents, residents had a hard time selling their homes. One person described his land as "cursed." In addition, farmers who had a hard time selling livestock started offering insurance on stigmatized cows to alleviate consumer worries (Anthony 2018).

Ritual enforcers have the power to control others by eliminating RSPs. The military did this when forcing evacuations near Titan II sites. SRT research helps us better understand this process. When people in power disrupt lab task groups, disorientation happens. Group members reconstitute RSPs afterward to reestablish stability. If a group experiences a negative disruption, they will reform procedures and move toward task completion with less disagreement (Sell, Knottnerus, and Adcock-Adzill 2013). Actions such as these also exist in the "real world." Consider the aforementioned literature showing that people in communities have greater cohesion after a disaster. Like task groups, they altruistically engage in shared goals directed at helping others. Reflect on Nazi concentration camps. Written accounts show significant numbers of people experienced disorientation after capture. However, captives would engage in RSPs from their previous lives to help, including impromptu prayer groups developed in spite of guard supervision and the blasting of air-raid horns. Food provided was loathsome, but women would do their best to construct recipes from it. They even staged commutative cooking festivities. People with medical knowledge would assume caretaking roles for captives suffering from severe health conditions (Knottnerus 2002).

I imagine Titan II evacuees went through somewhat of a parallel process. Away from their homes, they probably relied on the resources available to them to make life normal. Educated youth forced to leave their homes during China's Cultural Revolution in the 1960s did the same. The government relocated them to different parts of the country. Isolated from their former existence, they experienced psychological tension and a stripping away of old rituals. However, they reritualized with diary writing, studying, new pets, playing games, and storytelling (Wu and Knottnerus 2005, 2007,

2008). In addition, think of the communist party of Cambodia, the Khmer Rouge. They took over in 1975 and immediately eliminated former leaders, soldiers, intellectuals, and artists. To increase their power, the Khmer Rouge attempted to wipe out old RSPs in private and public spaces. This included dance dramas, family ceremonies, and religious activities (Delano and Knottnerus 2018).

With disasters, one SRT study examines the Dark Ages in Eastern Asia. This was a period of social and economic distress following the fall of the Roman Empire. Starting in the fifth century, many civilizations expanded. They maintained development by using natural resources more than ever. This put a strain on the land. As such, it triggered environmental shifts. Soon natural resource depletion existed, along with weather changes prompting, among other things, rampant flooding. However, over hundreds of years, certain RSPs continued in the area. People found alternative resources and modified RSPs dependent on old ones (Sarabia and Knottnerus 2009; see also Chew 2007).

Titan II disasters did not create this kind of disruption. Besides livestock issues, Arkansas citizens had little concern over the environment. This could be due to a lack of widespread awareness associated with environmental concerns but also because the consequences of technological disaster as compared to natural disaster are not always as apparent (Gill and Ritchie 2018). Regardless, after the Damascus incident, the USAF pumped 100,000 gallons of radioactive water from the silo. They let it drain into Van Buren County soil. California soil studies near former sites found significant amounts of trichloroethylene. That is what they used to clean missile sites after the Freon mishap in Arkansas. Some areas required new filtration systems because the water was not safe. Arkansas locations may have the same problem (Gruver 2009). What we do know is that the release of toxic gas from leaks had consequences. People from areas with leaks reported medical and mental health problems. With the 1978 Damascus leak, Anthony (2018) speculates that nitrogen oxide (N_2O_4) filled local air. Anything above .12 parts per million is problematic. He believes the area around 374-7 had 31.4 parts per million, 262 times more than the acceptable number.

Other SRT work confirms natural disasters disrupt life. As with people in concentration camps, survivors feel helpless, stunned, and anomic. Awareness of deritualization sets in after they realize resources used to engage in previous practices are gone. Lack of activity related to RSPs leads to life losing meaning. However, people soon reconstitute RSPs via religious practices, informal visits with others, family interaction, recreation, and gatherings involving food (Thornburg, Knottnerus, and Webb 2007, 2008). This opposes disaster research findings that religion impedes recovery but supports work showing it helps (see Gaillard and Texier 2010).

One SRT inquiry uses interview data from people who lived through the 1934 earthquake in Lalitpur City, Nepal. It tries to understand modern-day experiences of survivors (Bhandari, Okada, and Knottnerus 2011). It defines coping as how individuals interpret situations and respond to stress (see also Lazarus and Folkman 1984). It tells us people engage in various ritualized activities before, during, and after disasters. Moreover, when high-ranking behaviors emerge via reritualization, survivors have more of an ability to cope with disruptions and deritualization.

Disruption from the earthquake led to anxiety and fear. These triggered RSPs of prayer, traditional humming, seeking out family for emotional comfort, and discussing astrological beliefs in order to explain why the disaster occurred. Survivors also rushed to sites with the most destruction in order to check on the welfare of family and friends. High priests carried out special sermons emphasizing how deaths by accident in Hindu are inauspicious, subsequently symbolically dedicating each of the lost 1,000 cows. With loved ones gone, survivors would frequently return to the area of devastation, wander the streets, and mourn the dead. Interviewees also discussed the relevance of funerals. They created order when there was none. They helped dazed survivors orient themselves to the reality of loss. Interviewees did not understand much of what was going on or what to think about it after the earthquake, but they had funerals before. Funerals made sense. Overwhelmed with infrastructure damage and an inability to carry on with previous RSPs, people volunteered locally to help search for bodies, care for the injured, and rebuild homes. Those rituals provided purpose and solace. Interviewees stated that months later they began engaging in typical daily activities, ensuring reritualization. Two salient RSPs valued by survivors involved government funds set up to reconstruct homes and build a memorial in the center of the city for closure (Bhandari et al. 2011).

Years after the event, citizens still memorialize the dead. This includes practices in the house where family members will organize separate displays for those gone. It also involves community festivals. With one, Nepali people build huge chariots to push through the streets. Some participate to remember those who perished during severe drought, while others commemorate people lost in the great earthquake. Another ritual involves people clearing certain parts of streets for safety. With so many citizens on the roads, lingering memories of disaster make open areas valuable as potential evacuation routes. Interestingly, the Nepal army was having a parade when the 1934 earthquake struck. It was somewhat of a blessing since so many government responders were already in communities ready to help. Reritualization of this, and other response aspects related to the earthquake, happened through the years during chariot festivals. Volunteers set up emergency shelters and watched over visitors and tourists. Citizens helped clear debris afterward too.

To this day, these RSPs help with the parades but also keep a volunteer army of responders trained for another earthquake (Bhandari et al. 2011).

Ongoing SRT research reviews tornado sites in Joplin, Missouri, and Moore, Oklahoma (Johnson et al. in progress). It argues that SRT gives a new way to conceptualize disaster stages (Drabek 1986). For example, disruption represents onset, deritualization response, and reritualization recovery. For survivors, disruption takes place when tornadoes destroy domains of inter-action, such as home and work. It happens when family, friends, and pets die. Disruption emerges when businesses that sell food and provide regular medical services are gone. The cancelation of festivals and athletic activities is applicable too. This makes sense in a COVID-19 world.

As with the current pandemic, the elderly appear more vulnerable than most with tornadoes. The Joplin tornado shut down the senior center for an extended period. For many elderly, this was the only domain of interaction available for socializing with others. Research shows the stress pushed many over the edge. Again, as with COVID-19, domestic violence cases increased in these tornado-ravaged communities. Reritualization took place when resi-dents engaged in RSPs such as flying state and U.S. flags. Reopening summer camps, attending school, and publically celebrating holidays also applies. Additionally, RSPs related to cemetery rituals took center stage. Maintenance of headstones served two functions. It united people in a traditional domain of interaction and enabled control. It also restored places for the dead in time for Memorial Day. Those recently lost could receive community-based recogni-tion (Johnson et al. in progress).

DISASTER AND THE 53 FAMILIES

More wildfires are coming, but not just the kind that burn grasslands and forests. I am talking about the quick and intense growth of technologically related disasters. They have been increasing for years, as evident with the LC 373-4 incident, which happened over five decades ago. We now know that disasters are more than "acts of God." That does not mean we need to stop studying events like tornadoes and hurricanes. However, it is increasingly important to focus on sociological-based, human-oriented disasters. The development and use of new technology are not decreasing. As contemporary disaster researchers have done, we need to continue digging deeper into the details of previous technological disasters to know more about how to handle future ones, especially in an age of "normal accidents."

Regardless of new work on "natech," previous research shows natural and technological disasters are different. For example, with natural disasters, peo-ple emerge with stronger communal bonds and in better positions financially.

With technological disasters, conflict arises from debates on incident causes, both between powerful entities and the public and within public groups as noted by maximalist and minimalist positions. We also know that technological disasters are more likely to produce chronic effects on survivors, though studies in this area are currently limited (for a discussion of this issue, see Gill and Ritchie 2018.) This includes, but is not limited to, guilt, isolation, avoidance, drug/alcohol abuse, and domestic violence. Children who live through technological disasters experience poor academic performance and forms of social withdrawal. Moreover, we know that technological disasters do not follow the typical disaster stages. This is, in part, due to the special kinds of hidden damages survivors deal with for years following the event. It is easier to prepare evacuation infrastructure, rebuild structures, and mitigate tangible losses than to address social psychological issues.

Vulnerable populations are more susceptible to negative effects of technological disasters. Research also reveals that powerful entities try to elevate perceptions of controllability, but when things go wrong, governments, businesses, and the legal system do not always follow through with obligations to make survivors whole, if that is even possible. Therefore, trust breaks down between the public and organizations overseeing our lives. Blame and counternarratives create even more problems and distrust, with the powerful often dictating the truth. It may not be that all of this is intentional. It may just be a byproduct of the complex organizational divisions characterizing our culture. Regardless, survivors connected to technological disasters end up relying on other survivors or their own personal fortitude to manage altered lifescapes the best they can. Others, yet to experience the consequences of technological disaster consciously or unconsciously wait for what seems to be the inevitable. Hoping fantasy documents are right; they have little control over their life spaces and potential environmental aftermath.

How does this all connect to families of the 53? Did they emerge from the incident better or worse off socially and financially? Did they debate the cause of the incident with powerful entities? Within the group of surviving family members, did some take maximalist positions and others minimalist ones? Did they experience chronic, negative social psychological damage? As related to their lifescapes, how did their everyday rituals change post-disaster? How did children of the 53 navigate their losses? Are they still on a journey trying to come to terms with the catastrophe? What specific ideas rooted in disaster research apply to them directly? For example, are aspects of recreancy or secondary trauma applicable to their experiences?

With SRT, studies on the Nepal earthquake and tornadoes are important to aspects of DDR. Occasionally disaster research pays some attention to rituals, but it does not systematically examine how people who lose loved ones manage changed lifescapes, enhance their resilience, and address recovery with regular, symbolic behaviors (for an exception, see Post et al. 2003). As a teacher of death and dying, I find it compelling that it does not focus on long-term sorrow and loss either. As McManus, Walter, and Claridge (2017) argue, there is a clear absence of literature looking into bereavement and disaster, with Jakoby and Anderau's (2020) analysis of autobiographies involving the Indian Ocean earthquake and tsunami being a standalone piece, and one that only focuses on natural disasters. We need research on technological disasters to advance our knowledge. Hearing from family members of the 53 can help to fill the void. This is especially pressing with scholars now arguing that recovery is not an end in and of itself, but a "new normal" as we continue to experience "normal accidents." Fascinatingly, reritualization might be an open-ended process. It could be something that lasts a survivor's entire life (see Abrams, Albright, and Panofsky 2004). Would families of the 53 agree?

Chapter 5

Sociology of Sorrow

Unfortunately, more COVID-19 deaths are coming. It is late September 2020, and U.S. disaster declarations exist in every state. This virus will become endemic, perhaps never going away. In a short time, it became the third leading cause of death in the United States, with only heart disease and cancer to surpass (Gowdy 2020). People are talking about a possible cure. Sociologists Lee Clarke and Rick Phillips (2020) wrote an op-ed for the New Jersey *Star-Ledger*. The piece clarifies that science has never developed a cure for a virus. It only develops medicines to build immunity and treat symptoms.

With more death, comes more anguish. Thankfully, there are people willing to broach the topic of death and dying in their studies. We call them thanatologists, after Thanatos—in Greek mythology, the personification of death. Thanatology is diverse but traditionally involves psychology, sociology, or some blend of both. Grief is a worthy concentration area. It is an emotion, traditionally aligned with the sadness and stress associated with loss (DeSpelder and Strickland 2020). The world is grieving for the nearly 1 million lost so far to COVID-19. As I write, many are grieving for the way our everyday lives existed before social distancing and quarantines. Families who never had loved ones return after taking their final breaths in an underground silo on August 9, 1965, grieved.

Some say grief is a detachment process. We lose something—"bereavement." We react in the short term—"grief." We adapt with adjustment rituals—"mourning" (Neimeyer 2011). There is something unique about Americans using those words to define death circumstances. Jacobsen and Petersen (2020b) say one word covers the meaning for bereavement, grief, and mourning in many countries —"sorrow." They use all four words interchangeably. Following their lead, let us survey the "sociology of sorrow." This chapter reviews the history of death-related rituals in the United

States, discusses psychological and sociological aspects of grief, and considers a specific collection of other issues associated with sorrow and death. All of this provides a valuable basis for understanding what families of the 53 have to say about their lifescape changes after the Launch Complex (LC) 373-4 disaster.

A HISTORY OF U.S. DEATH RITUALS

Death-related rituals tell us who we are. For our purposes, death rituals within the United States are important. American practices have considerable variation. We will pay attention to Judeo Christian ideology, a belief system that frames most of the lives of descendants of the 53, and focus on four designations—death is life, ignoring death, death returns, and postmodern eras.

The "death is life" era stretches roughly from 1600 to the late 1870s. Homemade medicine dominated, death was everywhere, and no one shielded you from it. Parents refused to build close bonds with children due to high infant mortality rates. A *good death* was one involving being old and suffering from illness. Open fires for cooking and cleaning frequently kissed the fabric of women and children, rapidly engulfing them in flames. In war, wounded soldiers made their own life and death decisions, asking comrades to kill them if mortally wounded. At home, most people lived in small communities or on farms, with family living close by. Animals were for food. Religious ideas implied human death was punishment for sin. Funeral rituals were basic. Obituaries listed people at the deathbed, family and friends dug graves, and children participated in "laying out" the body, washing it with water and soap before covering it in a simple shroud. Etiquette books and readers for young adults provided lessons on how to manage loss and accept the presence of "bitter tears." Sometimes children would use hair from the dead to make rings and lockets. Coffins were utilitarian, seldom having ornamental features. A local church bell tolled following death, with the number of rings designating the deceased's age. Wakes were common, with bodies remaining in the home until the day of burial. Flowers would help mask the smell of decay as someone stood "deathwatch." With no technology to determine cessation, sometimes people would "come back" to life. A procession to the gravesite involved a carriage carrying the coffin, where after arrival a town preacher gave a eulogy minding the phrase, "Don't speak ill of the dead." At the end of this era, ritual memento mori photography began. If affordable, someone would take a picture of your loved one with eyes open, body in a lifelike position (Burnett 2015; Henger 2015; Sterns 2020).

The "ignoring death" era extends from the 1870s to the mid-1940s. A substantial shift involving technology and medicine emerged, and science refuted religious ideology. Americans pushed death out of sight. Terms like "life insurance," "beneficiaries," and "wills" emerged. The dead were worth money based on speculation of contributions in the future. Elaborate headstones reflected status. As Kearl (1989:52-53) points out, "The relative sizes of the stones have been taken as indicators of the relative power of males over females, adults over children, and the rich over the poor." They also reflect the importance of certain groups over others. Consider military memorials. No longer exclusively working for themselves in rural environments, those without wealth had to "take off work" when their employers allowed, which was typically a few days. As you know, this ritual continues. People did not always live close to family. They moved for economic opportunity, traditional social bonds diminished, and fragmented life proliferated. Organizations were critical to this. As there is now an app for everything, in the early twentieth century there were organizations for everything, including death. The sick went to hospitals for care, and Americans normalized dying in medical environments. Obituaries provided graphic details. Undertakers turned businesspeople processed the dead for burial in cemeteries outside of the community's everyday view. "Professionals" processing the dead carefully named their businesses to sound non-business like. In funeral "homes," an embalmer would drain a person of bodily fluids to preserve the body. With loved ones geographically spread out, the living needed plenty of time to drive and fly in before interment. Again indicating status, the departed needed nice clothes. Costing extra, they also needed fresh makeup, need they remind people they were deceased. Coffins became "caskets," with an original definition meaning a case for valuable property. You could go to a supermarket for food, and most certainly did not have to kill for it. Besides, animals should be pets. Telephones transmitted death news and newspapers supplied information about the lost, sometimes glorifying the existence of even the worst scoundrels. Cars delivered the dead to their "resting" places. Traffic on the opposite side of the road pulled to the side out of respect. Strangers may not have known the dead, but they were still part of a collective conscience. A preacher delivered a cemetery sermon, void of doing so in a church if the surviving family opted to have a more secular service. Shielded from emotional trauma, you did not see many children around (Mitford 1963; Kerrigan 2017).

The "death returns" era covers the mid-1940s to the 1980s. Reflected in earlier chapters, people no longer had the luxury of ignoring death. In the summer of 1945, the United States dropped atomic bombs on Japan. The arms race heated up, and Americans started building fallout shelters. Schools handed out comic books to accompany a short film called *Duck and Cover*. The movie pushed the ritual of children hiding under their desks if a nuclear blast occurred nearby (Matthews 2011). The term "Mutual Assured Destruction" entered the lexicon. The logic was, "If everyone has nuclear weapons, would that stop everybody from using them?" Then, the Vietnam War came, and television brought death back into homes everywhere (Stearns 2020). Eddie Adams's "Saigon Execution" image caught the essence of the war with the top of a gun pointed at a prisoner's face moments before a bullet pierced his skull. Reporters were on the frontlines showing us firsthand the "realities" of combat. Still, for Americans, the war was not physically close to them. Through the end of the Cold War, we let proxy wars consume the military while avoiding the death of our own. Rumors of rogue groups with nuclear weapons were concerning, as were trends involving the normalization of collateral damage resulting from attacks on civilians. For an emerging religious right, death was associated with sin again as the AIDS epidemic raged. People still wore black clothes to represent mourning. Things were different compared to the previous era, but aspects of ignoring death lingered. People suffering from loss made others so uncomfortable, social isolation was inevitable. Widows wore black, and kept their grief to themselves. Public sorrow was too morbid for others to process and deemed unhealthy (Shilts 1988; Schlosser 2013; DeSpelder and Strickland 2020).

The "postmodern" era of death began in the early 1980s. For some, the term "postmodern" simply denotes a period after the "modern" era. I see it as a time when meta-narratives of good versus evil fell. It also embraces hyper-narcissism, extended childhoods, and oddities like the advanced anthropomorphism of pets (in life and death). It is a time when news and entertainment merged and drones deliver purchased goods to our doorstep, including COVID-19 tests. We debate truth and let contradictions saturate our existence. We intentionally make private lives public (often with monetary motivations at play), manipulate images of reality to fit our Goffmanesque needs, and let the normalization of tech-driven personal communication with a sprinkle of virtual reality increasingly dominate (see Baudrillard 1994; Gergen 2010; Egan 2020). Death is everywhere, but nowhere. With health-care advances, it regulates itself to the old, but the young "see" it all the time. By 18, a person has viewed over 16,000 simulated murders on television alone. We all have the option to watch "real life" death in progress, whether a school shooting or terrorist act. As the pandemic reflects, some use all of this "pornography of death" as a tool of profit for a variety of things, from tourism to maniacal social control (Lake 2015; Kastenbaum 2016; Morse 2017). With the end of the death taboo, people fawn over books like *It's OK That You're Not OK* (Devine 2017). Popular death songs win awards (Kaufman 2016).

Aspects of this current era are intriguing. People are more open to hospice care and dying in their homes again. Social media posts inform us of deaths. There are fewer traditional obituaries and phone call death notifications. Memento mori photography is coming back. When my aunt Linda was on her deathbed, I was captivated when a relative began taking selfies with her. Some funeral homes promote this new ritual to increase funds. Platforms like Facebook are "memorializing" accounts. Physician-assisted suicide is growing. More academicians are teaching and researching death, this work included. That is opening up new doors of thanatology-based inquiry. Reflecting our detangling social fabric, individuals are now creating their own uniquely fascinating private grief rituals and opting out of traditional public ones, including funerals. Consider memorial windshield decals and roadside shrines, or virtual cemeteries. Even the public rituals are very individualized. Some funerals are now multimedia extravaganzas, feigning traditional religious messages. In this era, we are what we purchase, in life and in death. I have seen headstones with Dr. Pepper logos and Lego Star Wars figures. For better or worse, people now accept wearing your grief on your sleeve, not behind a veil. You could argue grief is normalizing itself, which I see as a good thing (Church 2013; Jacobsen and Petersen 2020b; Valentish 2020). However, there may be nefarious motives behind the trend.

PSYCHOLOGICAL GRIEF AND SOCIOLOGICAL CONSIDERATIONS

Clinical definitions of grief involve feelings. They also include physical, mental, and behavioral responses. With feelings, grief relates to sadness, anger, blame, guilt, and anxiety. Loneliness, fatigue, helplessness, shock, and yearning exist. Emancipation, relief, and numbness do too. Physically, especially in the short-term, the bereaved have stomach discomfort, chest tightening, throat contractions, and noise hypersensitivity. Breathlessness, muscle weakness, and a dry mouth can occur. Accompanying thoughts entail disbelief, confusion, and obsession with the dead. Some see the dead via hallucinations and dreams. Sleep disturbances, eating variation, absentmindedness, and social withdrawal are common. As is "calling out" for the dead, hyperactivity to redirect thoughts, and crying. Grieving people carry objects that remind them of the dead and visit places associated with them (Worden [1991] 2018; Holinger 2020).

The Origins and Fragmentation of Grief Studies

Throughout early history, grief had the name "melancholia." Before the fifth-century BC, mourning for short periods was perfectly acceptable. People who mourned for extended periods carried stigma. Others thought there was clearly something wrong with them. Premodern "doctors" claimed melancholia led to a lack of sleep and irritability. They believed these symptoms happened with cause, such as the death of a loved one. They could also take place without a cause, emerging from deeper mental disturbance (Horwitz 2020).

In the early 1900s, Sigmund Freud made a distinction between what psychiatrists now identify as "normal" grief and melancholic disorder. He argued in his essay "Mourning and Melancholia" that some take longer to achieve results when working through grief. Yet, he cautioned that medical intervention in such instances can create considerable costs ([1917] 1957). According to Jacobsen and Petersen (2020c:209), "Freud's many heirs, epigones and successors, explicitly as well as implicitly, incorporated the central premise of the grief work hypothesis" into their ideas. It became popular to see grief as an individual issue people work through without others. Future scholars sought to support his position or work hard at disproving it (see Granek 2010). This includes Lindemann's (1944, 1979) ideas on letting go, adjusting to life, and forming new relationships, some of which emerged with the study of grief after a nightclub disaster that killed 491 people. The idea was if you cannot work out grief on your own, you definitely need psychological help. As you might expect, pharmaceuticals came into play.

Many contributions on death and dying theory reference working through stages (see Stillion and Attig 2015). Kübler-Ross (1969) gave us a well-known five-stage model of grief. It contends that after loss, people deny the loss occurred and then become angry about their situation. Afterward, bargaining leads the bereaved to, sometimes with supernatural deities, ask for the person back in exchange for better behavior, maybe even the survivor's own life. Once the reality of the death sets in, the bereaved manage depression and eventually accept the loss. Though often thought in a linear, sequential manner, moving back and forth through stages is possible. Parkes ([1972] 2001) argues loss leads to shock, yearnings for the lost, disorganization with despair, and then a recovery process. The difficulty lies in the bereaved carrying a load of responsibilities while striving for emotional rehabilitation. As Bowlby (1977) implies, the more attached you were, the greater the grief reaction and harder the process of personal restoration. Rando (1984) gives a six "R" model of mourning, which includes recognizing loss, reacting, remembering, relinquishing attachments, readjusting, and reinvesting in new activities.

Worden ([1991] 2018) points out that losing someone important knocks your life equilibrium off balance. The first three tasks leading to the conclusion of grief sound similar to others mentioned—accept your loss as real, work through your grief, and adjust to a new environment without the deceased. However, his final task specifically concentrates on building lasting connections with the dead, something he suggests you never finish doing. Stroebe and Schut (1999) provide a "dual process model." Emotional lows and highs for the bereaved exist. Two different types of individual responses drive this—loss orientation and restoration orientation. Loss orientation takes place when people withdraw from others, engage in sorrow-based physical responses such as crying, and repetitively focus thoughts on the decedent. Restoration revolves around emotional labor that goes into developing new skills, like learning how to manage tasks the dead used to oversee, along with forming new relationships to complete those tasks. Like others, this theory concedes dealing with sorrow is not sequential. This includes fluctuating from avoiding the loss and challenging it directly (see also Rubin 1999). Overall, avoidance is a legitimate, healthy practice and more of an extended adaptive coping strategy. This is very applicable in situations involving special types of unanticipated losses such as homicide, suicide, and in the case of this book, disaster (Worden [1991] 2018).

For sociologists, it is faulty to concentrate on individual grief without concern for interaction dynamics. Alluded to by some thanatologists outside of the field (see Zaumseil and Schwarz 2013), the sociology of sorrow contends processing grief, even within a disaster context, is a social exercise. From the sociological principles provided to us by Mills (1959), we might consider grief a "public issue" in some, if not all, cases rather than a "personal trouble." We socially share, shape, and sanction grief (Jakoby 2012). Jacobsen and Petersen (2020c) make three excellent points related to this. First, personal identity, or sense of self, ties into others. When we lose a loved one, we lose part of who we are (see Kearl 1989). Second, social stratification is blatantly associated with grief. Some lives are just more valuable than others are, as indicated by the extra care and cutting-edge treatment given "important" people after a COVID-19 diagnosis (Lim, Kenen, and Morello 2020). Related, organizations will sometimes provide better safety measures for highly trained people greatly invested in by the agency. It is not shocking then that employment-related deaths happen more to people from lower ends of the socioeconomic scale. Reflecting recreancy issues, organizations also intentionally subcontract to distance themselves from labor issues, including worker deaths (Kearl 1989). Note too that some lives are more grievable than others are. Pay attention to what happens when a celebrity dies, or compare media coverage variation related to the cause of death (see Morse 2017). Third, though culture now openly recognizes grief and many accept that people grieve differently, it is hard to deny continued stigmatization.

Sociologically, we also know that grief "rules" exist (see Goffman 1963). People may not feel like weeping at a funeral after the death of a loved one, but might feel social pressure to try (Hockey 1992). Culture, though bending a bit on the issue, historically stigmatizes men who cry. After Lucille married my dad's adoptive father, she left her son with his grandmother Minnie. She was a mother to him afterward. I was young when she passed, but I remember the day clearly. My dad received a phone call. Afterward, he put the receiver down, walked down the hall to his bedroom, and shut the door. My brother and I slowly crept to the door and stared at each other in confusion after hearing a typically stoic man inside sobbing.

As Doka (1999:37) explains, culture attempts "to specify who, when, where, how, how long, and for whom people should grieve." Going beyond this, he explains that society also tells us some people's grief is more justified. This creates what he calls "disenfranchised grief." Consider miscarriages and the ambiguity people still experience with them (Worden [1991] 2018). With a recent controversial postmodern example, former model and leading social media mogul Chrissy Teigen is recovering from a miscarriage. Along with the roll out of a new ad campaign for Chex snacks, she posted numerous photos related to her loss, including shots of her inside of the hospital room holding her child alongside husband John Legend. The Daily Soap Dish website discusses this controversial happening with the headline, "Chrissy Teigen Shares HEARTBREAKING Photos of Deadly Miscarriage, But Fans Divided over Public Grief on Instagram" (Mazewski 2020). Regardless, some believe our grief rules need to dissipate. DeSpelder and Strickland (2020:337) sociologically assert, "There is no one right or universal way to experience and respond to loss. Grief is highly variable." Why then have psychology and psychiatry, intentionally or unintentionally, narrowed it down to a solely individual issue?

The Medicalization of Grief

The World Health Organization has a guide that includes psychological problems. It is the International Classification for Diseases. It, and American military mental health classifications, caught the attention of the American Psychiatric Association (APA) years ago. Then, they created the Diagnostic and Statistical Manual (DSM). Several versions of the DSM existed since 1952. The APA now advocates the DSM-V. It includes several controversial changes, including clinical definitions for binge eating, caffeine withdrawal, hoarding, sex addiction, and restless leg syndrome. It also has a new Unspecified Schizophrenia Spectrum Disorder, which only requires you to have "some distress" from unspecified symptoms. Some people believe the APA opened the floodgates with its most recent manual. Psychologists themselves are now arguing that clinicians can "diagnose anybody with anything" (Sax 2013).

For years, psychologists and psychiatrists believed the grief symptoms discussed so far in this section were standard. When you lose something or someone close to you, symptoms associated with distress and depression are a given for most (Granek 2010). However, is it problematic when symptoms exist for a long time? Does that make grief a mental disorder? Some believe so (for origins see Engel 1961). In recent years, psychologists and psychiatrists have referenced "complicated grief," "prolonged grief disorder," and "persistent complex bereavement disorder" (Simon et al. 2020). This sort of grief corresponds with Major Depressive Disorder (MDD) in the DSM-III, and subsequent revised versions. In the past, if you had five of the following symptoms, two related to poor mood and lack of desire to accomplish tasks, you had MDD. Related to previous discussion, the specific symptoms are depression, diminished interest in activities, weight fluctuation, issues with sleep, feelings of worthlessness, indecisiveness, and a preoccupation with death. According to the DSM-III, if you have a few of these and do not experience them for over two months, you probably have normal, "uncomplicated grief" (Jacobsen and Petersen 2020c).

Admitting the validity of sociological perspectives, the DSM-V notes that with an MDD diagnosis "a major depressive episode . . . requires the exercise of clinical judgment based on the individual's history and the cultural norms for the expression of distress" (APA 2013:161). Regardless, the DSM-V removed the bereavement exclusion, making grief abnormal. It indicates symptoms related to grief occurring after just two weeks, regardless of loss type, are suitable for clinical diagnosis and drug treatment. Critics claim this was a mistake. Sociologist Allan Horwitz (2020) argues human responses consistently show grief following loss is a normal, natural healing process that can take some time. Research shows that the bereaved have more in common with people who have never been depressed, compared to those with serious depressive symptoms (Wakefield and Schmitz 2013). What is most fascinating about all of this is that the DSM-V contradicts itself. Early in the manual, it overtly states that response to the "death of a loved one, is not a mental disorder" (APA 2013:20).

It appears all of these moves were not for science, but to appease the interests of powerful groups (Greenberg 2013; Frances 2013), most notably the pharmaceutical industry. These shifts expand opportunities for drug treatment. More people qualify for anti-depressants if more people fall under the MDD umbrella. This commodification of grief is especially compelling since nearly three-quarters of the APA committee that recommended grief-related changes in the DSM-V had ties to pharmaceutical companies (Horwitz 2020). Again, what does the sociology of sorrow say we should do? We should move away from our excessive engrossment with grief in terms of a checklist of symptoms. We should broaden our limiting views of grief, minimize judgments of grief variation, and build innovative perspectives (Jacobsen and Petersen 2020c).

OTHER ISSUES OF SORROW AND DEATH

Studies of sorrow are expansive, and there is not enough room to cover them here. For a deep dive into this area, other sources exist (see, for example,

Brennan 2016). Nevertheless, I do want to highlight a few thought-provoking issues—the ritual use of inner narratives, the ritualized development of personal narratives, the importance of communal memorials, and childhood grief. They all apply in some way to a spectrum of personal-public grief.

It is hard to separate internal sorrow from external, social experiences, public displays of grief included (Hockey 2001; Jacobsen and Petersen 2020b). The best we may be able to do in order to isolate internal sorrow from the external is to look at communication with the dead. This is not a reference to attempts to contact relatives via spirit mediums, though some do try (see Hodges and Ulsperger 2005). This relates to the living talking to decedents to keep them in their social circle. Research on "social convoy" models is applicable. It suggests you have social networks comprising your relationships, illustrated by circles within circles, with you in the center. Networks shrink as we age. In other words, peripheral relationships making up outer circles dissipate, especially when loved ones die. When we get older, bonds with those close to us become stronger, and we hold on to loved ones lost by talking to them, aloud or in our heads. A majority of people, at least in the short-term, create continuity by interacting with the dead after a loss. Therefore, keeping the dead in your social convoy, "presence in absence" as some say, is a natural process (Fuchs 2017; Stemen 2020).

With the development of personal narratives, emotions related to loss come from personal feelings, but also social interaction with others, sometimes in public domains (see Anderson 2001). In other words, the person represented in your convoy after death is partly what you remember of them, but also something new that emerges when talking to others about the person. The process for this ritualistically occurs in a variety of areas, but is particularly evident at memorial services, during, and after funerals. Lofland (1985:173) references this practice as the "social shaping of emotion" and the synthesized creation of the other. Through this process, there is a tendency for some to build overly positive images of the dead. Literature references this as a "sanitation" ritual. Whether conscious or not, we renegotiate who the lost was and have a tendency to push positive stories when shaping memories we, and others, carry forward. This ritual gives us clarity during a time of disruption, helps us make sense of the death, and gives hope for the future. Note in the postmodern era, this practice may be fading (see Tiller 2002; Walter 2008; Raphelson 2018), with new rituals related to tweets, snaps, and YouTube informing us who a person really was once they are gone (see Widmayer 2018).

Communal memorials are more likely to exist on the public end of the grief spectrum. They are not monuments. Monuments represent great achievement, or as some contemporary critics argue abuse and tyranny of the past (Zaretsky 2020). As seen later in this work, sometimes people use the terms interchangeably or are referencing a memorial when they say "monument." Regardless, as opposed to monuments, memorials do not tout triumph. They symbolize tragic loss, making them applicable to disaster and death. Survivors ritualistically visit them to be close to the dead. This commonly occurs on important dates, like anniversaries of the event tied to the memorial. Like visiting a grave, survivors leave "linking objects," such as flowers or items associated with the dead, to maintain bonds (Allison 2018). Some scholars analyze memorials through the ideas of text, arena, performance, and wound (Alderman, Brasher, and Dwyer 2020).

The text seeks to unearth the various forms of discussion surrounding a memorial. The goal is to pinpoint the kinds of people a memorial wants us to remember, but also who and what it wants us to ignore. Reading between the lines, they are tools of power (Bellentani and Panico 2016). Notions of recreancy and patterns of inequality tell us much about people and groups controlling the framing of reality around a disaster memorial. Arena involves the location of a memorial. With this, it is relevant to know who called for its construction, what contributed to site selection, whether it is open to the public, if someone took it down, and why. According to Davies (2005:164), memorials "evoke a universal acknowledgement of wrong." Removing one rescinds that recognition. Performance concerns how people use a memorial. As with the development of personal narratives, they are a place for remembering and negotiating what we should remember. As a repository of feeling, they have ties to collective rituals that help build narratives of understanding and reinforcing authoritative, official narratives of death and disaster. Sometimes they generate money for historical societies or other organizations that benefit from recounting tragic events. Wound pertains to legacies of physical destruction, displacement, and harm. A memorial has the ability to create transformation through tragedy (see Marcuse 2010).

"Memory work" revolves around emotional wounds, with recognition that marginalized people injured by disaster should have a say in a memorial's development, use, and maintenance for empowerment. This is especially important when survivors, experiencing secondary trauma, put their private grief on display for public consumption. It is also possible for a memorial to increase public awareness related to safety and risk (Alderman et al. 2020; Cross 2020). A memorial can serve "to warn or remind with regard to conduct or future events" (Bonder 2009:62) and as some propose, create closure for survivors (Eyre 2001).

There was a 7-foot-tall memorial built for the 53. All of their names were on it. On August 9, 1986, over 400 people attended a ceremony to dedicate it. It was located outside of the Little Rock Air Force Base for years (Stumpf 2000). I was surprised to find that it was only 7-feet tall. In my mind, I swear it was three times that height. As a child, I vaguely remember my mother driving me through the back roads of White County on our way back from swimming at Greers Ferry Lake and swinging by the deserted LC 373-4 site. I have more crystallized recollections of her taking me to the memorial on shopping trips to Little Rock. Sometimes we would take the exit to it, park the car, and walk up to read the names of men, like my grandfather, who died. As with others who visit memorials, this was a comforting ritual for us (Francis, Kellaher, and Neophytou 2001). One day I noticed the memorial was gone, seemingly vanishing overnight.

Working through material for this book, I started to realize that it would be hard to talk to wives who lost their husbands in the LC 373-4 disaster. Preliminary tracing of survivors led me to believe many had passed themselves. The logical thing to do was to focus on daughters and sons of the 53. A potential intergenerational advantage existed. Children of the 53 could provide insight into how the incident affected their mothers, them, and their children. The literature I reviewed up to that point, discussed in the previous chapter, strongly suggests some children have intense experiences when living through the disaster. Research looking into sorrow for children shows the same. Early on, grief involves "experiencing the deceased." In other words, kids "feel" the lost parent around them. This sensation morphs into directly speaking to the dead parent. Then, the bereaved intrasubjectively tangle with what life would have been like if the death did not happen. Survival guilt also emerges with sentiments of "never having known" the parent. These emotions are particularly salient when kids left behind visit gravesites or memorials. They sometimes feel a sense of relief when talking to people who knew the deceased or reading about events leading to the loss. However, this often applies to those who are seeking to know more about their loved one. Again, everyone grieves differently. It should not come as a surprise that not every child wants to know more about the dead. Regardless, gender identification, strength of relationship with the deceased, environmental support levels, and sibling/peer reactions make a difference with childhood grief. Increased responsibilities from the vacuum created from parental loss might distract from or compound grief when it further disrupts everyday life. Of course, age is a prominent variable. Most children do not have "personal death awareness," also considered a "mature" concept of death, until the age of 10. Social class is a factor. Wealthy families have higher levels of "death awareness," meaning they talk openly among each other about loss (Silverman, Nickman, and Worden 1995; Tyson-Rawson 1996; Hatter 1996). Mental health intervention can come into play as well. Rando (1984:155) notes, "All the available evidence suggests that not to assist the bereaved child in actively confronting death is to predispose [the child] to significant pathology and life-long problems."

SORROW AND THE 53 FAMILIES

Consequences of death for survivors go by many names in the United States—bereavement, grief, mourning. Some analysts believe these words should fall under one umbrella, sorrow. Different eras reflect different death rituals and subsequent adjustment to sorrow. Fields such as psychiatry and psychology have moved toward defining "grief," creating specific parameters for it, and shortening the length of acceptability for behaviors associated with it. It is too soon to see if the most recent trends will influence those adjusting to loss in a positive way. It does seem clear certain powerful entities, including the pharmaceutical industry, will benefit. Critics, including those in sociology, recommend taking a broader approach to the study of those experiencing loss and call for a continued recognition that there is considerable variation in the way people grieve. This could benefit areas outside of thanatology, including disaster research.

We currently have questions related to the 53 pertaining to rituals and life post-disaster. With this chapter in mind, let us consider some more. Did the era the incident happened in have an influence on how surviving daughters and sons managed their sorrow? As children, did they feel any effects of disenfranchised grief? Did they all experience their losses the same? What force did sociological factors, such as family dynamics, religion, and age, have? Do they remember their acute responses to the disaster? Did their grief seem to stop after a specific point, or do they agree with Jacobsen and Petersen (2020c:209) that closure is a myth and grief "emancipation is perhaps never fully accomplished?" How did they work through the deritualization? Did specific rituals help? Did they, or do they still, talk to their fathers? Did they, or do they, still talk to others about their fathers? What hindered their efforts to reritualize? Did any receive clinical care related to the event? If not, do they believe they should have? Do children's grief responses have any connection to other children who lost their fathers in the disaster? What do they think of the memorial built for the 53, and do they know what happened to it?

Before hearing from daughters and sons of the 53, let me briefly review issues on data collection.

Chapter 6

Research Approach

Sociologists use a variety of research approaches. Most of us recognize a traditional divide between quantitative and qualitative methods. The former uses statistical analysis of data, often collected through large surveys. A simplistic interpretation is that this procedure focuses on what people think and do. Consider a national telephone survey gauging public opinions on COVID-19 precautions. Though often complex, it is possible to use statistical data in a noncomplex way. Sometimes, sociologists use simple statistics to describe a group of people studied. The latter method, as a complement to statistical analysis or a standalone method, occupies itself with what people think and do, and why they think it and do it. The goal is not to administer questions in an attempt to calculate associations between variables. It is to concentrate on specific aspects of communication to gather "thick descriptions" of participants' experiences. Consider rooting yourself in an emergency room during the early phases of a pandemic. You familiarize yourself with the context by analyzing informal action and formal bureaucratic procedures, but also extensively interview medical personnel to get their perspective on COVID-19. Scholars often discuss this as an ethnographic process, recording and analyzing the human condition with vivid details (Berg and Lune 2018). This project leaned heavily on qualitative dynamics, though it did produce quantitative, descriptive statistics related to interviewee traits.

CASE STUDIES

As with other research on the aftermath of disaster (see, for example, Erikson 1976; Levine 1982; Kroll-Smith and Couch 1990; Edelstein 2004; Pardee 2014 Kroll-Smith 2018; Straub 2021), this project is a case study. It represents in-depth, multifaceted inquiry using qualitative methods, while focusing on a single event—the Launch Complex (LC) 373-4 disaster. No other studies thoroughly review the event, specifically in terms of structural ritualization theory (SRT) and long-term sorrow. That makes this research exploratory in nature. Case studies allow researchers to depict multiple realities not easily quantifiable, and this is relevant with research on topics like grief (Orum, Feagin, and Sjoberg 1991; Neimeyer and Hogan 2001; Hancock and Algozzine 2006). As discussed before, stage models and psychiatric quantification provide valuable information on sorrow responses, but recent arguments for creating more qualitative work exist. They imply the essence of sorrow lives in perceptions often unobtainable via statistics (Jacobsen and Petersen 2020a). For this case study, I used a blend of qualitative techniques, including content analysis, autoethnography, and interviews.

Content Analysis

Content analysis involves methodically extracting themes in communication. With this research being exploratory, I mined deep and varied sources to lay a foundation for understanding the LC 373-4 disaster. I systematically reviewed media sources, previously written accounts, and government documents. The information came from sections of the few books that mention the incident, Internet databases, newspapers, and documents from museums dedicated to Titan IIs. It all helped me to frame circumstances leading up to, during, and after the disaster. This was critical mostly because it educated me on pertinent political/military issues, facility design, terminology, historical nuances, and legal processes. Be aware that one of the challenges of working with a variety of primary sources is irregularity. Take into account imprecise information on the causes of the disaster (see Searcy Daily Citizen 1965c). With this in mind, I made some judgment calls to create consistency for the reader. I did my best to get everything as correct as possible and apologize for any oversight. The content analysis phase also helped me construct early ideas on rituals associated with disaster and sorrow. Many sources included interviews with people immediately following an event, but several included interviews with people many years later (see, for example, Hicks 2000). After using this data to guide me early on, I put it to the side knowing it would accent data from interviews.

Autoethnography

Autoethnography focuses on personal experience to enhance our understanding of other people's experiences. As a research tool, you position yourself as the subject of examination (Hughes and Pennington 2017). The goal is to provide deep insight into avoided or unexplored issues, while expanding our ability to empathize with others (Adams, Jones, and Ellis 2015). The process uses aspects of autobiographical writing and ethnographic dynamics, making analysis simultaneously process and product (Ellis, Adams, and Bochner 2011; Rambo and Pruitt 2019).

In agreement with Raab (2013:6), I believe the finest way to examine and describe something is "to be a part of it." As noted, two of my grandfathers worked at LC 373-4 when the disaster occurred. While researching and writing this book, I kept a journal. It reflected on my experiences as someone who lost family in the incident. I did not haphazardly create entries. I used a meticulous classification scheme to categorize them. The three main types of entries were on the research processes, theoretical dynamics, and self-reflection (for more information, see Ortlipp 2008). Some will question this methodology, mostly based on reduced objectivity. Would they question classics in sociology, including W. E. B. Du Bois's *The Souls of Black Folk* (1953), because they rely on personal experience (for contemporary extensions, see Buggs 2017 and Hurd 2019)? Do scholars in death studies believe Thomas Joiner's (2007) innovative work on suicide is illegitimate since he discusses his father's suicide? Regardless, autoethnography is trending, and there are clear advantages (see Hancock, Allen, and Lewis 2015; Luvaas 2017).

I believe my position as an insider created a higher level of access and made children of the 53 more open to sharing, while at the same time my status as a surviving grandchild, not a child, provided a buffer. This elevates the legitimacy of the research in this book. I believe my personal experiences allow you, as a reader, an elevated ability to understand the issues discussed. I think my ability to transition from an insider to outsider equals a better read. Moreover, I am also not sure anyone else would have interviewed surviving family members of the silo disaster. With many children of the 53 men now in advanced age, time was running out (for more information, see Méndez 2013).

Interviews

Ethnographic interviews, rather than survey interviews, take place in a setting where the interviewer and participant are together. They do not use a large amount of standardized questions for purposes of quantification. Instead, they use a set of questions geared toward open-ended responses. This maximizes the opportunity for respondents to provide profound points reflecting their thoughts and experiences (Spradley 1979; Berg and Lune 2018). For this project's interviews, I had a narrow focus. I wanted to speak with as many daughters and sons of the 53 as possible. I did not want to interview anyone from the same family. Preliminary analysis indicated that many spouses had already passed and grandchildren, far removed from the disaster, did not have much to say.

As the aforementioned review of sources and documents occurred, I worked with coinvestigators building a list of potential interviewees. We developed a matrix of potential contacts. At times, even with snowballing, this was harder than expected. As noted earlier, historical records provide conflicting accounts of the disaster. They also provide inaccurate information on the 53. Moreover, there is inconsistency with current online information, including data presented on genealogy websites. Expending a profuse amount of effort, coinvestigators and I tracked down children from 34 families, sometimes turning to social media with success. Several did not respond to telephone calls, social media requests, or written correspondence. Several refused interview opportunities, but provided contact information for siblings. Three potential interviewees were managing COVID-19 effects or highly involved with providing care for loved ones with the virus. Eventually, 20 people agreed to participate. I should disclose that I had one family member interviewed for this book. I did not interview the person. Coinvestigators cleared for data collection through my Institutional Review Board did. That person, as with other interviewees, provided consent.

I again mention COVID-19 barriers. I planned to complete interviews face-to-face, but university policy restrictions on such interaction made that impossible. Telephone interviews during a pandemic would have been my alternative preference anyway. I mailed consent forms to all respondents. Eighteen mailed them back signed. Two were not able to sign and return their forms due to pandemic-related limitations. However, they both provided verbal consent, which I digitally archived.

This book uses the names of the 53, but does not identify interviewees by name. I did my best to transcribe interviews verbatim, but I did some editing to reflect regional dialect and create fluidity. I remained aware of ethical challenges. This included a hyperawareness of the potential to trigger pain long repressed. Though I could not avoid my own feelings, throughout the research, I drew clear boundaries. When talking to participants, I attempted to avoid any comments supporting family or personal dysfunction. I should add that several interviewees sent me written correspondence after we completed our interviews. They said that there was information they held back or failed to recall during the interview that they wanted documented. I inserted that information into the findings where appropriate.

PARTICIPANT CHARACTERISTICS
AND INTERVIEW QUESTIONS

Each interviewee came from a unique family of the 53. This is not a project warranting judgments on quantitative standards, but I did want some level of diffuse representativeness. Fifty-five percent of interviewees were female. Forty-five percent were male. The average age for each respondent was 69. The average age at the time of the disaster was 14. I recorded 1,212 minutes of conversation, with an average of 1 hour and 6 minutes per interview. Questions revolved around SRT dynamics. I designed them along with the coinvestigators. We had an external scholar familiar with SRT review them afterward for suitability. Avoiding the term "disaster" to minimize preloading respondents with bias, the research team worked back and forth with that person until reaching a consensus on the pertinence. Excluding biographical questions for demographic data, the result was the following 35 questions.

Disruption

- Did your loved one have any other employment opportunities at the time of the silo incident?
- Did your loved one, or anyone in the family, have reservations about silo work?
- Do you have an opinion on who was responsible for the incident?
- What do you remember about the first time you heard about the incident?
- How did your family members react?
- How do you feel about the incident so many years later?
- How do you believe other family members feel?

Deritualization

- What changed in your everyday life after the incident?
- What important things did you do before the incident that stopped?
- Of those things, what was most important to you in your life before the incident?
- Do you believe much changed for your family members after the incident?
- What important things did your family do before the incident that stopped?
- What stopped that you believe was most important to your family?
- How long did it take before your life returned to normal?
- How long did it take before your family life returned to normal?
- If you have children, did not having your father around affect them?

Reritualizaiton

- Is it important to remember the loved one you lost?
- As the years have passed, do you think about him more, less, or about the same?

- What helped you manage your loss?
- What helped your family manage loss?
- What hindered your ability to manage after the incident?
- What hindered your family's ability to manage after the incident?
- What new activities became important to you after the incident?
- How often did you engage in those activities?
- What activities related to your father became more important to you as you aged?
- Which of those activities do you still engage in the most?
- What activities became important to your family after the incident?
- Which of those activities do they still engage in the most?
- Are there family members who do anything different than you do to remember your father?
- Outside of your family, do others do anything that makes you think of your father?
- What helps you manage your loss now?
- What helps your other family members manage the loss now?
- Is there anything that currently hinders your ability to manage your loss?
- Is there anything that currently hinders your family members' ability to manage the loss?
- Did you build bonds with anyone outside of your family who lost a loved one in the incident?

Reviewing data on disruption, coinvestigators and I noticed grounded, emerging themes allowing for the collapse of data from the seven questions into four categories. This included fathers' employment history/concerns about silo work, thoughts on the disaster/perception of cause, immediate disruption, and ongoing disruption. The same happened with deritualization data, but with more complexity. Responses from the nine questions directed themselves toward three categories. Family turmoil included maternal activities, sibling issues, relocation, interaction with relatives, and religious practice. Personal disturbances pertained to paternal activities, social impact on psychological disposition, education, role shifts, religious practice, and employment. Intergenerational dynamics did not produce subdivisions. With reritualization, data from the 19 questions settled into two categories—family and personal rituals. Family rituals connected to spending money, family activities, traditional grief practices, community/friend interaction, disaster-related interaction, and pharmaceutical consumption. Personal rituals fell into subcategories of family activities, maintaining possessions, site visits/memorial activities, community/friend interaction, disaster-related interaction, cemetery activities, funeral activities, spiritual/religious practice, and spending money.

As with the theories of grief discussed earlier, *I do not believe disruption, deritualization, and reritualization associated with technological disaster happen sequentially*. However, the next three chapters attempt to discuss these categories separately to enhance our understanding of each area and enlighten us on their relationship to disaster literature. You will see occasional references to overlap.

Chapter 7

Disruption

King COVID continues to conquer. I now know daughters and sons of the 53 struggling to beat it. I recently read that deaths from the virus toppled 3,600 per day in the United States (Sheets and Crane 2020). Exaggerated or not, it is a staggering statistic. Thanksgiving just passed. Many people, especially the vulnerable, are isolated. Limiting contact with others, being cautious about social distancing, focusing on hygiene, and feeling the effects of sickness and death, most of us continue to deal with daily pandemic-related disruptions. As I write this, two vaccines are competing to usher an end to it all—one from Moderna and one from Pfizer (Allen 2020). Ironically, I just finished interviews and the last was with a child of the 53 working as a pharmaceutical chemist. He expects a slow roll out of vaccinations and high probability of mutations.

This chapter focuses on the disruption of the families and children who lived through the Launch Complex (LC) 373-4 disaster. Again, disruptions involve the interruption of ritualized symbolic practices (RSPs), a breach of everyday, taken-for-granted life. They reflect a challenge to social order and related psychological responses. They signal frustration of loss, blame related to change, and prompt shifting social dynamics, including those related to family relations. People can experience the waves of disruption for days, months, and even years (Vollmer 2013; Knottnerus 2016). As a reminder, with this research categories emerged on fathers' employment history and concerns about silo work, thoughts on the disaster and perception of cause, immediate disruption, and ongoing disruption.

EMPLOYMENT HISTORY AND FAMILY CONCERN

Employment history and concern about silo labor give a feel for the comfort level men had with their work. Employment trajectory and worry about hazardous work can be disruptive forces themselves. An equal distribution of employment type existed. Of the 20 interviewees, 16 had some idea of what their fathers did at the site. Four said their fathers were sheet metal or general construction workers. Four told me their dads welded. Three said electrician, and three said pipefitter. Two interviewees said painter.

Several respondents discussed their fathers as "uneducated" but "hardworking," having spent their lives working around livestock and agriculture. One respondent talked about his father coming in for dinner. He recalled his dad saying to his mother, "Where is the meat?" She started crying and said, "There is no meat . . . We can't make a living on this farm. I know that's what you want to do, but we can't do it." That is when he started looking for alternative labor, like working in the silos. A different person explained, "My parents never owned a home. They never had a checking account. . . . We had to build fires for heat and never had a full meal on the table. It just seemed like there was never enough money." A few of the men had military backgrounds. This was a beneficial resource. One son explained, "Since dad had been in the Navy on ships, he was used to working in confined spaces." Military experience may have been a disadvantage to others' lives. One son detailed his father returning from war with what we now know as posttraumatic stress disorder.

Ten respondents said their father or someone in the family expressed worry about silo work. Six interviewees believed no one in the family had concerns. Four were unsure of how to reply. With those who pointed out someone had reservations, several argued financial necessities trumped safety. One daughter, 26 at the time of the incident, explained her father needed the money for his post-employment years. She said, "It was going to be the last job dad had before he retired." She asked him once, "Why do you want to go work in that place?" Relying on family stories, one daughter, five months old when her father died, told me her dad had a less risky job driving a backhoe before. She said, "None of my family wanted my dad to take the job. He took it because it paid more money than what he was making. He was simply trying to do more for us." Discussing her father's meticulous dress and cautious disposition, even as a construction worker, an interviewee who was 15 at the time of her father's death noted, "He had reservations about working the silos. Yeah, he did. He knew it was very dangerous, and they did not have proper safety measures or equipment."

A daughter who was 11 remembers her mother telling her father the morning of the incident, "Please don't go! I have a bad feeling." The interviewee said, "They talked it over, and mom went ahead and finished fixing his lunch, a sandwich and some cookies. She put it all in his lunchbox, the kind that was a little black box with the rounded top. He put his coffee in his thermos, left, and then never came home." A daughter who was 10 at the time told of how her mother was constantly on edge. The respondent stated, "Mother told him it worried her sick. . . . She only told us that later, but we knew. I guess she was trying to shield us."

A son, 24 at the time, said shortly before the disaster his father ended a conversation with, "I will see you soon, if something doesn't blow up." Another male interviewee, 12 at the time, reported his father telling him he put fires out at LC 373-4 before, and commented, "It's dangerous out there." A different son, 15 when his father died, explained, "He was making good money, more than bailing hay, or when he picked cotton. I think they were even paying his gas mileage to drive back and forth." Questioning the benefits, he asked his father, "Daddy, what are you doing out there?" After his father told him about his welding, the boy cautioned, "If you keep working in those silos one of them is going to blow up." His father replied, "Well, if I got to go, that's as good a way to go that I know of."

Not all men provided their families with specifics when asked. A daughter, 12 in 1965, explained that her dad learned how to be an electrician in the Navy. She elucidated:

With his military background, my dad took the approach that his work in the silos was highly confidential. I believe that he had a specific clearance. I believe he came to Arkansas for this specific job. I know that he had a gas mask for it, but with other jobs too. We were not allowed to even tell people at school specifically where he worked or anything other than he was an electrician. I would say it was kind of confusing for other people and me. They would ask you at school, we went to many different ones, "What does your dad do?" I would say, "Well, he's an electrician." And they'd say, "Is he a civilian contractor?" I wasn't allowed to say "yes" to that question. I felt very close to my dad. I would ask him what I could say. He eventually said, "You can tell them that I work for a contractor, and that's it." Part of it was that he was really protective. I think it was the Cold War angle. He was working in a missile silo, and felt that it just wasn't anybody's business. The secrecy was very powerful within our family. I'll just say that.

Still, her father had apprehensions. Her sister told her that he once said, "We almost lost the hole." The interviewee revealed that before her father died, he ascertained certain forms of life insurance to pay off debts. She said, "He didn't tell anyone about it." She also said in the early morning of the disaster her father came home at 2:30 a.m. He was working at a different site and his supervisor was sending him to LC 373-4. Her mother told her that he was only home long enough to get a cup of coffee and his gas mask, which he did not have much faith in at the time. Earlier, he told some family members the gas masks were completely inadequate for the type of substances the site would expose him to in the event of an accident.

With some respondents, the military background of their fathers restricted open talk about the silo. Cultural standards involving male emotional expression may have contributed to a dramaturgical wall limiting conversations related to work rituals. With interviewees not reporting risk concerns, responses included, "Well no, he didn't have any reservations," "I want to say no," "He wasn't ever too worried about working down in the silos," and "I don't remember him or anyone else discussing the dangers."

THE INCIDENT AND PERCEPTION OF CAUSE

The actual event is the obvious key disruptor for families of the 53. However, each interviewee's perception of what caused the accident is highly important. Fourteen rejected the welder explanation. Consider their theories. Keep in mind, the goal is not to judge accuracy of their statements but to appreciate them as alternate narratives or definitions of the situation. One female respondent stated, "I don't feel like we ever got many details. I'm sure there was a lot of stuff about it that would have changed the way I feel about it if I'd ever been able to hear or see what really caused it." Another daughter said, "There's a lot of people that do not believe that the government was forthright. The alarms had gone off twice that day. The third time, when it all happened, most of the men just sat down waiting for the lights to come back on. That's what they trained them to do. When they started suffocating is when some started heading up the ladder." A different female interviewee explained, "I've read that they maybe should have had a better elevator, a better ventilation system, a lot of other things. I remain suspicious about a lot of information that was provided." Other daughters said, "They intentionally closed those doors to smother the fire out, and my understanding is that workers were not even supposed to be in there because the sprinklers were not working," and "The military danced all around everything. They said the missile wasn't armed. I don't know if I even believe that. They were really just worried about national security issues and not the men. They've hidden the truth from the people." Yet another contended:

> The government was responsible for not seeing that they had updated equipment. The masks they had were from WWII. The Air Force personnel there were confused. They didn't know whether the missile was armed or who was

in charge. Therefore, men died. They should've had better built-in safety measures. I guess they were more concerned with saving money than they were concerned with those men's lives.

One son told me, "They just tried to blame the welder. If they wouldn't have done that, things might have turned out different for people. Here's the deal. They closed those doors on them all, and then they swept it under the rug. If it wasn't armed, why did they close the doors?" Echoing that sentiment, one son said, "Saying somebody with a torch caused it, there was probably more to it," and a different one noted, "It is my understanding that several safety protocols were not necessarily followed very well. That is probably what led to the incident to begin with." Another alluded to pressure to finish refurbishing the silo as quickly as possible. He indicated, "They were pushing their limits to get the work accomplished for some reason." Three male interviewees claimed to have inside information, or asserted they had completed their own research on the disaster. One who had access to the Little Rock Air Force Base and Air Force personnel said:

> They would not open the doors and let them out. . . . Someone could have authorized it. Some little old lieutenant, or whatever, didn't push the right button. But, then what happened is you had some Air Force people, probably still in training or whatever. They didn't really know what to do in an emergency. So, they closed all the doors. After those doors closed in situations like that, you had to wait a certain amount of time before you could get them back open. The Air Force made a terrible mistake, and that mistake killed my daddy and 52 other men. They tried to blame it on the welder. They said he punctured a hydraulic line. I don't know if you've ever welded or been around hydraulic fluid, but it just don't burn the way they said it did. . . . The Air Force has certain procedures and sometimes they just follow those procedures, and it's not always in the best interest of human life. In this case, they was worried about the cost of the equipment that could get damaged, the millions of dollars it would cost if everything caught on fire. They've always said a welder made a mistake. The people in the silo were at fault. That's not true. That's not true by a long shot. Even with fires in there, they had a sprinkler system. It could have put the fires out. That tells you something, right? If it was just fires that they were worried about, I believe those sprinklers would have done the trick. They had procedures, and they were to focus on suffocating the fire. You know, that was not the first fire they had down there.

One son, relaying information from a union representative, said:

> The Air Force was in a big hurry to get that work done. You know, they were trying to make the silos stronger. They had to do some internal modifications

and some outside ones. While they were working on that silo, they said they had
all of the fuel out of it so there wouldn't be any fires. They didn't. I believe they
left the fuel in it. The way I understand it, different crews were doing different things. Some welders were putting metal on the sides. Some were working
on the big doors where you went into the control center. They had hydraulics,
stabilizers, and sensors that controlled a lot of things. Part of it was that they
kept the missile from moving around in the silo if a Russian missile hit close
by. In case of an emergency, some of these things were heat sensitive, smoke
sensitive, and vibration sensitive. One of the welders was doing a modification
up right close to the door that takes you out of the bay and cut a hydraulic line.
That fluid was flammable. It created heat, fire, and then smoke. Sensors went
off. You had over 50 men down there without air. They had oxygen masks,
but they only had a few pounds of air in them. They couldn't wear big ones.
They had a ringed ladder to go up and down between levels and a bigger tank
would've kept them from using it. Even the tanks they had were too big. If they
wanted to keep their tanks with them, they had to wear them on their chests to
move up and down the ladder. The doors at the top, the big thick doors over the
missile itself, they were on ground level. Two of those, they slid together and
met in the middle. Typically, those two doors were open so the workers could
have some air and a little bit of light. It also helped them a little bit with the
claustrophobia down there. Some of the guys had a problem with that. Those
doors were open before all this. There was no crew handling the missile right
when this all happened. If there was, they could have reset the alarms and
opened the big doors over the missile that closed. I know the top of the missile
wasn't in there, but they shouldn't have had any type of fluid or fuel in there and
then it would have been an absolute safe environment for these people. They
were in such a hurry to get the modifications done. Was the field truck busy at
another site? Did it have a flat tire? Who knows? Maybe it was in the maintenance shop having a spark plug change or something? For whatever reason,
the missile was still fueled. Now, when the guy burned a hole in the hydraulic
line, that started a small fire. They were pushing oxygen from outside into the
silo with something like a big air conditioning unit. What happens when you
put a strong amount of oxygen down in a hole like that with a fire starting? It
accelerates everything. So, there you go. The sensors detected the smoke, the
big concrete doors to the control center close, the doors over the top close,
and the vents for the air conditioning do too. They closed that thing down to
protect the missile. There's no air for the men. They're locked up in there and
then electricity goes off because that was a safety thing. Now, they have no
lights. Their oxygen tanks last maybe five minutes. You have 53 men scattered
up and down that black tunnel. Some start climbing up the ladder to get out of
that place, but they find out they have nowhere to go. Everything was locked.
They basically drowned, not because they didn't have water but because they

didn't have oxygen. I was told there was a lot of hollering and screaming going on. . . . I don't know.

Reflecting dislike between military divisions and the need to skirt bureaucratic protocol, a different son explained:

I deep down didn't buy what the Air Force said back then. I think it was the government's fault. I think it was a bigtime cover-up. They were supposed to go by government standards at the site. If you've ever been in the military, you know those don't always hold up. If anybody is responsible, it's probably the Air Force. I was in the Marine Corps. Even we let some things slide, but not as much as the Air Force. If one man was working sheet metal or whatever, there was supposed to be another observing him. They were supposed to wear airtight oxygen masks. They never did because it was too bulky for them to go into tight spaces. There's always shortcuts. Like I said, I was in the service for three years, and I know how things like that go. There is a tendency to take shortcuts as long as other people don't see you doing it. Some people say the men were under pressure to finish the job fast. Now, I can't see the government being in a hurry to finish anything, but stranger things have happened. . . . The Air Force guys who were supposed to be on duty were topside playing checkers or cards. The contractors might have been running the show and maybe the Air Force just had a skeleton crew there. I just finished reading the book *Flags of Our Fathers*. One guy in it says the Air Force messes up so much you can't ever tell if they're on our side. A foreman over the sheet metal workers went down into the site shortly after they cleared all the 53 men out of it. There were so many ashes around it felt like walking in snow. He asked some people in there with him about a cable that looked cut, not burned. Nobody answered him. They just gave him some looks and someone said, "If I were you, I wouldn't ask any more questions." The warhead wasn't in there. A lot of stuff had been taken out so they could get compressors and things like that down in the silo to finish the upgrades. But, the Air Force left a million dollars worth of stuff down there. It would have been safer with it all out, but it would have cost more money to do it. They could have opened the big doors over the silo, but a Full-Bird Colonel in charge said, "We've already killed 53 men. We're not going to open the doors. We don't know what's going to happen if we open those doors." The electricity went out and so did the lights. The only way those men could have gotten out was up the ladder. They had an elevator, but even if it had electricity running to it there wasn't enough room.

With questioning in this area, one person indicated "a wrench or some type of tool was dropped." She confused the event with what happened at the Damascus facility.

Interestingly, respondents who rejected the welder explanation also had a preoccupation with the locations of their fathers' bodies post-disaster. They said things like, "Daddy was at the bottom with his mask on," "My dad was one of the ones on the stairs close to the top trying to get out," "When they found my father, his leg was broken," and "My dad wasn't even supposed to be at that site that day." One told me, "My dad had been on a smoke break and had just gone back down when it happened. He was on the first rung of the ladder when they found him."

Six interviewees accept the government's narrative. Respondents said the primary or sole reason for the disaster was a welder's mistake. Responses here contained statements such as, "I've always heard that some welder hit a hydraulic line," "They say a welder nicked a hydraulic line," "It was a spark from welding," "A welder hit a hydraulic line, and it started a fire," and "There was a small fire, and it got bigger and bigger." One interviewee even noted, "I truly think it was a fire, because I saw a man at the funeral home that had an imprint on his face where he had been laying on a hot surface, like a metal honeycomb looking floor." Overall, these interviewees did not appear to have as much turmoil through life connected to the disaster.

IMMEDIATE DISRUPTION

Sixteen interviewees provided details on how they heard of the incident or their fathers' deaths, their dispositions, and family reactions. The others reported no recollections, but not because of memory repression surrounding trauma. It is more a product of age at the time. The average age for respondents absent of recollections was 1.3 years old. As you would assume, adults are often void of specific memories from this point in life, though language development, discussions with others during early years, and traumatic experiences do come into play (see Tessler and Nelson 1994).

Nine interviewees said they discovered, or first heard about the event, via media outlets, specifically radio and television. This is interesting since you would assume learning of circumstances leading to the death of a loved one would come from people within a close social circle. An interviewee told me, "Looking back, I can't believe they had it all on the news before families knew what was really going on." Regardless, the circumstances had an influence, with it being too grand of an occurrence for media to keep under wraps even in the 1960s. Respondents noted, "It came on the radio," "The news broke into the show I was watching. They said the silo had blown up," "Something about it was on the news," "We were all home together waiting for daddy, and it came over the news," and "I remember it being on national TV." Providing details related to that last comment, one son recalled, "My wife and I sat down to watch the CBS Evening News with Walter Cronkite. It was around six o'clock. He said there'd been an accident at a Titan missile complex outside of Little Rock." Five interviewees found out via family and friends. They noted, "My brother called me," "People started calling my mom," and "I had worked at my granddad's all summer. The day it happened, I came walking in and he met me at the driveway. He told me what happened." Others said, "I was over at my friend's place and my first cousin showed up. He had found out" and "A good friend found out and then informed us." Two others heard through coworkers or coincidence. One daughter, 16 then, explained:

> It was just a fluke. Our preacher had been sick and was in the hospital in Searcy. My dad, who had preached before, filled in for him the Sunday before. Just us kids went to see him. It was my brother who was 16, my 17-year-old sister, and our little sister, who was 9. Our cousin who lived next to us went too. My mother was at work. While we were there, they brought in Mr. Saunders and Gary Lay. They were burned and had smoke inhalation problems. They put them in a room right across from our pastor. We all talked about the two men brought in and wondered what was going on. There was a lot of commotion amongst the staff. We listened in and found out they had been in the silo. Everyone was saying an explosion took place. We came on home and my mother got home from work. We asked her where dad was working. She said it was outside of Searcy close to Pangburn. We told her there had been a fire and maybe explosion.

Eight respondents in this category reported shock and disorientation. Interviewees said things like, "It was amazing, horrible shock." One 14-year-old daughter said, "I remember going into town that day, and we saw daddy's white car parked where he caught his ride to the silo. After I knew about the accident, it was very late into the night before we really found out anything. I was in shock. I remember my mother crying. I remember everyone crying." An 11-year-old daughter provided this compelling commentary:

> I remember seeing a lot of people standing around and cars parked everywhere on the TV. I didn't even know where my daddy went every day. Envision this. Film is rolling on a projector and all of a sudden it breaks. The film is going, flip, flip, flip, flip, flip. . . . That's what it was like, a movie going that just stopped. Like most, my family had drama going on. School was getting ready to start, and just all that stuff. Then all the sudden, bam, and daddy's gone. Flip, flip, flip, flip.

Another female respondent, 12 then, commented, "The television show *Sugarfoot* was about to come on. My mother was taking a nap in the other room, and the news broke into the show. I knew my father was up there. I went and woke my mother up. It was not until late that they confirmed the men perished. It really struck hard." In terms of disorientation, some respondents noted, "I didn't understand what was going on" and "I just didn't want to accept it." Reflecting a tone of confusion and disbelief, a different 12-year-old daughter said:

> I remember it all like it was yesterday. The day dad died, he was bringing home a supervisor with him that he really liked. That man owned the home that we were renting, and we were going to buy it. They were going to finalize the deal that night. Having moved around so much, dad thought it would be good to stay in place for once. My twin brother and sister were outside playing. I was sitting at the table and helping my mother prepare for dinner. She expected dad and our guest at six o'clock on the dot. We didn't entertain very much, and I was surprised she turned on the TV while we were waiting. Within seconds, I heard her scream. She was just absolutely hysterical sitting on the couch. I'd never seen my mother cry. I'd never seen her behave that way since my parents were not particularly affectionate. I asked her what was going on and she told me there was a silo explosion in Searcy. I was completely calm and told her that it wasn't a problem because he was probably at a different silo. She said he was there. There were already reports that the men inside were screaming and trying to get out. After that, I went outside to get my brother and sister. My mom talked to some other people on the phone, maybe the wife of the supervisor. She finally insisted later into the night that we all go to bed, but she woke us up at some point and told us dad had been killed.

This respondent went on to say that it took her years to accept her father's death as reality. In follow-up correspondence after our interview, she told me her sister felt the same way but they did not discuss their feelings about it until recently. This chapter will elaborate on this denial of reality later. Related to the disruptive force of an unseen emotional display, a brother of one of the 53 commented in a media source, "My mother was a real stoic person who never showed emotion." However, he also pointed out, "I saw her break down and cry. I had never seen that before in my life. It made an impact on me."

Five respondents discussed what I would identify as "stoic practicality." All were male. Without referencing any specific emotional disposition, they told of hearing about the disaster and their fathers' deaths and subsequently responding by completing necessary tasks to move themselves and others forward to create needed order. This implies aspects of reritualization to create structure occur very quickly among families following a technological disaster. For example, one 22-year-old son noted:

I called my mom after finding out. My granddad answered. He told me my mom wanted to talk. I told her dad was tough and the government probably didn't want a bunch of secret information getting out to the Russians. I hung up and called my boss, got me some clothes, got in the car, and drove all night through Alabama and Mississippi. I helped mom with the funeral plans and financial things after I got back to Arkansas.

A 21-year-old son explained how he pulled everyone together and organized a caravan of family to drive to the silo site so they could gather more information. Others' sons told similar tales and even discussed obligations to calling other family members to share information. In discussing their male family members, female interviewees commented on stoic practicality, including the completion of tasks such as picking up their fathers' cars from locations where the men met to carpool to the site.

Three remaining people in this category commented on anger. Driving to his mother's house upon finding out about the disaster, one said, "I was mad. I just had my first kid, and I couldn't stop thinking about my daddy holding him on his lap. He was only six months old when daddy passed away."

ONGOING DISRUPTION

Responses varied on whether the event continues to disrupt lives. Eleven people discussed some form of trigger related to memories and disruptions. Seven did not mention anything specific with recollections. Two respondents said the incident did not disrupt their lives beyond when it happened.

With those who discussed disruption and triggers, some mentioned specific holidays such as Christmas, but a majority discussed pausing and reflecting when exposed to missile defense issues. Here, and in other places during the interview, respondents invoked comments related to the Damascus incident. One female respondent told me, "I'm 71 now, and all this still literally sticks in my mind. I've thought about it an awful lot through life. Did you know that missile in Damascus that exploded was the same missile in the silo where my dad died? Many men were injured and one died in that explosion." A different 71-year-old said, "I've never gotten over losing him. He was an amazing, wonderful father and husband. I still just feel like I missed out on a huge portion of life. I've always had such a sense of loss after it all and remained afraid of loss my whole life. When my brother died, I had a heart attack . . . You know, I think that Damascus explosion got more attention, and I don't know why."

One 55-year-old daughter said, "We had a young lady at our house a few weeks ago. She's probably 25 or 26 or something, and she'd stopped by to do something. Missile bases came up for some reason. She had no idea even what they were. I told her, they're all over the state of Arkansas. She had no idea what used to go on, especially concerning something like this accident!" One 71-year-old son said, "I still think about how the government failed. It bothers me that you always hear about the one in Damascus. What about this one? Some good people got killed and every year when August is coming, I think about it. On that day, I watch the clock roll around to one. I've never gotten over it. I've got a bad taste in my mouth until the day I die." A 72-year-old male commented, "It's been 55 years ago, and I still stop to think about it every day. Nobody wants to talk about it. Everyone wants to talk about Damascus. There's been a movie and all that on it, which was very well done. I respect what it was, but for some reason you don't hear about this one. It's just something I'll never get over." Noting safety concerns now versus then, he said, "You know, I think about this sometimes. You had kids in this state sitting on their granddad's pond fishing feeling like they were in the safest place in the world, and there could've been a nuclear missile within 15 minutes of them. Things just seemed safe, but maybe they weren't." An 80-year-old son stated, "Sometimes I think about my dad during WWI working for General Electric. He was a supervisor and they built all kinds of military equipment, including artillery pieces. He died in that silo, but he made a contribution. He died serving his country. You might say he died with his boots on." Several others mentioned both the Damascus silo and the power of August, but in later lines of questioning. One noted, "My mother's funeral was on the same day in August that my dad died," and another pointed out that her father's birthday was the same day as the accident. His family was waiting on him with a big party planned.

Of those who did not mention missiles or other military-related triggers, a few discussed other triggers such as objects or rituals related to their fathers. An 82-year-old female told me:

> A few years ago, three maybe four, I opened a bunch of boxes that's never been gone through. They have some of my dad's things, so I'm having to go slow. I've been going through them one at a time. It is hardest when I run across something with his handwriting on it. It tears me up. . . . He had a very distinctive handwriting. When I see it, I always feel like his death was something that should never have happened. I wonder whether there was, something [the military] could've done. I just still feel like he was taken. . . . My dad was old then, but I still feel like they took years away from us.

One son commented, "I'm 67, and this still impacts me. Most people just want it swept under the rug. . . . My dad smoked cigars. Even to this day, if I'm around somebody smoking one, I start thinking of my dad. I have held all this stuff in me my whole life. It's still in me. I've never forgotten it. I will take it to the grave with me. It still bothers me to this day." A 77-year-old son relayed that straws make him think about the disaster. He pointed out, "That silo was like a straw. If you ever try to suck something thick up through a straw and can't get much through, it was like that. I think that you take 53 guys in a tunnel with that big missile occupying that much space and there just wasn't enough room." At a later point in questioning, someone discussed how her father's blue-collar "greasy smell" brought back memories of the disaster and her father.

Two respondents mentioned family as a trigger. One 55-year-old son explained that his mother was his connection to the disaster. With her not around, he does not think about it or his father much. However, he did tell me that he came across some boxes not long ago with documents containing information on the disaster. In terms of family, a 65-year-old daughter said, "I think about my daddy quite often. If I had to put a number on it, I would say a couple of times per month. I wish he wouldn't have died. I wanted him in my life as I got older. When I see my grandchildren, sometimes that makes me think of myself when I was younger, when he died." However, she also went on to explain that things at her job trigger thoughts about him that make her momentarily stop working. She noted, "There's a lot of welding going on where I work. I see those guys welding, and I think about that silo. I see them start welding, and I think about that man starting that fire and all the smoke in everyone's face." She even went on to imply that some of her phobias relate to the incident. Referencing how her father died, she commented, "Stuff smothers me. I don't like things in my face, water in the shower or anything else. I sure don't like going underground or anything like that." One son brought up that he had anxiety when he was younger and worked a construction job going into a deep hole to pull dirt up from the ground in order to lay a concrete foundation.

With the respondents who discussed ongoing disruption but did not comment on specific triggers, nearly all focused on their loved one's status as a dad. Considering how it changed their lives, they emphasized how their dads did not get to see fatherhood to completion. It caused them to have "consistent" sorrow and to "grieve for years after" the disaster. One 68-year-old daughter explained that losing her father altered her life, but "There's nothing you can do to change it." A different interviewee, just one year older, always directed her rage at supernatural forces. She said her mother constantly wanted her to embrace faith and consider the accident as part of some sort of cosmic plan, but she has always been "very angry at God for taking her father," a point we will revisit later. Another female interviewee explained:

I don't know if I'll ever stop wondering, even at 58. It took my father. I missed having a father. I always remember just yearning for that father. I desired one, that male that has your back with unconditional love. I'm sure I've romanticized what a father is. In my mind, my father was a strong man, and he would've been there for me. I can imagine his arms around me, holding me, saying, "It's going to be okay." I don't know. I didn't have any of that. I thought about those things as a child, and I still do. I've got a wonderful husband. But in my mind, that father's love is something just no one else can fulfill.

A 55-year-old daughter commented, "I still feel like nobody ever cared that I lost my dad. His death still affects me, and it has always bothered me. Through the years, I've just internalized it and just tried to wrap my brain around it. There's not a day that I don't think about him. I didn't get the opportunity to know him. I've always felt like a forgotten child." Of the respondents who said they have no ongoing disruptions in their lives due to the event, comments indicated feelings such as, "It's already been around 55 years. I just moved on, you know."

SUMMARIZING DISRUPTION

The 53 were not site supervisors or active military. They were civilian sheet metal workers, welders, electricians, pipefitters, and painters. Their families had limited resources. At the silo site, they certainly held the least amount of power. This created a lessened ability to avoid risk-based work, which has a higher potential for death. Primarily uneducated and skilled in manual labor, many of the 53 believed silo labor suited them. Ritualized strain associated with financial necessity coerced them into working at LC 373-4. Echoing vulnerability, you could classify numerous as poor, living in substandard housing, and at times struggling to feed their families. They needed the work, even if it was risky.

Some followed cultural rules of ritualized emotional expression. As men, they hesitated to discuss concerns about hazardous conditions with family. Several had military backgrounds and carried over RSPs of secrecy related to their work lives. However, 50 percent of interviewees told me their father or mother voiced concern. With a show of homologousness, some respondents disclosed their fathers also took out policies designed to supplement their family's financial situation in the event of death. Some of the 53 prepared their loved ones for future loss with ritualized discussions of risk. This symbolizes a ritual of anticipation related to disruption, with parallels to anticipatory grief. Though not considered in this exploratory research, there may be grief variation for disaster survivors who engage in anticipation loss rituals before the disaster.

Data reveals that survivors' beliefs on the cause of the disaster influenced their grief trajectories. Reflecting recreancy issues, a majority of respondents failed to believe that the cause of the accident was the welder. These interviewees have repetitively questioned government explanations through their lives and rejected fantasy documents on origins of the event. They speculated for years that the darkside of bureaucracy lurked within the walls of the silo making their fathers expendable. They think organizational RSPs, such as pressure for project completion and loose safety standards, are undeniable. There could be a correlation between the sorrow people have and the acceptance of "official" explanations. Those taking a minimalist position on disruption were the same ones who supported government explanations for the disaster.

A majority of interviewees felt comfortable enough to discuss their family member's or their own immediate reactions. Expected responses included shock, disbelief, and tears. Interpersonal relationships as a form of social capital played a part for some as they managed the initial disruption, though this primarily limited itself to family. Several interviewees discussed frustration finding out about their fathers' deaths through media outlets, prompting me to speculate that survivor relationships with media sources are worth extracting from the original data at some point. Some respondents indicated secondary trauma by way of witnessing their mothers' acute, physical reactions to news of the disaster. Male scripts of grief response apply once again as interviewees explained that brothers, uncles, and others became task-oriented after the event, pushing emotional reactions to the side as they moved toward creating order.

Pointing out the lack of research on long-term effects, Norris et al. (2002:241) say the effects of disasters "may be quite enduring." With this research, 90 percent of respondents noted lifetime issues with sorrow and the disaster. It was clearly a part of who they were as they navigated through life. Rest assured it still is. This left me eager to find out about RSPs related to acute and chronic lifescape changes. Not yet discussing litigation, respondents opened the door for considering more aspects of secondary trauma with talk of poor government responses. There is more on this to come. They also detailed memory triggers via holiday rituals, the month of August, and coming across stories on missiles and silos. Triggers coupled with sensory perception events prove interesting. I did not expect so many to detail ritualistic, salient experiences specifically involving sights and smells associated with their fathers and the disaster.

Chapter 8

Deritualization

Last night, I was thinking about Christmas, Hanukkah, and the other holidays just ahead. It is December 2020. Though not all are following pandemic guidelines, people will experience things differently this year. In the face of the disruptive pandemic, deritualization is happening. Traditional practices are falling to the wayside. The holidays will take place without extended family and all the typical accompanying fanfare. For some adults, there will be no face-to-face gift opening. For some children, there will be no sitting on St. Nick's lap.

My dad's mother, Lucille, had a sister named Mary Mae. With my grandmother Lucille in Indiana during my youth, Dad would take us to Aunt Mary Mae's house during the holidays. I always enjoyed seeing her husband, Uncle Raymond. A member of the Arkansas National Guard for over 40 years, he died a few weeks ago. One of his granddaughters wrote on the funeral home "tribute wall" that she would never forget his "corny jokes and warm hugs." I feel the same. Suffering from other health conditions, COVID-19 proved lethal. I wanted to go to the visitation, especially to be there for my dad. Raymond meant a lot to him too, but I have been distancing for public health and personal reasons. I did write my aunt Mary Mae a letter. I told her that her husband had one of the warmest smiles I have ever seen. You can see that smile on the tribute wall I mentioned earlier (Smith Family Cares 2020). I do not know if my aunt ever read my letter. Her husband was in hospice care toward the end. Nothing could stop her from leaving the side of her husband of nearly 70 years, but she and several immediate family members contracted COVID-19 while at the hospice facility. Her health was ailing too, and she ended up passing soon after Raymond. There was a joint graveside service, no traditional rituals in a sanctuary. I stayed home with my thoughts and recollected the last funeral I attended. It was my mother's sister, my aunt Linda, whom I spoke of earlier in the book. I use "attend" loosely. My mother had a wonderful relationship with my aunt, but years of animosity existed between so many family members. I always attributed the genesis of it to August 9, 1965. The police ended up escorting my mother and all of her children, including me, out of the funeral home before the service started. At my uncle's request, I was on the program to speak. He told me a few days before that was what my aunt wanted. I worked hard crafting words that reflected her generosity, love for family, and adoration of life. I never spoke those words. Undoubtedly, disasters leave behind years of tangible and intangible devastation.

This chapter is on deritualization. Recollect that it involves the breakdown or loss of previously engaged in ritualized symbolic practices (RSPs). Thoughts and actions comprise RSPs, both dissolve with disruption and lead to deritualization, the collapse of life meaning and associated behaviors (Knottnerus 2005, 2016, forthcoming). Dealing with responses related to deritualization was complex. Almost all interviewees gave multiple examples under each designated question. Therefore, statistics pertaining to responses in this chapter will not equal the total number of interviewees (N = 20), but the total instances of deritualization commented on by respondents (N = 149). As compared to the previous chapters, tables will steer us through the information. Knottnerus (2016) argues that RSPs involve larger social arrangements as well as thoughts and behaviors unique to everyday lives. Therefore, it is no surprise to see bifurcation with interviewee responses. One category emerged including 74 references (50 percent) to family turmoil - see Table 8.1. A second category with 48 references (32 percent) to personal, individual-based disturbances appeared. A final category arose with 27 references (18 percent) to intergenerational dynamics.

FAMILY TURMOIL

With deritualization and family turmoil, interviewees discussed the post-disaster breakdown of rituals associated with maternal activities, sibling issues, relocation, interaction with relatives, and religious practice - see Table 8.2. Maternal activities related to changes in disposition and behavior with interviewees' mothers. Sibling issues connected to dynamics between

Table 8.1   Deritualization Post-Disaster

Category	Number	Percentage
Family Turmoil	74	50
Personal Disturbances	48	32
Intergenerational Dynamics	27	18
Total	149	100

brothers and sisters. Relocation pertained to families moving soon after the disaster. Interaction with relatives related to decayed social bonds between family members, including extended family. Religious practice referred to the collapse of spiritual endeavors.

Maternal Activities

Thirty-three responses (44 percent) existed for family turmoil and maternal activities. Themes on role shifts, social impact on psychological disposition (SIPD), overprotection, and money became apparent. With role shifts, interviewees discussed mothers decreasing maternal activities and increasing traditional paternal behaviors. This was especially challenging for those who did not remarry in an era where society stigmatized single mothers more than now. Often citing "toughness" and "strength," consider comments like, "She always worked hard at being a mother and father," "She was just totally focused on us kids and doing the job of two parents," and "It was difficult, but she was totally focused on all aspects of getting her kids raised and educated." Role strain increased with this shift, especially for mothers engaged in efforts outside of the home. One interviewee explained, "At the time of my father's death, my mother was driving back and forth working on her master's degree at UCA. She had her hands full." Another said, "Mother tried to keep her job in town and run the farm. Cows would get out and neighbors complained. She would have to hunt cows down and then go to work the next morning."

One daughter discussed how her father always took the family on road trips but that stopped. Her mother tried to take up the mantle but had a hard time. The respondent noted, "She put us all in her car, and bless her heart, by herself she drove us up the Alcan Highway into Alaska. But, it wasn't the same." Interviewees commented on how their mothers started to reduce displays of emotion, detailing how they often "fought back tears" and "tried not to cry." One person explained her mother always tried to "keep the pain in her eyes" from the children. Mothers taking on traditional fatherly rituals frustrated many interviewees. A daughter commented on courtship, "I had a

Table 8.2 Deritualization Post-Disaster: Family Turmoil

Subcategory	Number	Percentage
Maternal Activities	33	44
Sibling Issues	22	30
Relocation	9	12
Interaction with Relatives	8	11
Religious Practice	2	3
Total	74	100

date one time with a guy who went to my church. He came in to pick me up and my mom told him that if he mistreated me she was mom and dad both, and she would beat the hell out of him. He never asked me out again." This theme of overprotection came through in other interviews. Some explicated, "Mom may have been too overprotective," "Talk about a mama bear," "She had a pretty tight grip on us all," and "My mother watched us all like a hawk." Regarding overprotection and a move away from her father's loose rules, one interviewee said, "I can remember telling my mom one time it had been hell since dad died. I had marks for a while over that. She was just trying to protect me I guess."

Norris et al. (2002) report mothers have a much harder time post-disaster while juggling caretaking for others. You can imagine the pressure many of these women felt. If not, responses on deritualization and SIPD make it clear. Interviewees made comments such as "It took mother a good while to get over it all," "She shut down and didn't talk much," and "I knew something was really wrong around 3rd grade when I noticed she had started drinking really heavy on the weekends." One made it clear that "Living with my mother after my dad died scarred me for my whole life." Other respondents said things like, "The day it happened I lost both parents, my daddy to the silo and my mother to a nervous breakdown" and "She was just trying to survive, but she became vulnerable and [people] took advantage of her." One daughter detailed how her mother ritualistically tried to put on a happy face in spite of the disaster, but everyone could tell it was a performance. Her mother lost her father the year before her husband died in the silo. The interviewee told me, "My mom had a great sense of humor, but I think she overdid it sometimes just to cover her true feelings." Financial strain did not help. Discussing life post-disaster and rituals involving eating or extracurricular activities, respondents said things like "We just barely made it," "Dad's paychecks stopped, but we did get a little Social Security check," "Mom managed to keep her garden going and save up $20 for groceries," and "Money was tight."

Sibling Issues

Twenty-two replies (30 percent) concerned deritualization and sibling issues. As with maternal activities, role shifts were relevant, along with SIPD and monetary factors. Role shift comments were minimal, but powerful. For example, with animosity toward her older brother, one person explained, "My older brother tried to take charge of the household. He moved his wife and all three of his kids in with us after daddy died. He said he was doing it to help my mother, but it was chaos. All of our old routines were gone with all those new people in the house." As with mothers, siblings felt the weight of deritualization by way of SIPD. Interviewees commented "My five-year-old brother really missed his father," "My brother and sisters went crazy over all the changes," "My sister was traumatized not having my dad around anymore and had nightmares for years," "Not having dad be a part of our lives anymore hurt my sisters bigtime," and "It was devastating for all of us children." Variation in managing deritualization could have existed due to mental resources.

One interviewee explained that his autistic sister had a worse time managing than him since their father was such a big part of her everyday life. Norris et al. (2002) state that maturity buffers some of the stress that comes with disaster experiences. Accordingly, some interviewees noted that older siblings probably had "more awareness" of what was happening and managed the event better. However, his older brother, possibly missing routine displays of affection his father gave him and those his mother withheld after the incident, turned his attention to promiscuous behavior. The respondent told me, "You have to look for ways to forget the way things used to be and overcome what you're feeling. I think that is what he was doing." Another person said her sister, who did like to talk about her dad all the time, turned inward and just never talked about him again her whole life. Another said her brother turned his feelings outward and became wildly aggressive throughout life. Shortly after the disaster, he drove to a town nearby and picked a fight with some people "probably knowing he could not win." He ended up with a broken glass bottle shoved up his nose. After she and her mother picked him up at the police station, she said he remained bedridden and "bled terribly for weeks." With her mother out working, the interviewee, 10 at the time, elucidated, "I tried to watch him on my own. We finally had to take him to the hospital." Regardless, situational events yielded lifelong responses as well. One daughter told me:

My oldest sister was in a fight with my dad that morning. He had been at my grandmother's house and came over to give her the last $5 he had in his wallet. She told him that she hated his guts and hoped she never saw him again. He died that day, and it changed her whole life, every aspect of it. She has lived so miserable because of that day. After that, she lived different. It is sad for me to see her today. It's just pitiful.

Mirroring this case of lifelong turmoil, a different interviewee noted:

My brother was exactly like my dad. My dad didn't always make the very best choices and neither did my brother. I think it cost him his life. He didn't take care of himself. He did not live a very healthy life, and he kind of isolated himself from the rest of the family. Some of it may go back to this event. I think it had a lot to do with it, I really do. We were at the age when I think it was so important to have a male figure around to show you how to be a man. He went from having that every day, and then all of a sudden he didn't have it.

One person said of her brother's disposition post-disaster, "My brother became an alcoholic, married like four times, and went to prison three times." Discussing an older sister who previously had nothing peculiar about her behavior, one daughter told me that her sibling started obsessively accumulating material possessions. She no longer interacted in a way reflecting people as important. She became overly concerned with things. She recounted, "She always had what I would call a hole in her heart from all this. She started buying, almost like a hoarder. She has like 40 dogs. She buys so much she doesn't need. If I handed her $500, she would just blow it on something she doesn't need. I believe she had a mental break." Though minimal, others commented on similar behaviors with siblings. However, some discussed siblings hoarding items that used to belong to their fathers. That created ritualized conflict. Interviewees said this was due, in part, to jealousy. Some respondents stated that they were their father's "favorite" child, and the deritualization of their father's protection left them susceptible to sibling exploitation. One daughter explained that her mother, especially after receiving the financial settlement, spent lavishly on her siblings. This especially occurred with her older brother. She did without like never before. They knowingly took money designated to her after the disaster leaving her with hardly anything for her transition to adulthood. Reflecting this theme, a different daughter said:

> My sister and I have hard feelings toward my brother. When my dad died, we had two new vehicles. We didn't own a home, but my dad always wanted very nice cars. My mother was driving a fairly, brand new Ford Galaxy. My dad's truck was a Ford pickup. Well, after he died, my mother gave my brother the pickup. She let my brother have my dad's truck! Well, he ended up selling it, and then he got a very expensive, very fast Dodge Charger that he raced. Then he got deployed to Japan, and my mother made payments on his car for him! He got his portion of the money after dad died, but he also got two vehicles out of it. My sister and I had to buy our own. That sticks with me.

Some of this may be due to gender dynamics and mothers associating their sons with their dead husbands. As one daughter detailed, "After my dad died my mother showed a whole lot more partiality to my brother. She didn't do as much for us girls. . . . Maybe she saw my father in him." Regardless, sibling issues among those with the same gender designation occurred too. One son I interviewed called his brothers "greedy." He told me that before his father died, his dad bought him a horse saddle. His brother took possession of it after the disaster and said, "It's mine!" He would never give it back. The same thing also happened with his father's tractor.

Relocation

Nine responses (12 percent) involved relocation. A daughter who was 12 at the time of the disaster told me, "We ended up selling the farm and moved out of the country to Beebe and built a house." Relocating to a new house or new town can be part of a process associated with building a new sense of self after a loss. As seen in the next chapter, if you move to a location where family support is more available, the potential for positive social bonds can create higher levels of emotional support (DeSpelder and Strickland 2020). A daughter interviewed stated, "My mother moved us back to Oklahoma very soon and my grandmother moved in with us to help out." Several others explained how they or their families moved to Texas after the event. One son, who was 23 at the time of the disaster, implied the disaster did not influence his everyday life much since he had only been back to Arkansas a couple of times since it happened. However, shifts in living locations, whether represented by one big move or a series of them, created a collapse in RSPs (Ulsperger et al. 2017). One respondent, 11 then, moved with her mother to Texas and started school in a major metropolitan area within a few years of her father passing. She explained her mother wanted a fresh start, but also decided her daughter needed a place where she "could get a better education." I will address her personal struggles pertaining to educational adjustment shortly. Another female interviewee who was 10 when her father died indicated, "We moved out of our house we lived in with daddy to a new one. It took us time to adjust." There was one instance where a son explained to me that his father and mother were building a new house around the time of the incident. His father was not able to work on it with his wife anymore, but she put in the effort to complete it on her own. His dad never lived in the house, but his presence lingered. The son recalled a conversation he had with his mother after the completion of the project. He told me he was sitting with his mother in the house one day and said to her, "What's the one thing about this house daddy would've liked the best?" Swaying in her rocking chair, she replied, "He would have liked the commode." The mother went on to detail how she and her husband "had to go out to the barn" in the old house to urinate and defecate. That ritual was gone. Though the husband never experienced the pleasures of modern sewage, the mother explained he would have loved indoor plumbing.

Interaction with Relatives

Eight replies (11 percent) concerned deritualization and interaction with relatives. Some deritualization overlapped with relocation here. For example, one daughter who was 26 then explained, "Before it happened, I came home four times a year even with me living in Texas. We would always come in for

Christmas and family reunions. After dad died, we would come to Arkansas maybe once every year. Visits never got back to normal. We always just ended up talking about how somebody's neglect killed daddy." Another daughter, then 15, stated, "My dad dying cut me off from a lot of family. Things changed a lot." Keying in on celebration rituals and family interaction, someone who was 14 told me her mother tried to pull everyone together for a sense of normalcy, but "Birthdays and holidays were not special anymore. Before losing dad, we had lost my sister a few years before. It all took the joy from us in so many ways." Back to August 9 as a reminder, one person told that her family was having a birthday party for her father the day the disaster occurred. Everyone was "expecting him to come home to a birthday meal that never happened." Returning to mothers, a daughter, just a few years old when the event took place, suggested that her mom's tendency to "shut down" and cut off interaction with others left her feeling isolated. She told me she was active in a variety of areas through her school-age years, but she could not remember many people coming to support her. On her mother, she stated, "I can remember her maybe going to one game." A different daughter explained how her mother would take certain family members on shopping trips, leaving her out. Her father's death fresh on her mind, she desired interaction with others, especially since all the quality time she spent with her father abruptly stopped. She expressed, "I would just stay back at home when they would go . . . I was by myself with nobody having time to talk to me. I would lock up the house. If it was at night, I would try to go to bed, but always ended up staying awake and crying."

Previous acknowledgments of the military and its importance changed within families. Everyone was not always on the same page. One interviewee explained that tensions in this area emerged immediately after the death of his father and uncle in the disaster. He pointed out:

> My grandpa had a rough time since he lost two of his sons. We was at his house afterward and a car come up. It was somebody from the air base. Two guys knocked at the door. One said, "Sir, we just want to tell you that your son was killed in the missile silo." Grandpa said, "We already know that, it's time for y'all to leave because y'all killed my son." They had the nerve to walk back up, knock on the door again, and ask where my uncle's family lived. They didn't even know we were the same family. Grandpa said, "No disrespect, but I'm going to go in the back to get my shotgun. If I come back and y'all are still here, I'll kill both of y'all for my two sons that y'all killed."

One daughter told me this kind of animosity may have played into her family "nearly disowning" her. She enlisted in the army, and her family "thought it was horrible."

Religious Practice

Two responses (3 percent) involved religious practice. A daughter explained that through her life, her mother shifted discussions on religion to her dead father. Trying to convince her daughter not to blame God, she would encourage her to see it all as "an accident" with no connection to the family religious beliefs. A different daughter told me that church was "important" to her family, but "none of us could ever go back in that little church dad's funeral was in. It was just too painful." They eventually moved their membership to a different town.

PERSONAL DISTURBANCES

With deritualization and personal disturbances, interviewees discussed the breakdown of rituals associated with paternal activities, SIPD, education, role shifts, religious practice, and employment - see Table 8.3. Paternal activities relate to changes directly involving the interviewees and their fathers. As with a theme previously discussed, SIPD connects to individual deritualization's impact on psychological disposition. Educational deritualization pertains to personal experiences with scholarship and learning environments, and role shifts to an aforementioned theme involving the changing of family expectations. Religious practice relates to personal beliefs and spiritual behaviors, while employment refers to work activities.

Paternal Activities

Twenty-four responses (50 percent) about personal turmoil involved deritualization and paternal activities. Several respondents argued that without their fathers, special moments of "inspiration," "encouragement," and "learning" ceased because they had to "finish growing up without a dad." Trips to the "sale barn" in towns like Beebe abruptly stopped, as did participation in certain recreational activities.

Table 8.3 Deritualization Post-Disaster: Personal Disturbances

Subcategory	Number	Percentage
Paternal Activities	24	50
SIPD	11	23
Education	6	13
Role Shifts	3	6
Religious Practice	2	4
Employment	2	4
Total	48	100

Ten at the time of the disaster, one daughter explained, "I was probably closer to my daddy than I was any other adult. He was probably the only adult who ever took me seriously." Interviewees often explained how admiration for their fathers shaped daily routines. Fifteen at the time, one son stated, "Daddy was my hero, and life wasn't the same without him. I had a hard time going to the farm without him around, and I missed seeing him when he came home from work every day." He continued, "There wasn't anyone as good as daddy looking out for me and teaching me lessons after he was gone." One daughter said, "He wanted me to learn how to drive, so he would let me get in his lap and drive his pickup truck." Echoing sentiments of teaching, a different daughter told me:

> Everything changed. My dad was in the category of a teacher. . . . He was the person who wanted to make sure I saw and learned everything I possibly could. . . . I missed it. My dad inspired and encouraged all of his children. I will never forget it. He sat us down when I was around the age of 10 and told us we would absolutely be going to college. . . . He taught me to run. He taught me how to exercise. I would go running with him, and when I felt like I couldn't go on he would tell me I could. He would say, "Girls can run!" He always told me I could do anything in the world I wanted to do. I think especially back in that day for a woman it was unique to have a man encouraging you. Some women thought there were things they couldn't do. I never felt that way. That stopped, and I missed my dad teaching me things. The things he taught me before he was gone stayed with me. . . . He was very strict, but very loving. I missed the structure he brought to my life.

Perhaps a lost art, one son explained that his father taught him to never "talk about politics or religion" because "you're liable to offend a person." Maybe I should have heeded that warning writing this book, though I am still perplexed as to how a public health crisis became a political issue. Regardless, that interviewee said his father taught him so much more though. He let me know how his dad showed him to tame horses, train dogs, shoot guns, drive a tractor, and make his own money. Amazed at the things he learned from his father, he stated:

> There was a man who couldn't tame his quarter horse so he gave him to daddy. He took him out into a pond, hopped on his back, and started riding him. He done that two or three times and broke him right there. A man had a gun shy dog that he told daddy wasn't any good. Daddy brought him home, put him in the boat with him on the pond, and shot his gun. There was nowhere for the dog to go. Before long, he wasn't gun shy anymore. . . . My uncle couldn't kill some ducks on a pond once. Daddy went out there with a .22 instead of a shotgun and got them all. Then he said, "Now go get your ducks." I swear that is true . . . . If daddy took one step, I took three. . . . He was working some land one time and

had me get up on the tractor with him. Eventually, I was driving it by myself. I made a round and he stopped me. He had that look, and I knew I better get my rear end off that tractor. He pointed down the line I had driven and said, "That looks like a snake crawled through there, but we'll straighten it up. I think you can do a better job than that." I said, "Yes sir!" Right there, he taught me how to drive a tractor and take pride in my work. I was 10 and right then I learned how to get to the clutch, stop a tractor, and take it out of gear . . . . I did something to make $20. Daddy told me to hang on to it. The next day he drove me to the dairy. Daddy picked out a bull calf and helped me buy it. Later, he showed me how to sell it to buy more. I eventually ended up with 16 head of cattle!

A daughter, 16 then, discussed "little moments" when she learned things nobody would have told her about otherwise. She mentioned, "I had picked up a matchbox somewhere just lying on the ground. For some reason, it had a 50-cent piece in it. I always remember dad telling me that was good luck. There are other things like that he told me." Other interviewees discussed everything from respectfully turning your lights off when turning around in someone's driveway at night to learning about baseball.

A few interviewees missed traveling with their dads, whether cross-country or just a few towns over. One daughter stated, "I would travel with daddy. Up on the hill on Highway 64 right before you get to Conway there was a rest stop. We would go to a country store before we got there, get bologna and a bottled Coke. I didn't have anything like that anymore after he was gone. I still think about all that every time I drive to Conway." Besides going on drives, many recreational rituals ended. Children of the 53 indicated to me, "I never got to go fishing with my daddy again," "My daddy and I went fishing a whole lot and that stopped," and "I remember he took me hunting with him and fishing. That never happened again." Someone noted, "My dad would take us waterskiing, but after he died my mother sold the boat. We didn't go waterskiing anymore." Another said, "I never got to hear his music again. He played the fiddle, and I believe he taught himself. I was learning how to play the piano and my brother was learning how to play the guitar. We would all play together. The music stopped." Of all interviewees, only one person strongly suggested an absence of deritualization in terms of paternal activities. He told me, "I didn't have a father growing up, so that kind of is what it is. I don't remember ever thinking that it was odd. I don't think it was traumatizing." He did explain that his memory of his childhood is limited and that could be due to living through this incident.

Social Impact on Psychological Disposition

Eleven replies (23 percent) concerned deritualization and SIPD. One interviewee commented, "As a kid, I may have been mentally sick" because dealing with the disaster "was just really hard." Other participants noted, "With dad's chair empty, life felt empty. I felt empty" and "I didn't feel secure with him gone. I still have that empty void." Mirroring these comments and explaining the lifelong impact of the event, one son said:

> I've held on to what it would have been like if my dad would've been here all my life. I think I would've felt a bit more secure. I just have always had that empty void. I can break down at any moment thinking about him. They say time heals the pain. It does in some cases. My mom's been gone now for about 10 years. I don't think about her as much, but you know, I still think about my dad because of the way he died.

Reflecting survivor's guilt, a daughter, 15 at the time of the disaster, told me, "It is crazy to think this way when you are a kid, but I thought to myself if I would've died everybody could've gone on a little better. Why did it have to be dad?" Several interviewees compared themselves to their siblings to gauge the impact of the disaster on their own perceived psychological disposition. One respondent stated, "I don't think it all hurt my brothers like it did me" and another, "I was the one who became codependent." Reflecting resource variation with age, one daughter, 12 when her father perished, explained, "They were working and had their own families. It didn't impact them like it did me." She went on to say, "I've been married 47 years now to my second husband. All of this may have influenced my first marriage. I lost my mother a few years after dad. I was searching for some family connection. I thought my first husband was going to be it, but he just wasn't." Also seeking to fill the void of a fatherless life, a daughter who lost her dad at three explained, "I was always longing and looking for that father figure. I'm married to a wonderful man and all my expectations for him have maybe been too much through the years. I realize now that my father would have been human like any other person."

Education

Six responses (13 percent) involved education. The disruption of the disaster and deaths of their fathers created problems with academic success, which Ulsperger et al. (2017) point out is a serious detrimental outcome that can compound stress that is already accumulating by way of ritualized strain. Ingrained in responses at this point of interviews, participants commented, "I think I would've went to college if not for all of this," "It just ended up being hard going back to school," "My grades dipped," and "After the accident, my grades did suffer. I had nobody to help me." Some tension resulted from mothers encouraging daughters to fall back on traditional gender roles when fathers previously fought for the alternative position. One daughter specified:

My mother wanted us to live our lives, but I guess my partial resentment was I had this expectation from my dad that I would go on to college and have a career. At one point, my mother insisted that I take Home Economics. She wasn't nasty about it. I did what she wanted, but resented it because I fell behind in math. She thought all I needed to do was train to be a homemaker. She didn't consider herself well educated, and she was a very pretty woman. She just focused on different things than what I valued because of my dad.

Disruption appeared to be a double-edged sword with education. Aware of relocation dynamics, one daughter cited her move to Texas and said, "When I started school there, it was in a bigger city. The kids would tease me. They would call me a country girl, say I was a hillbilly, and ask me why all the people in Arkansas went barefoot." She then explained things improved, and she ended up getting better grades than ever and benefited from exposure to diverse peers. Parental employment may have cushioned the educational deritualization blow for some. One interviewee pointed out that his mother was a teacher and always placed a value on education no matter what. Focusing on her son, she never remarried, and he went on to obtain a PhD.

Role Shifts

Three replies (6 percent) concerned role shifts, with interviewees feeling like they had to adopt matronly responsibilities to help mothers who had added paternal duties. One daughter said, "I felt like it was my responsibility to take care of everybody." Another had clear resentment, partially due to feeling forced to care for younger siblings. She told me, "My older sister didn't have any of the responsibilities I had to take care of our younger brother. When it came to taking care of my brother, my mother would say my sister's nerves wouldn't let her help out. Nerves? Of course, she was going out on dates, and I didn't get to." One respondent explained, "I became my brother's caretaker. I mean, I would talk to his teachers or the principal or whoever when something was going on with him at school." Reproducing previously discussed rituals of mothers safeguarding children, the interviewee further detailed, "I didn't really mind taking care of him though. I probably spoiled him too much and was overprotective." One older son provided an in-depth analysis of how he felt the need to look after his family after his father's death. He recalled that it was difficult for him to leave the house and start his own life when he reached a certain age. What made it even harder was his mother remarrying shortly after and finding herself in a bad relationship. He made it clear that his siblings did not look after their mother appropriately. He said, "I didn't think she would ever get married. I went to my little brother and said she wouldn't have married that man if I would've been home. Nothing good came out of that marriage and it all turned out to be a living hell for everyone."

Religious Practice

Two references (4 percent) were on religious practice. One daughter said to me, "When I think about him not being around, I think about God. I tell myself he lived out the life God expected him to, but I still think to myself that I got cheated out of so many years of his company." Reflecting a higher level of salience, a son commented, "The whole thing made me very angry and changed my religious beliefs for a long time . . . I have been off and on with religion for years and years. I still struggle with anger, especially when August rolls around."

Employment

Two instances (4 percent) of employment-related deritualization existed. One discussion focused on the period immediately after the death of the interviewee's father. Reflecting employment-based rituals, a son explained, "My dad baled hay for a lot of people. Me and my brother helped him. All that work went away." A different son had a remarkable, but unfortunate, more long-term experience with employment rituals. Detailing his experiences with deritualization and work, he told about joining the National Guard six years after his father died. He did not indicate to me any problems talking about his father to others during that time. However, things changed. He clarified:

I had the opportunity to go to work at the Little Rock Air Force Base. I had stayed away from it for so many years because I hated it so bad. They were responsible for this accident, but after a few years, I got a job there working for civil engineering. I ended up working for years around so many people who worked at the silos themselves. They made jokes. They would joke about certain things, you know. One time they put a shoe by one of the places where you could get out of a silo. They made it look like there was somebody who was trapped in the silo accident and was trying to escape. They would take pictures of stuff like that and show them around. They would show me stuff like that, but nobody knew my dad passed away out there except a couple of people. I put up with that so many years, these things happening. They have like a newspaper they put out through the Air Force. I have one that talks about what happened with this silo. It has pictures and everything. I made a promise to my dad that when I retired I would read it to everyone. I did it. I retired a year ago in October. In front of about 150 people out there, read them the whole article. When I was finished I said, "You've all known me for 25 years out here. This is not what happened at that missile silo. I will drop it at that." I cried, so did a lot of other people.

INTERGENERATIONAL DYNAMICS

Eight interviewees explicitly said they never had children, or failed to mention children at any point in the interview - see Table 8.4. Explaining that her sister never had children either, one of these people did spend some time talking of how disaster changed the lives of her brother's children. Twelve respondents discussed 27 aspects of deritualization related to their children. This involved seeking answers, absence of narratives, traumatic narratives, rejection of narratives, and activity voids.

Seeking Answers

Seven responses (26 percent) conveyed that grandchildren had taken time out of their everyday lives to devote attention to the disaster. They were compelled to have a better understanding of it, as reflected by specific behaviors. An interviewee commented that one grandchild, "Having a lot of questions, very recently developed quite an interest in trying to understand my dad's and our family's military history, including what happened to dad." Others made comments such as, "My son has shown an interest in it all through the years" and "My kids are always reading articles about it." Discussing a son, a different respondent noted, "He is always seeing what he can find on the internet." When looking at background information for this project, I found grandchildren posts on various internet sites related to the disaster. Also, similar to my work on this book, one person told me, "When my daughter was in, I don't know, 7th or 8th grade, her school project one year was on this incident. She put together a 25-page or so document. It had pictures of my dad, newspaper articles, and just different things. It means a lot to me that she did that. She is 28 now and lives close by."

Absence of Narratives

Six responses (22 percent) detailed how interviewees suffered because they had nothing about the 53 they wanted to pass along to children. They

Table 8.4 Deritualization Post-Disaster: Intergenerational Dynamics

Subcategory	Number	Percentage
Seeking Answers	7	26
Absence of Narratives	6	22
Traumatic Narratives	5	19
Rejection of Narratives	5	19
Activity Voids	4	14
Total	27	100

also said they did not know how to talk to their children about the disaster. Respondents gave comments such as, "I never could explain to them why granddaddy wasn't around," "There wasn't ever too much I wanted to tell," "I was just trying to get on with my life," "I didn't know how to talk about it," and "I didn't talk, but just cried when my kids brought it up."

Traumatic Narratives

Five responses (19 percent) pertained to a need to have profound discussions on the details of the disaster with their children. In this area, interviewees made comments like, "They know about it, and they know how he died in that missile base," "I talked to her all about how it happened," and "I always took my daughter to the cemetery and talked about her granddaddy's death as much as I could." One said, "I always told her about it, and she always had really hard experiences with that." As you would assume, not all grandchildren wanted to know the specifics.

Rejection of Narratives

Five responses (19 percent) involved the ritualistic rejection of narratives. Participants said, "I've always tried to talk to my kids about it, and they just turn a deaf ear," "I try to tell them about it, but they never asked me questions," and "Only one shows much interest." Extremely perplexed and blending in pessimism about younger generations, one respondent said, "I took my son one day to the cemetery. I always thought he had a little sense. I told him from where we were standing he could see his granddad's grave. I tried to talk about the accident . . . I might as well be telling him about pinecones on the tree. Younger people don't care. They scare me."

Activity Voids

Four responses in this category (14 percent) concerned activity voids. Here, interviewees said things like "My children missed out on doing things with my dad" and "They missed having a grandfather."

SUMMARIZING DERITUALIZATION

For surviving families, rituals broke down post-disaster. Interviewees mentioned family turmoil more than personal disturbances. Perhaps participants were more comfortable discussing the breakdown of rituals experienced by others compared to the collapse of their own personal life meaning and associated behaviors. It is also possible that the family domain of interaction, once offering a sense of security and identity, evolved into something menacing and made a serious imprint on the children's cognitive frameworks (see Edelstein 2004).

With family turmoil, lifescape changes for mothers topped the list. Women abruptly became the sole head of household and struggled in the absence of their husbands. They attempted to deal with loss of structure with the family. Managing grief, immediately they had to address role conflicts, juggling maternal and paternal tasks. This occurred homologically in the home and outside of it. Mothers inherited the position of ritual enforcer. They took the lead with family activities, generating rules related to interaction with those outside of the family (e.g., dating rituals) and initiated an overprotective disposition. Moreover, stay-at-home status deritualized for mothers. Some started new jobs, primarily to generate family financial security. However, this led to more disruption when employment responsibilities were at odds with home obligations. Struggling with sorrow, some mothers emotionally withdrew from salient maternal RSPs involving support for their children. This lifescape shift escalated feelings of isolation. Also echoing already discussed disaster research, some surviving family increased practices involving substance abuse to manage added stress.

In terms of structural ritualization theory, sibling troubles have a high frequency in the family category too. We again see lifescape changes revolve around a vacuum created by the death of fathers. However, in this case, siblings such as older brothers stepped in to exert control. This led to family animosity. Sibling divisions furthered when mothers allocated more resources to sons. This RSP may have occurred because sons reminded mothers of dead fathers or due to traditional rites concerning patriarchal control. Older children, already out of the house, may have experienced less grief and deritualization. In some ways, they had already started to create emotional distance between themselves and their fathers. Moving to new houses prolonged disruption after the disaster. Perhaps feeling threatened by their local environment, families ended up experiencing additional strain because they had to adjust to new domains. This even applied to cases where new homes had better amenities than the old ones. Also of note are salient examples of relocation involving major geographic shifts. Moving to a new house supported survivor recovery if resources in the area, such as extended family, existed. Conversely, it increased isolation for some because they were "cut off" from the family who could offer support. Transfer of church membership is applicable here as well.

On personal disturbances, the highest frequency of deritualization concerned paternal activities. Therefore, respondents most often mentioned the sorrow and the deconstruction of RSPs involving shared conduct with fathers. This included lifescape changes linked to recreational practices, conversations yielding emotional support, and behaviors of encouragement. The second most noted theme corresponded with SIPD. Interviewees felt a "void" without their fathers around. Hinting at increased insecurity related to lifescape changes, children felt uneasy knowing fathers were not coming home from work, not sitting at the dinner table, not taking them on trips. Months after the disaster and throughout life, interviewees would ask themselves, "What would it be like if daddy was still around?" Some struggled with survivor's guilt. Several still do. Less frequent in this area were comments on educational changes. However, accounts of poor school performance and lack of parental help with schoolwork are compelling. They represent recreancy-related distrust in the legitimacy of a previously valued institution and lowered sense of support from authority figures in the home. Reports on mothers who encouraged their daughters to stop pursuing male endeavors and seek out traditional female behaviors instead are equally potent. With mothers abruptly stopping certain maternal RSPs, some children did not have a choice. A small number of interviewees discussed fulfilling maternal roles to keep their families functioning. For example, they increased RSPs related to household maintenance and tending to younger sibling's educational affairs. With limited presence, interviewee comments also indicated deritualization by way of the rejection of religion and lack of employment, which linked to the father's personal network.

Deritualization findings also showed difficulties with intergenerational dynamics. Forty percent of respondents said they did not have kids or failed to mention them during the interview process. For those without children, you have to wonder if the trauma they experienced as children influenced their childlessness, either consciously or subconsciously. For those with children, some of the 53 would be proud to know their grandchildren ended up expressing an interest in their lives. With many, it was probably a ritualized rite of passage for grandchildren to hear stories about their grandfathers, listen to their parents talk about the disaster, and research the event on their own. The disaster defined their parents' sense of self, and it defined many of their lives too. However, some of the 53 might be disappointed to know that their children have tried to share memories with grandchildren, but they suffer rejection. Ancestors and death-related events carry no meaning for some. This surely generates frustration. Some daughters and sons feel like they lost the opportunity to have a father. Homologous to that, they feel like their children missed having a grandfather as an important life resource. They want to create an enduring legacy around their fathers, but many cannot.

Chapter 9

Reritualization

Keeping an eye on the world while working on this book, I did not think things could get more surreal. It is January 6, 2021, and some still refuse to believe the pandemic is real. Those who perceive ongoing dangers patiently await answers. The U.S. government is distributing vaccines, slowly. State agencies, with almost a year to plan, are confused as to how to inoculate the public. There are other issues. Just a few days ago, some health officials in Tennessee turned vulnerable people away after saying they ran out of the vaccine. Some report that was a lie, with workers calling their family and friends to give them remaining doses (Rawnsley 2021). Today, citizens stormed the U.S. Capitol building (Ferris et al. 2021). One had face paint and a horned fur hat. A different man, who lives close to me, sat in a representative's office chair with his boots kicked up on her desk. It is evident that for a certain segment of America, distrust is at an all-time high. I could feel it flowing from the mouths of just about everyone I interviewed for this book. Perceptions of injustice were apparent when they talked about government figureheads, contractors, and lawyers they dealt with post-disaster. Young mothers and their kids wanted to reconstruct their lives and move forward feeling those in power treated them fairly, with dignity and respect. "Moving forward" is an interesting concept. I wonder how the United States moves forward after the past year. This brings us to reritualization.

Remember that reritualization is the re-creation of an existing ritualized symbolic practice (RSP) or creation of a new one. This process softens the blow of lifescape shifts linked to deritualization. It creates cognitive clarity, reassurance, and stability. However, as you will see, it can have unintended consequences, including continued disruption (Knottnerus 2016). With reritualization, I totaled all instances discussed by all respondents (N = 387). As with deritualization, two categories emerged, with 77 (20 percent) concerning family and 310 (80 percent) focusing on individual actions of people interviewed – see Table 9.1.

FAMILY RITUALS

Interviewees discussed spending money, family activities, traditional grief practices, community and friend interaction, disaster-related interaction, and pharmaceutical consumption – see Table 9.2. Spending money related to exhausting previously unavailable streams of revenue. Family activities connected to behaviors within the core and extended family, including aspects of paternal alternatives. Traditional grief practices pertained to ritualistically visiting cemeteries, going to the disaster site, maintaining possessions of the deceased, and memorial activities. Community and friend interaction involved behaviors with people from the towns of the departed and elevated camaraderie with others in family social networks. Disaster-related interaction linked to activities with people connected to the disaster outside of family social networks. Consider visits with survivors of the disaster at Launch Complex (LC) 373-4 or other workers associated with it. Pharmaceutical consumption related to taking prescription drugs.

Spending Money

Twenty-nine responses (38 percent) about family rituals involved spending money. Most of the time, interviewees cited money from the lawsuit, but they did occasionally allude to other sources of income. This included Social Security monies or financial contributions from those outside of the household. Coinvestigators and I did not code instances of simply having new forms of income as reritualization, because sometimes families did not spend the money. As one interviewee said, "Mother got a $35,000 settlement. All that money was still in the bank when she died. She did receive Social Security checks for the kids, but she deposited them into the bank and never spent any of that money on herself." It is possible that saving money was a new ritual providing some sense of security. Regardless, when interviewees mentioned their families doing something specific with money they did not have before the disaster, coding occurred.

Table 9.1   Reritualization Post-Disaster

Category	Number	Percentage
Family Rituals	77	20
Personal Rituals	310	80
Total	387	100

Table 9.2   Reritualization Post-Disaster: Family Rituals

Subcategory	Number	Percentage
Spending Money	29	38
Family Activities	19	25
Traditional Grief Practices	14	18
Community and Friend Interaction	12	15
Disaster-Related Interaction	2	3
Pharmaceutical Consumption	1	1
Total	77	100

A 69-year-old daughter told me, "One of my brothers helped take care of us monetarily. We relied on that money, before the lawyers started hunting us." General comments on spending existed, such as "Momma got a little bit of money and used it," "My mother used any money she got to keep up with the bills," and "That money helped my mother live out the rest of her life since dad wasn't around." Retrospectively, disappointed with settlement terms, a 67-year-old son explained, "I think each family got something like $30,000. It seemed like a lot then, but for a wife with no husband taking care of four or five kids, that's no money." Reflecting aforementioned relocation, respondents discussed spending and housing accommodations. Interviewees noted, "The house we bought after it all was from the money," "We moved into a nice home in Beebe with central heat and air," and "The home my mother bought with it was a nice three-bedroom, two-bath brick home on an acre." Some mothers used money as an investment opportunity for their children and used it for potential home locations for their children to use later in life. A 58-year-old daughter reported, "Mom wasn't going to just hand money off to us, and let us go blow it. She made us each buy five acres of land."

With money designated for the children, respondents said things like, "All of us children got some settlement money to spend." Several people discussed new money helping with educational expenses. Respondents said, "My sister, who was brilliant, got her master's degree," "For us to go to school there was a small amount," "We used that money to go to college," and "Because of that money we were able to finish college." Note that some respondents discussed limitations placed on their reritualization due to what they perceived as not receiving enough money post-disaster. The two paramount lines of thought here deal with contractor/attorney behavior and the actions of some adult family members.

Representing recreancy and secondary trauma, many interviewees had strong words on contractors and attorneys connected to disaster litigation. These did not count as RSPs involving spending, but I believe are important to mention. A female respondent noted, "The settlement seems off compared to how much money they put into building the sites. I was looking through some old papers on all this, and I found the actual cost of what the government was paying to have the site upgraded. They were paying those 53 men pennies compared to the total cost. I was floored. It was ridiculous. It was an injustice."

On lawyers, one interviewee explained, "Those lawyers then are like they are now. They see an ambulance, and they go running for it." A male respondent elaborated, "An attorney from Conway came around, but everyone went with another guy. I think he was the one who tried to run for governor, or he was a governor once. He had a big firm in Little Rock." Specifically referencing Sid McMath, one son, 23 at the time of the incident, was dazzled with his family's representation. He stated, "Mom and I visited with that bigtime attorney. I was impressed with him. He told us how many other families had already gone with him." Others did not give similar responses. A son, 15 in the year of the disaster, said:

> Do you remember Sid McMath? He was the lead lawyer on the settlement. Momma got $35,000 out of it. That's all she got. Some of them got more, some of them got less. I heard her talking one time and she told someone the lawyers told her after awhile, "Take it right here or leave it." Momma didn't know about all the legal mumbo jumbo. Only place she'd really been in life was to town and back. The government took advantage, and she knew it. I heard her once crying to family and telling them she didn't know what to do. McMath and all of them, they was nothing but crooks. When someone says, "This is all the government is going to pay you, take it or leave it." What do you do? We were all just country folks. I'm not going to say ignorant or dumb, but the government had the upper hand.

A different son stated:

> My mom was older. She didn't get much, only like $30,000. It should have been a lot more than that. I think the lawyers took a lot. Mom had a law firm represent her. Do you remember Sid McMath? I don't know if he represented everybody or what. He had just been the governor back then. I don't know if he directly dealt with the families, but I believe it was his law firm. His name was all over it. He had a very prominent name because of the fact he had been a politician one time. . . . All the wives weren't like highly educated. It's not like many of them had been to college. They came from a background of poverty, so they maybe didn't have a lot of money. Some people I've talked to think the attorneys kind of took advantage of those women in the situation they were in. They basically told mom, "Here's how much money you're going to get." Somebody told me that at one point the law firm approached the families with a particular settlement number. The families were not happy with the number. They thought it should

be higher, but the attorneys told those women, "Well, it's not worth the fight for us. Here's what you're going to get, and you can take it or leave it." The government wasn't originally involved in the payout, but for some reason they came on later and said, "OK, we'll put up the money since it was an Air Force property." I guess the government decided it was their problem and not the contractors'.

Interviewees brought up Henry Woods too, implying he was the one their family had direct contact with via the McMath Law Firm. They questioned the decision of allowing the government to pay out so much of the lawsuits and not contractors. In this vein, some made critical comments of legal counsel but did not specify names. Regardless, their words echoed the thoughts discussed earlier. A daughter told me, "My mom always said the lawyers got more money than our entire family got. I do have one copy of a check that went to my mom from the lawyers for $39,000. I think the attorneys got like 70 percent of what we got. Really, we got nothing." A son, I have not mentioned yet furiously, pointed out, "They were starving the survivors out. They knew we all needed the money and waited until we couldn't wait any more. Then the lawyers told everybody, take this money they are offering now or wait a long time." One daughter, not knowing where to seek answers about the settlement years later said, "I called the contractor who employed my dad, and they couldn't tell me why the settlement was set up the way it was. There was no college funds set up for any of the children I knew. It was just done so improperly. They should have paid for the kids to go to college, set up a specific college fund." In the McMath Law Firm's defense, it appears Sid made sure the children of the 53 he represented had trust funds to pay for the future educational endeavors (McMath 2003). It is possible adult family members, perhaps represented by other attorneys, decided to divert such funds elsewhere.

Several interviewees commented on wanting to buy their first car or home, and the desire to buy a home when they entered adulthood. However, they were shocked to find out money they thought they had did not exist. Some mothers, maybe managing families less fortunate than others, clearly spent money designated for their children. One son argued that adults involved in the lives of children post-disaster "may have just been greedy." Regardless, one daughter told me:

> There was a trust set up for each individual kid. I don't know exactly how much I got, but it was really next to nothing. When I turned 18, I got the printout from the bank with the check that they sent me and what the money had been spent on. My mother had taken out $500 for clothes one year, $200 for this, and $300 for that, . . . When I got my money, it was only $1,200. . . . My mother should not have been able to access my account.

Another voiced her frustration saying, "Mother spent my money on my brother's medical bills. . . . She spent so much on them. I remember her sitting me down one day and telling me that she was going to take some of my money . . . I think mother used it for herself sometimes too. I didn't end up with much at all." I believe these types of responses represent structural isomorphism as related to recreancy and secondary trauma. Powerful entities took advantage of vulnerable families following the incident. However, once adults in some of those families had access to monies not designated for them, they took advantage of people the money was supposed to go to—vulnerable children who lost their fathers. As adults today, some interviewees implied they are still working through distrust and mean-spiritedness that characterized the period of their childhood surrounding the disaster. They feel betrayed by people they previously viewed as dependable, selfless, honorable, and loving.

Family Activities

Nineteen reritualization responses (25 percent) in the category of family rituals were on family activities. Instances of paternal alternatives appeared the most, typically involving the importance of a mother's new husband. Generally, if a surviving spouse remarried, it was within a few years after the disaster. For example, some interviewees said, "It helped my mom to remarry four years later," "Mom remarried three years after dad passed," and "It happened in '65 and mother remarried in January 1970." With the line of questioning in this area, respondents praised paternal alternatives noting, "Mom remarried, and he was another amazing man," "We were blessed with a wonderful stepfather," and "God blessed me with a really good stepdad." One daughter, so young she only knows her father through stories others tell, detailed to me:

> I don't remember how old I was, but I remember my sisters calling my stepdad by his first name. They weren't calling him dad . . . I clearly remember thinking, "This man isn't my dad?" It was strange, but you know, he was my dad. I don't know, just hearing them call him that though . . . That is when I realized I didn't really have a father. He did a great job with all of us. Yeah, I have no complaints.

Unfortunately, some wives had compounded loss, as a 66-year-old daughter explained, "My mother met someone. They ended up getting married when I was a senior in high school. They were married for 13 years, but he died of cancer." She went on to detail that her second stepdad continues to this day to help cushion the effects of not having a biological father for over 55 years. With great pride and introspection, she elaborated on being happy to pay back the care given to her throughout life. She clarified, "My mom is still alive. She lives nearby over in Arlington with my stepdad. I go over there all the time to see them and help them out." As noted previously, paternal alternatives were not always optimal. Consider aforementioned issues with new boyfriends or husbands already discussed in this book, in addition to statements like, "Mom only stayed married to her second husband for a couple of years. She was looking for someone to fill the void, but he was not it." A different person said, "When I was in college, mom did date someone briefly. My brother and sister were still living with her. They didn't care for the guy she was seeing. I think she was just lonely. She didn't end up remarrying." One component linked to unnecessary paternal alternatives was the presence of extended family. One son told me, "Mom didn't remarry. She was living around Ft. Smith at the time and decided to move back to Clarksville where all her relatives were."

Indeed, social capital had positive consequences for many families. A 68-year-old female reported, "My mother and siblings weren't going through it alone. We helped each other. My mother's children from her first marriage suffered, though they had a different father. Their dad thought he was going to be a big Hollywood movie star and abandoned them. Dad treated them like his own." A daughter, three when she lost her dad, stated,

> Mom had some help. I had a cousin who was my mother's age. She had one daughter that was a year younger than me, and she had gone through a divorce. I remember when I was growing up, she was very good friends with my mom . . . I don't know what they talked about or shared, but they talked and shared a lot. She became my mother's close friend. We all even vacationed together.

Others commented, "Luckily, mom's parents lived right up the street from us. She definitely had family around to help," "Mom's sister lived nearby," "Mom had extended family all around," and "Mother moved us from Little Rock back to Bald Knob to be around family so they could help her out."

A small number of interviewees expressed regret that they did not engage in new activities with the families enough, failing to ease the pain of others. Focusing on her mother, a daughter told me, "I couldn't support my mother emotionally. I was too selfish, just concentrating on my opinion that she wasn't paying enough attention to me. I don't think any of us children appreciated the grief she was going through. So, I feel somewhat guilty years later. I was so self-absorbed. I don't think I contributed to helping her." A son, who was a young adult when his dad died said to me, "I could have done more for my mom, but my ex-wife did not get along with her. She was jealous of my mom. She needed to consult with me about things, like what to do with the cows, the house, the car. Anyway, my wife was very insecure and that kept me from doing a lot I should have done."

Traditional Grief Practices

Fourteen responses (18 percent) involved traditional grief practices. Cemetery visits applied, as a 71-year-old interviewee noted, "My mother had a hard time recuperating and going on with her life. She went to the cemetery every day." Not all children were receptive to this, because it disrupted their own lives. One daughter told of how her brother demanded her mother stop going to the cemetery because it was not good for her or the children to be there so much.

Backing up disaster literature referenced in a previous chapter, families of the 53 visited the location where loved ones perished. Some went immediately to LC 373-4 before the government confirmed the death of the beloved. A daughter, 15 then, commented, "My brother went to the silo right when we all heard about what happened, but they wouldn't let him get as close as he wanted. He badly wanted to help with the recovery, to go in and get dad." Another said, "We all went over there shortly after, but they wouldn't let us in." A son, 24 then, told me, "My family went to the silo site as soon as we heard something happened. We spent the night up there. We tried to find out some information at the site, but of course, they had it sealed off." They told all the families there, "There's nothing to see. Come back later and we'll let you know." Though there is not much there anymore, some continued to visit the site. A 71-year-old interviewee commented, "You know, there's a marker there. A lot of people cannot find where the silo site is, but my sister and I have driven out there some. The last time, we actually drove as far as we could down that road until we got to where it is blocked." One son, wanting to go years ago, discussed his mother persuading him not to do it. He said, "I never went to the site itself, because mom never went to the site. I tried to get her to go out there, but she just wouldn't go." Detailed later, many interviewees kept their fathers' possessions and ritualistically integrated them into their lives after the disaster. Just a few mentioned other family members doing the same. This encompassed statements like, "My sister always kept a lot of his stuff."

As with cemetery headstones, one traditional grief practice pertains to family visiting memorials. Here, the memorial built for the 53 is important. Individual reritualization and the memorial will come up later. For now, just note interviewee comments such as, "My brother would go to the memorial. He told me all about it" and "My family went to the dedication. There is a photograph of all of us there." On erecting the memorial, respondents made statements like, "My sister dealt with the lady that started all that," "My family added a little bit of money to help build it," and "My older sister and my mother, they were really into that. They talked a lot to the woman that pushed to make that all a reality. We gave money."

Community and Friend Interaction

Twelve replies (15 percent) concerned social capital accompanying community and friend interaction. With patterns of community behavior, people in hometowns of the 53 knew which families lost loved ones, especially in cases where multiple men died from the area. Someone remarked, "It was hard for my family's community. You have three or four of yours buried in the same week, it's just hard." People in some towns made efforts to make surviving families feel at ease.

Illustrated in the interview process, respondents made statements like, "We'd go to Conway, to Penney's or Franklin's or wherever, and everybody would talk to mom" and "Mom had a little dress shop after dad got killed. She did quite a bit of business, but part of it was that everyone wanted to come in and visit with her." Participants told me things such as, "People would come up to my older brother all the time and say that they knew my dad. They would tell him how much they respected him. That happened for years and years after dad died."

According to respondents, these ritualized occurrences put their mothers at ease. However, they sometimes created a disruptive tone and secondary trauma. A daughter explained to me that once a woman approached her mother in a public location and started talking about her father. Nothing seemed that out of the ordinary until the woman said, "Your husband was such a good man, unlike mine. Why did it have to be him that died?" The interviewee relayed to me that her mother did not know what to say in response. Building on that strange incident, other community-based conversations took ugly turns. One respondent elucidated:

People usually watched what they said about my dad when they wanted to talk about his death, but sometimes people would say things to my family and it wasn't very nice. One time someone tried to talk to my mother about him. They thought they knew more about the accident than her. They told her he'd lost his hand in the accident because the people outside of the silo closed the door on it or something. Those kinds of conversations were horrible, and put my mother into a funk. That time I told her, "Well mom, you know that's not true because we had an open casket and he had his hands." Of course, back then guys would trade rides. We lived in Little Rock. Someone tried to tell my mother one time that their relative was not going to go in that day, but my dad insisted on it. The person said dad called that man and said he was depending on him to get to work. So, the man got dressed and went that day. I guess they blamed his death on my dad. Of course, there are a lot of stories like that where somebody missed and didn't die or wasn't going to go to work but ended up dying.

Still, most of those in the community made it a point to help families of the 53. One daughter told me that a prominent business owner in Beebe who owned a Ford dealership paid off her father's truck so the family would not have to manage that debt. That same person owned a popular restaurant and hired family members of the 53. Note that wives of the 53 did not just take, they gave back to the communities attempting to provide relief. One daughter elaborated:

Mom would do stuff for other women in the community. She liked helping black women, white women, anyone. It didn't matter to her. She seemed to know everybody in the community. She usually helped people that she knew didn't have husbands. Even though we didn't have anything, she would take what we did have and buy toys and things for people like that who needed help around Christmastime.

Other mothers took jobs helping disadvantaged children in their communities. Many put effort into keeping grandkids more often or children of extended family members. With social capital, surviving wives also informally created support networks. Respondents mentioned "good people" from "the other families" as being "great help." They also contended other families "were supportive" and "still close" after all these years. With considerable admiration for other families of the 53, one interviewee said:

Other people who lost men in the silo helped us. . . . They helped my mom. One wife became her good friend. They became very, very close. I mean, it was like best friends all the time. They stayed with each other overnight. They went shopping together. They went on short trips. They were just trying to deal with life. I think that helped my mom a great deal. And I think it helped mom deal with the loss. She had somebody to talk to that could fully understand what she was going through.

With long-term bonds in mind, another explained:

Other families who lost men from my hometown are still friends with my family. We still went to church with some of them through my life. One of the women who lost her husband in the accident passed away not too long ago. I went to her funeral. Another one, she died 15 years ago or so. She was a very strong woman, a 1st grade teacher. She had a strong personality. I just knew her when she was older. During her funeral, the preacher even mentioned August 9, 1965.

Disaster-Related Interaction

Two reritualization responses (3 percent) involved disaster-related interaction. One female respondent recounted a union representative would come visit her family after her father's funeral. Explaining the ease that it created for her family, she stated, "I could tell he felt so bad. He apologized and all that kind of stuff. He told us the union had a legal team that was working to make sure there was at least some sort of compensation for the spouses and kids." A son discussed the benefits of his sister "talking to Gary Lay in Searcy at Harding University when he was speaking to the White County Historical Society" a few years ago. He fondly recalled her passing information from the conversation on to him and others.

Pharmaceutical Consumption

One reply on reritualization in the family (1 percent) was on pharmaceutical consumption. A son told me that his mother went to her doctor to discuss the anxiety she had after the death of her husband. She took "something" afterward. The stigmatization of mental health issues was high 50 years ago, and in many ways, it continues to be. The percentage in this subcategory would have no doubt been higher if I included references to "self-medicating" and ingesting formally prescribed drugs.

PERSONAL RITUALS

With reritualization and personal rituals, interviewees discussed post-disaster individualized family activities, maintaining possessions, site visits and silo memorial activities, community and friend interaction, and disaster-related interaction – see Table 9.3. They also told me about cemetery activities, funeral activities, spiritual and religious practice, and spending money. A miscellaneous "other" subcategory existed too. Individualized family activities involved one-on-one behaviors within the core and extended family. Primarily, this related to routine conversations relevant to the deceased and with the deceased. You should reference definitions in the previous section for elaboration on community and friend interaction, disaster-related interaction, and spending money. Note there is not an exclusive theme for traditional grief practices, as was the case with family rituals. Instead, forms of traditional grief practices have exclusive designations within this category. This was necessary due to the plethora of responses with certain lines of questioning. For example, respondents spoke extensively on maintaining their loved one's possessions, visiting the site of the disaster and participating in memorial activities, cemetery, and funeral rituals, along with spiritual and religious practice.

Again, for specification purposes, family reritualization had more of a concentration on group dynamics and other larger social arrangements. This is not the case here. Personal reritualization concerned responses about individual actions, sometimes appearing in one-on-one domains.

Individualized Family Activities

Fifty-five responses (18 percent) focused on family activities. A few general references to family support via mothers, husbands, and grandparents existed. One female respondent extensively explained how her mother arranged activities that elevated her independence. Her mother wanted her to be able to "take care of herself" if she was ever "suddenly left alone." Other comments in this area included, "I married an engineer, and we've had the same interests through the years. It's helped," "Mother showed me pictures, which I adored how she explained past relationships and extended family," "Grandmother always told me stories about dad," "I had a lot of support from my grandparents," and "I leaned on my grandmother and grandfather." One male interviewee elaborated, "I had my granddad. He was more of a dad to me growing up. He taught me how to hunt squirrels, how to fish. I had the utmost respect for him." A majority of details in this area revolved around talking to family members and speaking to the dead.

With family talk, interviewees said they "didn't avoid it" and "talked with family about the accident openly." Referencing her mother, one person

Table 9.3   Reritualization Post-Disaster: Personal Rituals

Subcategory	Number	Percentage
Individualized Family Activities	55	18
Maintaining Possessions	54	17
Site Visits and Silo Memorial Activities	43	14
Community and Friend Interaction	36	12
Disaster-Related Interaction	35	11
Cemetery Activities	34	11
Funeral Activities	31	10
Spiritual and Religious Practice	13	4
Spending Money	5	2
Other	4	1
Total	310	100

told me, "I would talk to my mom about my dad, often when someone else passed." With an uncle, a male interviewee commented, "I had my uncle to talk to. He was younger than my dad was, and he had a hard time too. All of his hair fell out, but it all grew back." Many respondents did not talk to their brothers and sisters often, citing personality, age, and geographic differences. If they did talk about the disaster, it was one-on-one and mostly in later life. They indicated, "I never talked to my siblings about this much, especially not in a group. I talked to my brother about it most through the years," "I only started talking to my sister about all of this a year ago," and "My siblings and I never really talked about it then, but now I text or call them on the anniversary of my father's death." Reflecting the sentiment on electronic messages, one son said, "August 9th is just a black day on the calendar. You know, I always call or text my sisters on that day." Only one interviewee, an 80-year-old male, indicated speaking to a sibling frequently through the years about everything. He pointed out, "My brother is still alive. I've had a lot of discussions similar to the one I'm having with you with him." Interviewees who talk to their children about their father's death do so with kids who have also lost immediate family members. A couple of respondents commented on talking to their children, but said they only talked to them about their father "some" and "have done it less" as they have gotten older.

Not all interviewees brought up conversation-based themes with a relative. In fact, some contended that talking about the dead hurt more than it helped and that a lack of discussions "shielded" them from unnecessary pain. In media sources, one person discussed how her family only talked about her father when she was younger. Even then, she never discussed him much with anyone. Another explained, her mother had a specific rule for the children. Her mother removed her father's pictures from the walls and explicitly told her daughter and sons to "not talk about" what happened "too much."

Earlier, I referenced research that says talking to the dead is a natural grief process (see Fuchs 2017). Affirming this, multiple people commented on ritualistic communication with fathers. Statements such as "I had conversations with my dad once he was gone," "When I was younger I talked to him all the time," and "I used to talk to my daddy in my head" existed. Studies imply a majority of people talk to dead relatives in the short term as a ritual geared to create continuity in their lives. However, this project provides evidence that surviving children of the disaster continue to speak to the dead throughout life. Participants told me, "I still talk to him" and "I still talk to my dad. I might sound crazy, but I do." One son, 15 at the time of his father's death, said he talked to his dad through the years mostly when he engaged in activities they used to do together. He mentioned, "I do it when running dogs for hunting like he taught me. There's not one time I put those dogs out on the ground that I didn't think of daddy."

Stressful conditions trigger discussions. One daughter, a few months old at the time of the disaster, said, "I still talk to him. It sounds dumb, but with this election I asked him if he had any influence, and if he did could he help us." A son, 11 then, explained, "I've talked to my daddy through the years, especially when my brother would get in trouble. I would tell him what a mess the family was in and wish he was around." A daughter, a 3-year-old in 1965, stated, "I carry on conversations with him when I need extra support. I ask him what I should do."

Some people find this RSP suitable in specific domains, probably because they carry an aura of acceptability associated with "dead talk." An 80-year-old interviewee revealed, "I've talked to my dad when I was having family issues and problems, which I don't want to get into. I'd go to the cemetery and talk to him. I'd tell him how much I loved him." Believing his father was out of the silo when the disaster started, but went back in to rescue others, one person in his late 60s ritualistically says to his father, "Why did you go back in there? You could still be here with us."

Maintaining Possessions

Fifty-four (17 percent) of replies were on maintaining possessions. Respondents said things such as "I have his dress shoes, but they're old and deteriorated," "I have his union card," "I still have his battery clock and rocking chair," "I have a few items, like his medals," and "I still have some of his pipes." In terms of items related to the disaster, interviewees commented on watches and clothes. Participants noted, "He had on a Timex watch that never stopped running. It was still running when they brought it down, and I still have it. It still smells like smoke from the silo" and "I still have the watch he had on, and it smells like smoke." Others said, "I still have his clothes that he had on that day" and "I have a pillow my mother made out of the shirt he was wearing when he died." A few mentioned wallets, and one recounted, "I still got my dad's billfold and some other things he had at the time this happened. It is in a bag sealed up. I've got that locked up in my safe with my guns. I can open that bag and smell the smells from that day in the silo. It's got that smoky smell to it."

Clearly maintaining possessions, such as personal items, is important for surviving children of the 53, including an "old black lunchbox," a "bracelet," an "old cigarette stand," "wedding rings," "his old Bible in a cedar box," and the "Bible the iron welder's union" gave the family. Yet, engaging in this ritual is not as simple as you would think. We know from this book that people grieve differently and at different paces. While children may want to hold on to a dead parent's possessions, surviving parents may want to rid themselves of the items in order to move forward. In other words, secondary trauma related to grief variation is relevant. Flabbergasted at her mother's actions, one daughter told me, "My mother got rid of just about everything after he died!" Bureaucratic red tape also facilitated secondary trauma when the government withheld loved one's possessions for a while. One person said, "I had to go to a warehouse in Little Rock to get all of dad's things. That building is still there. It is a big, long building. It was just nothing but a warehouse then, and they kept just about all the men's stuff there for a year. I guess they kept some of it because they were still investigating." Two participants kept mementos from their dads' previous jobs. Both had fathers who helped construct the Gateway Arch. One explained, "You know, they hired him one time to go work on the St. Louis Arch. When he was gone working one time he brought me back some red patent leather shoes. I kept them. I still have them in the original shoebox." The other stated, "My dad worked on the St. Louis Arch welding. Every time I see it, I think of him . . . I've driven by it quite a few times. My son even bought me a tape on building that because he knew my dad helped build that." Though the interviewee values the video his son gave him, he has never been able to watch it. He told me, "I guess that's something psychological." Parents also kept children from accessing items related to their fathers. In one media source, a daughter explains that since her family rarely spoke of her father much after he died, she had to sneak around to "look at old pictures" of her dad that were "hidden away."

Keeping documents related to the disaster continues to be an important ritual. One son indicated, "I have a lot of newspaper articles that my mother passed down to me. Since I was just seven months old when this all transpired, she knew I would someday have an interest in learning more about it. I save that sort of information." On legal materials, one daughter noted, "I've kept papers from probate court, petitions for appointment of special administrator, paperwork from the actual court proceedings, and something on pursuing a wrongful death claim." Another said, "Having the documents has always been important to me. They have stuff blacked out. It's been awhile, I need to pull out my boxes." This respondent went on to explain her ongoing desire to put all of her documents together, so she can pass it on to her grandchildren. Others have completed this process already, systematically organizing "scrapbooks" with "clippings," "military discharge papers," "truck payment invoices," and "paychecks." Also, consider letters from Sid McMath and Lyndon B. Johnson. One person still has pictures of her father in his casket at the funeral, though she does not know where they came from or who took them.

Children of the 53 also described having videos with their fathers in them, and a video related to the disaster provided by those who organized the Little Rock Air Force Base (AFB) memorial. Cutting edge at the time, one son told me his brother managed to bring a video camera to his parent's house a few weeks before the disaster. The family always cherished the footage, but could not bear to watch it. Finally, after several years, the time was right. Unfortunately, water leaked on the stored film, and he was never able to watch. The respondent went on to say that to capture his father's essence, he had a painting made of him sitting on a horse. He keeps it in his spare room and still takes the time to go in and look at it when his father is on his mind. In a follow-up letter, a daughter told me that she "bought a die-cast metal pickup truck that resembles daddy's late 40s or early 50s model; one with rounded fenders, running boards, chain and hooks on the tailgate, large front grille, etc." To this day, she keeps it in her living room where she can walk past it and "remember my daddy driving it with me sitting in his lap." On the memorial video, one person said, "My mother who has since passed is on it, so are my two brothers and my aunts. They've passed too. They're all in that video." However, of those who brought the video up, none recalled the location of theirs.

Site Visits and Memorial Activities

Forty-three responses (14 percent) involved visiting the location where the death occurred and rituals related to the memorial. Comments indicated children went to the site soon after the disaster and throughout life. Respondents reported, "I went shortly after this all happened, but they wouldn't let me in" and "I went not long after the accident, but never been in it. I could see the concrete mound and the door that was over the missile." With social capital contractor connections cited, a daughter who was 12 at the time commented:

> My dad was good friends with one of the people who worked for one of the contractors. This man must have been over the whole project there on site. He came to our house the next day. He must've been friends with my dad, and he loved him a lot. This is hard for me. . . . He asked me if I wanted to go to the site and get dad's hardhat and his badge. My mother took me. They had a huge box sitting on pallets with all the men's hardhats and badges. I dug through all of them until I found dad's. I don't know how appropriate it was for me to do that then, but my mother let me. I think I'm glad, because it gave me closure in a certain way. Because I saw the place, I saw the top of the silo. I saw all those things.

She was the only person to mention this sort of activity.

Regarding visits later in life, interviewees and comments in media sources noted, "I used to drive by it, but gosh, it's been years," "I've been to like the road where you turned down to the missile base," "I've been there many times," and "I drove out to it in the 90s I think it was. I just wanted to see it, look around at it. It was just a flat piece of land surrounded by what I remember to be a black chain link fence. At that time, there was a keep out sign." A 65-year-old respondent told me, "I've been to the silo site many times through the years. I was there the day they shut it down. If I remember right, they blew it up just after 1:00, which was about the time the accident happened. After that, I kept going out there. I don't know why. The gate was always locked and that kept me from going in."

Discussed earlier in this work, a memorial and a monument are not the same thing, but people do use the terms interchangeably or are referencing a memorial when they say "monument." Instrumental in establishing the memorial at the Little Rock AFB, one person indicated, "Yeah, I've been to the site. I helped get money together to put a small monument there too. I have not been back in a few years. The monument there is at the edge of the road that turns to go to where the original site was. The government wouldn't let us put it any closer, because it was private land at the time." Again reflecting the power of social capital, this interviewee, along with a handful of others instrumental in establishing the Little Rock AFB memorial, even told of going down into the silo before the U.S. Air Force (USAF) deactivated the complex. One said, "Right before they was going to destroy it, I got to go down below. There was two or three other survivors that went down there with me. It was kind of a peaceful moment. I was where my dad was when he died. Before that, I'd never actually been to the site myself." Another specified,

> Somebody from the government who knew about me, I don't remember who called me and said, "We're going to be blowing it up. Would you like to go inside?" They told me to round up anybody else who would want to go, but told me I had to do it that day. I said, "That doesn't give me much time." He said, "Well, I'm sorry about that. But if you want to see it, it's going to be today." So I got a babysitter for my kids, and I called around trying to find others who lost their father. . . . Anyway, we all met out there. We were escorted. I only went into the command center with all the controls. There were a lot of panels, buttons, and video screens. There was a big door. I am assuming it wasn't locked and that is how the command people got out when the accident happened. It was like a vault. On that door, somebody had went in with white paint and drawn a picture and called it the ghost site. After seeing that, we had a lot of quietness just taking everything in. They only gave us a certain amount of time and then they ushered us out. That was it. It was emotional and sad. Yet, I was honored to be in the last place my dad was alive.

Going deep into the facility, a different person recalled:

> I was fortunate enough to go back in with a few other people. It was very informative. We saw the control panel, the launch panel. This really gets me. The telephone

was a rotary dial. When I was down there I took a little plaque that said Level 7, where my dad was working. We used the elevator when I went into the silo, and it was hard to fit five people in it. When they used it to pull bodies out, they could only put two at a time on it, and the floor was so small they had to lean those two bodies to the side just to fit them in. One of the Air Force guys with us, and I still got it in my mind just as clear as a bell all these years later, told us, "Some people try to sugarcoat it. I went down here the night of the accident. They flew me up from the base on a chopper. I was the only one who could turn off a valve that had water leaking into the elevator. I had to crawl down the ladder over two men crammed together. When I reached Level 7 there were two men sitting on a bench, a couple close to the bench, and one man just laying against it . . ." In the back of my mind when he said that, I just knew that was where my dad was. He told me, "When you see a diesel engine start and smoke rolls out of it, that was the kind of smoke down in that silo, except it was 10 times heavier." It was unburned fuel. After your first breath, you're gone. They may have all suffered a few minutes.

Not everyone had a desire to visit the site or have such experiences. A couple of people, perplexed as to why I would ask if they had ever been to the site said, "I've never wanted to go there" and "There is nothing there for me." Others wanted to go through the years but implied certain things kept a visit from happening. This included relocation to another state, not being able to locate the site, and the inability to find a relative willing to go to the site with them for emotional support. Related to visiting the site, a few people commented on the importance of visiting their old homes. One daughter said that she was working on developing a list of places she lived with her sister and wanted to visit them. In a follow-up letter, a different daughter told me, "Sometimes I drive out to the old home place where we once lived and reminisce the life we had living on the farm."

With the memorial at the entrance of the airbase, people made comments like, "I went to the dedication," "I went to the event in Jacksonville," "I remember going to the ceremony," and "I've been to the monument." Others responded, "I used to stop by it all the time," "I've stopped by to see the monument more than a few times," and "I drove by it every day on my way to work." One respondent involved with the planning for the initial placement of the memorial said, "We had great get togethers. We had refreshments and got to finally put family names with faces. It was wonderful." Another commented, "I was on the committee that dealt with all of it. There was a nice lady, one of the daughters, who called everyone to help. We'd meet at a restaurant to discuss it all. I told them if we are going to do something, it has to be nice. I didn't want to insult our fathers." Showing more signs of recreancy-related secondary trauma, a key player in setting up the memorial and funding for the memorial said:

I created a nonprofit group to raise funds for the monument outside of the base. Back in 1985, I was waiting for an oil change, picked up a newspaper, and saw where the government was dismantling all the silos. It just brought back a flood of emotion. The Challenger had exploded and several astronauts died. There was so much of a hubbub, and rightly so, for these lost astronauts. I'm thinking, "Hey, that was eight. We had 53." Our silo incident is still one of the most tragic episodes that has ever happened. The defense system of our country involved civilians like my father. They weren't given the fanfare. They weren't given anything. That day started me on my journey of trying to find families, develop a nonprofit organization, form a committee, and get something for the 53 men lost. I found out quickly that the government was, what is the word I want to say, non-cooperative? They wouldn't even talk to me. They wouldn't return my phone calls. Nobody would help, until I went public. The brother of a man who died with my father worked for the *Arkansas Democrat-Gazette*. He was a top dog there. He became a committee member. He put a story about us wanting a monument in the newspaper. After that, I did a television interview, and the government was all over me. Then they wanted to meet. We first met at the base, and I went by myself. After I was there, they took me into a room with a big, long beautiful oak table. Top-level people were there. They tried to intimidate me so much. Yes, it was intimidation 101. I left basically telling them, I'm doing this with or without your help, so we'll see where it goes. I started with a few people and finally found all of the family members. Most were excited to finally have their loved ones acknowledged. They liked the idea of having something that would last with their loved ones names on it. Some didn't want anything to do with it at all. Families, and several unions, gave money to build the memorial.

The dedication took place on August 9, 1986. Discussing it, the interviewee went on:

Let me tell you a little story. When they dedicated the monument, family members and all kinds of Air Force personnel were going to be there. They were going to have the base chaplain give the prayer. They were going to have jets fly over us. They were going to play taps. A colonel was going to speak. The day came and it poured rain, hard rain. The streets were flooded. It was that bad. I just bawled as my tears fell with the rain into the streets. We were going to have the reception with decorations and food after the dedication indoors at a hotel in Jacksonville. I had to shift everything to there. Anyway, I don't remember who came to me that morning, but it was one of the higher ups. He told me the Air Force reneged. They were not going to do anything for us - no prayer, no planes, no speaker, nothing. All the families gathered at the hotel anyway. The committee had to rush around and find speakers.

Obviously, the government did not want to cooperate fully with the effort of families in getting the 53 remembered. Things worsened when the USAF decided to remove the memorial from the base entrance and move it inside the gates. There was more disruption, more hurt, more confusion, and more anger. The interviewee just discussed told me:

> My daughter called me one day. She was living in the area and driving from Cabot to Little Rock. Like many others, when driving by the memorial she would look over at it. She told me over the phone that the monument was gone. I was like, "You've got to be kidding me!" I had to sign the monument over to the government after we dedicated it since it was going to be at the entrance to the base. At that time, they told me they were going to build a military museum beside it. The museum, like the monument, would be facing the freeway so people in cars passing by could see it. That never happened. When I signed it over, they said they would maintain the memorial site. They did not. I would come into town and the whole area would be all grown up. They even damaged it when mowing the grass around it. . . . During all of it, I came up against such harshness from the government, I still have a bad taste in my mouth.

Another said, "The Air Force would've never done a memorial on their own, and then moved it! The sensibility was not there. I would go by it when it was outside of the Air Force base at the edge of the freeway. Then, I went to stop and see it one day, and it was gone!" Viewing the removal of the memorial as another disaster-related disruption, someone explained, "I would drive out there with my oldest grandchild. I was so proud when we'd go by there and tell him that his grandfather's name was on that monument." Someone else elucidated, "They moved it and I thought nobody's going to know about the silo and what happened now." After calling to see what happened, the USAF told the person, "It's ours, and we can do what we want to with it." She, like others, did not have access to the base. Initially she tried to get in to see the monument, and the USAF turned her away "many times."

Some frustrated interviewees gave up seeing it, seeing the location shift as "a horrible thing." One son said, "I don't know what happened to it. I kept telling myself I was going to go find it, but I still haven't." Unsure of what to do others noted, "I remember going by all the time and then one day it was just gone," "I hate that they moved that monument off the interstate. I hate that. I can tell you that," and "I couldn't find out where it was!" Another pondered, "I don't know why they moved it. Was it in somebody's way where it was? Really? Come on!" A son commented, "Having it outside the entrance to the base made it easy to find, and made it a good place for families and the community to go, but that's the government. It should be at the state capitol in Little Rock." One said she tried to see the memorial, but "It takes an act of God to get on that base." Persistent family members found a way. One explained, "I eventually found a friend with base access." She finally found her way to the memorial "in a nice area." Others told me they only saw it if they happened to be on the base for unrelated reasons. One person said his food business was catering a USAF event and that gave him access to the memorial. Using the exact same phrase a different interviewee provided earlier, one son said his first reaction was, "You've got to be kidding me!" He then said, "After it moved onto the base I drove around looking for it and bam, there it was. It stayed there for a long time I think."

Signaling what some respondents interpreted as a sign of disrespect, moving the memorial around almost became a ritual itself. Just a few years ago, it moved to the Jacksonville Museum of Military History, established in May 2005. This created even more perplexity for surviving children. Regardless, the move was not such a bad thing, since families who could figure out where the memorial was could easily access it again. Descendants of the 53 indicated, "I can't believe they moved it around so much," "I really wished they wouldn't have moved it again. I don't even know where the Jacksonville Museum is," and "Is it still on the base?" For families privy to the memorial's current location, I was told, "At least they did a good job with the display at the museum in Jacksonville. My sister is in one of the videos they show there" and "My sister and her kids have been to the museum. They said it is nice." Strangely, the *Encyclopedia of Arkansas* entry on the museum, written by a senior employee, currently mentions having artifacts related to the Damascus event but makes no mention of 373-4 or the 53 (see Duggar 2014). Perhaps the memorial was not there upon submission of the entry. I tried to get information on the exact date of relocation on a few of occasions, once speaking to the curator of the Jacksonville Museum of Military History. He was going to talk to the curator at the base and get back to me. I never received a return call. Maybe it was just miscommunication.

Despite all this, some interviewees having minimalist positions either did not know there was a memorial or just did not seem to care. Some interviewees said, "I didn't even know they put a memorial up," "I only learned about that a few years ago," "I haven't seen it in a while," and "I never wanted to see it." One even said to me, "I went to the dedication ceremony. Someone played the bagpipes. It was very touching, but I was pretty cynical. It took so long for something like that to happen. I was just thinking through it all too little too, too late." In a media source, a brother of one of the 53 living in Louisiana recently explained, "I have no desire to go. It's just too sad. It's just something I would rather leave in the past." Also in a recent media source, a daughter explained her mother's disposition after being told her children were going to visit the Jacksonville Museum of Military History to see the memorial. The daughter said, "She didn't really have a reaction. She wasn't upset. She just files that away as trauma to never to be thought of again."

Community and Friend Interaction

Thirty-six personal ritual responses (12 percent) involved duologue with community members and friends. One-on-one emotional support helped. On people living close by, participants said, "I was glad to have a good neighbor," "My neighbor was real sweet and very supportive in helping me through everything," and "My neighbor had a daughter who helped me out." Norris et al. (2002) explain that formal school interventions are important for children experiencing disaster. Perhaps with no awareness of this in 1965, interviewees who did get help in this area received it informally and were glad. They commented, "I had a wonderful teacher, and we talked about what happened," "All the teachers were supportive when they talked to me," and "My bus drivers were a married couple who would talk to me about things I was going through." Referencing widespread community members, one son explained:

Talking to other people about my dad is always nice. I found out about 15 years ago from a guy nearby that he knew my dad. I was not a friend of his, but I had always known him when I saw him. Anyway, we just got to chatting and come to find out that he'd worked with my dad on some jobs. He thought my dad was a good guy. He said he was a hard worker.

A daughter indicated:

I've talked to people throughout my life who live around here and knew my dad. I've came across people and had conversations with them just by chance. I was at the Family Dollar and struck up a conversation with an older man. We were waiting in line. He asked me what my name was. I told him what it was before I got married. He gave me an odd look and said, "I knew your dad. You must be his youngest." He told me he was a heck of a baseball player and remembered seeing him play when they were younger out at Floyd. That conversation meant a lot to me. I never knew my daddy played baseball.

On friends, people commented, "My church friend helped me," "A girl at school talked to me about my dad," and "I had a buddy who talked to me about it all." Referencing a girlfriend, one son who was 15 in 1965 said, "There was a good family I spent a lot of time with after daddy got killed. I was dating a girl, and her parents took me right in. Having them made things a lot easier on me." Similarly, some told of how their friends were there for them when their families were not. One daughter, 14 at the time of the disaster, articulated:

> I talked to my friend about things, but never my mother. I had a friend who stayed with me after dad died. She was a great friend who helped me. Since my mom was not as available, I had to have someone come stay with me. I just couldn't be alone. I had my mom, but she was grieving. For probably two months, my friend stayed with me. The weird part about that is, several months after she stopped staying with me, her brother was killed in a hit and run. After that, I went and stayed with her.

Another daughter, 10 then, said:

> Through the years, I always talked to my friends more about my daddy than my family. When I have a good friend whose parent dies, that opens up the door for me to share a lot with them. That probably started after the accident. My family didn't pay attention to me much, but me and my best friend talked about everything a lot. Actually, her daddy worked out there with mine. He was a welder. I always believed he was the one who started the fire with his welding equipment. I don't know why I believed that. Even though we talked, we never spoke of blame. We just really talked about missing our dads.

This shows, as with family reritualization in this area, participants built bonds with other individuals who also lost fathers in the disaster. However, I want to reiterate that here interviewees referenced one-on-one personal connections not broader family-to-family interaction. Consider statements like, "I still keep in touch with people who lost their father to this," "People from other families who lost people are still kind to me after all these years," and "Over the years, I've talked to a lot of people who lost their dads when this happened."

Taking into account postmodern shifts in interaction, some turn to digital communities for continued support years later. One person let me know that every August she posts something about her father and the disaster on Facebook. I perused that social media site and found that others do the same. Last August, one person who was not a participant in this project posted:

> Fifty-five years ago today, and three days after we celebrated my 10th birthday, I lost the most important man in my young life. My daddy was killed in the 1965 missile silo disaster that happened about three miles outside of Searcy. So, today I honor my daddy along with 52 other brave men and daddies. I also honor the two survivors, Hubert Saunders and Gary Lay. I'm still bitter about it because in my opinion these men's safety was not the most important thing on

the site that day. My favorite part of the newspaper article that was published on the 50th anniversary is this, "Not all Cold War casualties were military, and not all of them happened on the battlefields of Korea and Vietnam. Some of them happened right here in Arkansas."

Disaster-Related Interaction

Thirty-five replies (11 percent) concerned disaster-related interaction. Recall that with the family reritualization category, this related to behaviors with people connected to the disaster outside of family and friends. There were a small number of references to this theme there, but considerably more here. Part of that is due to the inclusion of actions related to personal research on missile silos and the accident.

With interaction involving people associated with the disaster, a daughter recalled, "I happened across a union friend of my daddy's. He said my daddy never met a stranger and would do anything for you. He was supposed to go to the Searcy site on the day of the accident, but the union sent him to a different one. It meant so much to me to talk to that man." Chance encounters like that leave respondents "always wondering" who they "are around," and if any of those people are a part of their lives. A son commented:

> One time, a company was putting up power lines between Heber Springs and Russellville. My dad and uncle worked that job. Anyway, years later I was working a pipeline job in Clearwater, Florida. I was talking to a supervisor and he said, "Son, where are you from?" I said, "Conway, Arkansas." He said, "I know where Conway is." I said, "Well, I won't lie to you. I didn't think you would know where I'm really from so I just said Conway. I'm actually from a little town outside of Conway. "I told him the name, and he said, "I know where that is. I was a superintendent when they run that power line through there. I had two brothers that worked for me. One was a tall slim guy, the other one was short and stocky." I said, "I called the tall, slim one daddy and the short, stocky one uncle." He told me, "If you search your head right and try to be as good of a man as your daddy was, you'll be alright."

That story had to do with his dead father, but not necessarily the disaster. However, he told another one that did. He said:

> Let me tell you a story about a man I talked to one time when I was in the hospital in Conway. It was a couple of years after daddy died. I was there because I was moving a fence back and building another one. I was on a tractor and a part come up and shoved a piece of steel through my foot. They operated on my foot. A doctor down there in Conway did it. I was in the room with a man who started asking me about my life. I told him about my dad, and he went

to crying to the point he couldn't talk for awhile. He said, "I worked for one of the inspectors who went down into the silo after the accident. Them Air Force guys slammed the doors shut on those men. They should be guilty of murder. I would have paid to put them up against a concrete wall and shoot them down. There wasn't no explosion or need to shut those big doors, but they did and all the men suffocated and died. It wasn't armed. They could've left it open, and the smoke would've went straight up into the air. Then, at least some of the men could have gotten out." I found out that they marked where daddy was. He was right near the hole at the top of the ladder to get out. Two men were about to the top of the ladder wedged together, and daddy was right behind them.

A different son revealed:

Talking to other people who knew about it all gave me some answers. An inspector that worked the silo accident ended up in my Sunday school class one time. He married a girl who lived about a quarter of a mile from our house. I think I heard he lives in Alaska now. He was a super nice guy. We had a Sunday school party at our house and he told me all about everything. He said all the guys was out of the silo for lunch. The Air Force personnel were out of there too. There was supposed to be Air Force personnel watching over all the men for safety and all that, but after lunch the men went back to work and none of the Air Force personnel went with them. Well, a welder hit a hydraulics line and it caught fire. The Air Force people saw the smoke and shut all the doors to snuff the fire out. I believe if they would have left it all alone it would've quit burning on its own. Before that, I didn't really know what happened. Yeah, he went down there and told me where they were all sitting and how they looked. . . . I asked if those Air Force guys got punished. He told me, "Yeah, they didn't get court-martialed. That would have looked bad since they let the accident happen. But they did put them into some of the lowest jobs they could." He told me they had one running a little candy shop somewhere on base. Yeah, they made jobs to punish them, but they still kept them.

Another man stated:

One time, I worked at an Exxon station on that last exit goes toward Greenbrier. I worked the night shift, and they used to bring government vans through that were taking people to relieve other people at different silos. They always called the site where my dad died "the ghost silo." I'm not sure they were making fun of it or anything. When I was in it that day, one guy told us a couple of stories about things that happened there, switches thrown the wrong way for no reason and a lieutenant who was there to relieve another officer seeing a man just sitting on the floor. The person on the floor said he needed lunch. Later he told other crew about it, and said he didn't know there were civilians on site. They told him there weren't. They went back down into the silo to look for the man, but there wasn't anyone there. He was gone.

A daughter told me of an odd personal connection to the event that involved a more long-term relationship. She explained:

I worked at the Unity Health hospital in Searcy. I had been there 10 years. I worked in the engineering department. My boss and I were visiting. I don't remember how it came up. He asked who my parents were. I was telling him who my father was and that he was killed in the missile base explosion. His face went pale, and he said, "My father was a supervisor." Now, his father wasn't in the explosion. His father wasn't down in the silo when it happened. My boss was 12 when it happened, so he remembers it. We were just astonished that here we were. He hired me, and we had history together and didn't know.

Implying emotional benefits, several people spoke of encounters with Hubert Saunders and Gary Lay. One interviewee said, "Mr. Saunders came to the funeral home for visitation." Another noted his presence at his dad's service and said, "When Mr. Saunders came in he looked scared to death." Others commented, "I've talked to Gary Lay and think that helped me. I never met him until probably five years ago. It was a Christmas party over at a country club in Little Rock. It was just a coincidence," and "I talked to Gary Lay at one of the memorial events." Note that some participants recalled Lay at the memorial ceremony, while others said he did not come because it was too much for him to handle. Someone who did not think he was there said, "I know that he has lived with guilt, knowing what he knows and knowing that many men died." Many interviewees have a fascination with Lay. A few wanted to know if I had contacted him, and several had researched him and recited accounts Lay provided to journalists about the event.

On research as a disaster-related ritual, respondents told me, "I started writing a book about all this, but I never finished it. I just really wanted the world to know what the military did to my daddy," "I've looked through papers and called the company that employed my dad during all of this. They kind of freaked out," and "I've done a little research on the incident myself." One person discussed looking at virtual cemeteries online and inaccuracies presented on specific websites. Three people commented on reading *Command and Control* and watching the documentary based on the Damascus incident (Schlosser 2013).

Cemetery Activities

Thirty-four reactions (11 percent) pertained to cemetery rituals. Some comments reflected sporadic visits. This included, "I go to dad's grave sometimes," "I would go every year or so," "I used to go quite a bit, especially on Memorial Day and Veteran's Day," and "I only go when I am having a tough time with life." Several interviewees referenced recent visits and stated, "I go four times a year," "I was out there two months ago," "I went last month," "I just went out there a week ago," "I go weekly," and "I go quite often." Upon visiting their father's gravesite, respondents told me they "collect trash," "clean up," "take flowers," and "go to think." One son indicated he is on the "cemetery committee," which meets "the first Saturday following the first Sunday in April." Regular attendance corresponded to geographic location with many. People told me, "My dad and uncle are buried at a cemetery close by," "Daddy is buried pretty close to where I live now," "I go to where my father is buried frequently because it is so close," and "It is only two miles from my house." One 68-year-old daughter told me she was very comfortable visiting her father's burial location. She explained, "When I was younger I lived right beside it. It might sound horrible, but all the kids would go over there and play." One person who lived close by implied geographic proximity made no difference. He simply relayed, "It helped me at the start to go out there, but after awhile I just didn't feel like going as often." Geography also has links to feelings of sorrow. In one media source, a brother of one of the 53 insinuated acute grief was overwhelming soon after hearing of his loved one's death. However, long-term grief was not as prominent since the accident happened in Arkansas, and he lived in California.

In a media source, though she lives in Missouri, a daughter details traveling to Arkansas regularly to engage in various rituals associated with the disaster. A different daughter not living close to her dad's resting place indicated, "I still have family in Arkansas I visit, so I go to the cemetery more than you would think." All others made statements such as, "I haven't been to my dad's grave in a long time because I live so far away," "I haven't been to Arkansas in probably six years," "I just don't visit that area much," and "Since I live in Texas, I don't go to the cemetery very often." Two people mentioned visiting "virtual cemeteries," but both still live in the area and did not discuss their actions as related to emotional processes. As reviewed earlier, they said it was for researching the disaster or for genealogy purposes.

Funeral Activities

Thirty-one replies (10 percent) regarded funeral-related rituals. While participants indicated the funeral "helped," aspects of disruption existed.

Interviewees made comments about new activities they participated in before the funeral. For example, older children helped locate their parent's remains post-disaster. Secondary trauma continued via bureaucratic disorder. Statements were, "I had to find out where they had taken dad's body. It was total chaos, but I eventually found out he was up in Little Rock somewhere," "I tried to locate where my father was. One funeral home had 13 of the men's bodies," and finding loved ones was hard because "The government had their bodies a lot of different places, just scattered all over the place." In follow-up correspondence, one respondent said the USAF initially refused to let her family see her father's body. However, she insisted since, curiously, her late husband told her before the disaster if anything happened she must be sure to see his remains.

Even after finding remains, lingering death rituals from earlier eras created hard adjustments for those living in rural areas adjacent to the Ozarks. One older son told me:

> My daddy's older brother made the funeral arrangements. It was hard on me. He insisted on bringing daddy's body 22 miles back to the house and leaving it there before we buried him. They put him in the living room. For a few days, I would get up in the morning and go to the kitchen having to walk right past my daddy in the living room. I guess that's the way they used to do it when somebody died, but I still remember it and wouldn't wish that sort of thing on anybody. Yeah, that was hard on me, probably the hardest part of it all. There his body was, right there where I watched TV with him and all that.

Related to this generation gap and a lack of adult emotion, in a media source someone connected to the disaster said, "Our family had suffered a lot of tragedy. They were raised in a real backwoods upbringing. It was a different time with lots of death and illness. . . . But, this was just more of the same."

For younger children, funeral rituals were a new practice, but the internal dialogue accompanying fathers' funerals was an important part of moving forward. A son, 15 then, said, "The funeral let me know everything was going to be different." As one daughter whose name was spelled wrong in her father's obituary noted, "I remember telling myself no one ever acknowledged me or my grief until the funeral." She was 10. It was hard for daughters and sons to compare this funeral to others throughout their lives. Many of them felt overwhelmed by the number of people in attendance. They reported, "There were so many people there that church couldn't hold them all," "People were outside all the way to the road," "I couldn't believe there were so many people there," "Everybody said it was the biggest funeral they ever had seen," "I'd never seen that many people in my life," and "It was covered up with people." For comments in this area, all recalled thinking that high attendance was a "compliment" reflecting the level of care others had for their fathers. However, some interviewees were skeptical. A son, 17 then, said, "I think there were a lot more people at his funeral than probably would have been if he hadn't died the way he did." A daughter, 15 then, told me, "I don't know if all those people cared about me. I remember thinking a large part of it was that they were just curious about everything that happened." One person said his mother did not let the size of the crowd deceive him. Having previous experiences with the process, she said that after a few days they would be lonely because people would stop coming around. A different interviewee said her mother told her the same thing often. She remembers her remarking, "Everyone else's life will just continue on."

Respondents in their pre-teen and early teens in 1965 provided comments related to seeing their fathers' bodies for the first time after the disaster. They said things like, "I just remember looking at him wanting to see his tattoo, so I could make sure it was him" and "He still had his natural hair, his eyelashes, and all that stuff. I felt better knowing he didn't die the same way some did." On that note, one daughter explained going to other men's funerals. They had "honeycomb" burns on their bodies from the design of the platforms making up each level of the silo. She did not see those burns on her father and implied that was a good thing. Indeed, someone told me, "I still remember the black around my dad's nails. He also had a mark on his face. I remember wondering if he fell over on the walkway where the metal was hot and it burned an imprint into it." One daughter said, "When I saw him in his casket I could see he'd been gripping something. I told myself he must have been holding on to a ladder or something when he died." Related to that, another daughter told me, "When I saw him, he looked like he was just sleeping. Well, except for his hands. They were drawn. Later people said some of the men were hanging from the ladder. So looking back, part of me thinks that he was on that ladder." A different daughter stated:

> Whether tradition or she felt it necessary for any number of reasons, mother made it open casket. That was the best thing in the world that ever happened to me. It was just disastrous that we had lost him, but I remember thinking he looked perfect that day. He looked the way he always did. But, this is burned in my brain. The only thing that I noticed, because I would always touch his hands, was that he had some little burns or cracks in his skin. I don't know what the preparation was for the open casket, but I'm sure there were cosmetics involved. His skin was cracked where he'd been burned. I'm glad I touched his hand and his face that day, because I would think for months and months that maybe it wasn't him. . . . A few years down the road, I finally said to myself, "You saw him in the casket."

Only one person commented on the funeral being closed casket and wishing it was not.

Spiritual and Religious Practice

Thirteen reactions (4 percent) were on spiritual and religious practice. Dreams fell into this grouping. As grief literature reveals, this is something that occurs close to the time of a loss (Worden [1991] 2018; Holinger 2020). Comments reflect this. One person said, "I did dream about my dad for a few years after this all happened. After a few years, the dreams all went away." Another told me, "When I was younger, I would sometimes have dreams about my daddy. One night, on a school night, I had a dream and heard his voice. I raised up in bed and saw his silhouette. He told me not to cry and that he was watching over me. I never had a dream about him again." Disappointed with having just one dream about her father, someone else said,

> I hear about people who dream about their loved ones. I've talked to people that have multiple dreams over the years and still have dreams about their parents. After all these years, I've had one dream, one in 55 years about my father. I remember the details clearly. I'm going to start crying again. . . . Okay. In that dream, he is sitting on a tractor on our farm. He looks down at me, and I am just streaming in tears so happy to see him. I introduce him to his grandchildren and tell everything about them to him. He has this big smile on his face. I pray sometimes to have more dreams about him. I know he would be so proud of me. Sometimes I was a rotten little kid, but he would have ended up proud.

A different daughter revealed having more dreams of her father as she ages. She said:

> I dream of my dad more as I have gotten older. In the dreams, he just walks into the house, and we all say, "We thought you were gone for good." He says, "No, I've been around." He looks the same. In some of the dreams, we are just in casual situations, eating a meal, out in the yard, or whatever. Those dreams are so comforting.

Similarly, an 80-year-old son told me, "I dream about my dad when I'm having problems with the business. In one, I was sitting in the office, he came in, and I asked him for advice on dealing with my son, who I've worked with for years." Someone said, "I have dreams where I'm talking to my dad, and then I wake up. . . . I always want to go back to sleep so we can keep talking."

One respondent provided an eerie account riding the line between reality and a dream. Combining a spiritual encounter with disaster-related interaction, he testified to me:

I was at my soon-to-be wife's family reunion at a church several years after all this. Someone came up to me talking about this incident and said, "You know, that's over with. You need to let it go." About that time, another gentleman, he sells strawberries in a town beside mine, came up to me on the other side. He said, "Who was that you were just talking to?" I said, "Well, I didn't get his name." I turned around and the man was gone." I don't know if you believe in angels, or whatever. I was in my early 20s, and I cry to this day thinking about that.

On religious practice, interviewees provided statements on post-disaster behavior such as, "I will sometimes envision my daddy in heaven," "Through the years I always prayed to meet a man like my daddy," and "God helps me think that daddy dying in that silo saved him from suffering something worse." A 66-year-old daughter told me, "Praying to God helped me through everything. Sometimes, you just have to trust and believe. God keeps me going." Prayer rituals did not always work for respondents. One son said the disaster turned him away from God. He commented, "I've prayed to God. Not long after the accident, I asked God to help me because I had so much to bear without my daddy. I asked God to help me move on, to help me forget. I haven't." A daughter replied to this line of questioning, "I can remember my mother telling me if you have the faith of a mustard seed, miracles can happen. I remember praying that a miracle would happen. That my faith would take hold and my dad would wake up. That, of course, didn't happen."

Spending Money

Five responses (2 percent) corresponded with spending money. Interviewees discussed using settlement money for their own personal educational and housing expenses. They also noted contribution to the memorial fund, purchasing flowers for the memorial, and spending money from the nonprofit exclusively on memorial expenses. Again, all contributions for the memorial came from families and from unions. Returning to recreancy, litigation, and secondary trauma, respondents implied that the USAF and contractors refused to provide financial assistance after saying doing so would equivocate to "admitting guilt."

Other

Four responses (1 percent) related to therapy, employment, and relocation. The only person who discussed therapy told me, "One time I went to counseling. I was just always mad after the accident. The guy asked me if deep down I thought I was angry all the time because my dad left me. After he said that, I decided I had more sense than that idiot . . . I didn't stay much longer." With employment, one person hinted that the disaster may have propelled her into a career as a mortician. Another talked about how his coworkers turned supportive after the event. For relocation, one participant provided an abundance of details on how moving out of state post-disaster set her on a positive path. She cited new opportunities for educational achievement. Ironically, she also mentioned career success with organizations that had a hand in developing the technology that led to the birth of Titan IIs, including Boeing and Lockheed Martin.

SUMMARIZING RERITUALIZATION

This chapter is important because it helps us understand how families adjust to lifescape changes after a technological disaster. Literature exists telling us disruption occurs within a variety of domains post-disaster. It details aspects of deritualization and breakdown too. Yet nothing addresses specific sociological adjustments by way of reritualized behavior, especially in terms of long-term sorrow (for exceptions exclusively on natural disaster, see Bhandari et al. 2011; Johnson et al. in progress).

Grief is a family experience and an individual experience (Rosenblatt 2005). Therefore, it is no surprise that reritualization for people connected to the 53 involved family and personal rituals. We must view each category as a separate unit. Drawing comparisons with descriptive statistics is inappropriate. After all, everyone has a different grieving process, and each category had themes with different labels and a different number of themes. Yet, the door is open to draw comparisons in terms of structural isomorphism. Certain RSPs were important for families. Some of those were prominent for daughters and sons embedded in families as well, such as paternal alternatives and traditional grief practices. Despite this, respondents indicated some RSPs were more significant for the family unit as compared to the children within it. Spending money is the most obvious example and a powerful one that implies aspects of recreancy involving secondary trauma and litigation. However, it also brings to light issues with recreancy and secondary trauma via adult-child relationships embedded within the context of disaster. This definitely warrants deep additional scholarly exploration.

It is apparent that families, daughters, and sons experienced transformative rituals helping them to process sorrow post-disaster, with some RSPs ranking higher than other ones. On family rituals, compared to other themes in the category, RSPs related to spending money and family activities ranked high. With spending money, salient examples included buying new homes, paying for higher education, and paying bills. Looking back on the data, repeated comments with this theme implied a high degree of repetitiveness. Nearly 38 percent of comments on RSPs on family rituals concerned spending money. Homologousness became clear when considering overlap with other themes connected to relocating, providing resources to other families in need, and money directed toward traditional grief symbols, including memorials. It is evident that having financial resources, by way of the lawsuit, support from family, community leaders, or Social Security payments, provided the means to engage in the RSP of spending. Under family activities, salient instances involved paternal alternatives. Remarrying and stepfathers, along with extended family support structures, were important. Data revealed repeated comments on these sorts of behaviors, representing repetitiveness. Nearly 25 percent of comments in the family ritual category were on family activities. Homologousness existed by way of other themes with examples of non-monetary support given by people in the community, friends, and strangers via disaster-related interaction. Other people are the unmistakable resource needed to engage in new RSPs involving family activities. As insinuated with social capital, isolated respondents did not have an adequate number of people in their social convoy to help with sorrow and life readjustment.

Moderately ranked RSPs on family rituals provided interesting results despite lower status. Traditional grief practices had a strong showing, as did community and friend interaction. Powerful commentaries on cemetery and memorial behaviors existed with traditional RSPs of grief, some of which related to a paramount resource—other surviving families with a shared goal of building a memorial. With social capital again in mind, data points on community and friend interaction revealed that people with connections to smaller towns received greater support from people outside of the family. Though a low number of references existed, the relationship between community size and the management of sorrow is worth further exploration. In addition, the impact of disasters on community-wide grief deserves attention in the future.

Among reritualization and family, disaster-related interaction and pharmaceutical consumption ranked low. The obvious factor is a lack of repetitive references in each area. Moreover, the comments provided did not display much force. Regardless, they do create the impression that powerful entities involved in disasters can ease sorrow with personalized visits. One interviewee explained that a union representative visited with her family. That person displayed regret for the circumstances. It eased the minds of family members. Financial support from unions to help build the memorial later on did as well. Another person discussed a mother who took medications for anxiety. Perhaps the use of drugs to ease pain would not have ranked so low if the research had a concentrated theme looking at substance use and abuse from a wider perspective.

On personal rituals, RSPs associated with individualized family activities, maintaining possessions, and site visits/memorial activities ranked high compared to other categorical themes. Salient examples of family activities included grandparents talking one-on-one to interviewees about fathers. Grandparents also provided respondents individual attention via recreational activities. Some mothers refused to let children discuss their dads. Keeping their fathers in their social network, interviewees had conversations with the deceased dads for emotional support, a ritual that continued throughout life. On repetitiveness, nearly 18 percent of comments in this category concerned family activities, a high number compared to other themes. Homologousness with other personal rituals became clear considering continued bonds with fathers, including maintaining possessions, site visits, and talking to non-family members about the dead. The key resource with this RSP was having extended family willing to spend one-on-one time with surviving children and having people willing to talk openly. Under maintaining possessions, salient instances comprised respondents who kept and preserved their fathers' things. Through the years, many used RSPs to ensure the items upheld the smell, look, and feel they had at the time of the disaster. Seventeen percent of comments were on this theme. Homologousness existed by way of other themes, including the aforementioned family talk. Keeping disaster-related documents is similar to disaster-related research. Also, consider people who curate their fathers' old Bibles, which relates to spiritual practice. The crucial resource here is the stuff, which some had a hard time accessing. People mentioned the military holding on to items for up to a year post-disaster but also mothers hiding or throwing their fathers' things away. Some survivors found themselves ritualistically sneaking around to locate hidden items. With some children's post-disaster experiences, secondary trauma occurs due to bureaucratic dynamics and power disparities. However, unseen in previous literature, secondary trauma can also come by way of variation in grief rituals within the family domain.

Visiting the site was important after the disaster, but interviewees did not provide many details other than denial of access. There was one exception. A data point revealed that a friend of the family with access to the launch complex brought some people to the site within days of the disaster. A daughter told me that she had the opportunity to sift through personal belongings of the 53. She found her father's things and said that day was important to her recovery. If others had the same opportunity, it may have benefited them as well. Visiting the memorial was important too, but as discussed, it was hard to maintain ritualistic visits because of the relocation of the memorial and recreancy-related resistance ritualistically engaged in by the government.

With memorial visits, homologousness linked to cemetery activities. The vital resource for participation was site/memorial availability and knowledge of the memorial's location.

Moderately ranked RSPs yielded insight despite a lower status. RSPs on community and friend interaction, along with disaster-related interaction, had a commendable amount of evidence though there was lower repetitiveness compared to other personal RSPs. Cemetery and funeral activities did too. With community/friend contact, respondents discussed the importance of social capital through positive engagement with neighbors, teachers, acquaintances of the 53, church friends, and best friends. They also celebrated one-on-one relationships with people from other families of the 53. That indicated homologousness with memorial activities, which similarly brought families of the 53 together. Again, a key resource is the access to other people. Absent of this in recent years, some interviewees turned to social media to display their sorrow and connect with others in virtual environments.

Data points on disaster-related interaction lacked clear homologousness in terms of other RSPs involving personal rituals. They also failed to provide direct understanding of resources since they relied on chance encounters. Nevertheless, random interaction with LC 373-4 workers was exceedingly essential for some, especially if it involved one of the two civilian survivors. Cemetery activities were important to interviewees, and they continue to be. Respondents discussed visiting fathers' graves, taking flowers, cleaning plots, and serving on cemetery committees. With this, homologousness existed via silo site visits and memorial activities. With resources, proximity to the cemetery as a domain of interaction was influential. On funerals, locating fathers' bodies was important. As with material possessions, government bureaucratization hindered things. Many interviewees said seeing their father's body at the funeral proved crucial for two reasons. First, it created a reality orientation, which helped some deal with sorrow. Second, body condition informed respondents on accident details. As with researching the disaster later in life, injuries provided clues and gave much-desired answers no one else was supplying. Of course, not all had this resource. Some of the 53 had closed casket funerals.

Among reritualization and personal rituals, spiritual/religious practice and spending money ranked low. There was a limited amount of repetitiveness with each of those themes. With the theme of spiritual and religious practice, compelling comments revolved around dreams and prayers related to the 53. Homologousness here aligned with interviewee attempts to keep the dead in their core set of supportive relationships. Under spending money, the few comments provided referenced personal finances obtained via the disaster and using them to pay for educational expenses, housing, cars, and donations to the memorial fund.

Chapter 10

Remembering the Titans

Joining knowledge from past disasters with future events is essential. Accepting links between humans, environmental shifts, and natural disasters is not required to appreciate that. Obviously, nature is having its way with us, but technological disasters are just as important to watch. Scientists suggest COVID-19 has natural origins. Alternatively, some argue it came from a lab and made its way outside due to human error. As I write this, a team of World Health Organization scientists is trying to get answers in China. The government there, never fully cooperative in supplying pandemic information, is blocking their entry (Turnnidge 2021). With organizations and mistakes, it would not surprise me to learn that someone in the wrong place, at the wrong time, made a bad decision (for more information, see Baker 2021).

Whether a biological lab, NASA, a nuclear power plant, or a missile silo, technological disasters will continue as they have for decades. There are so many rules, procedures, and people willing to violate them for practicality's sake, catastrophe is always inevitable. The human mind can only handle so much information. An abundance of complicated technology is always waiting to fail or go errant. There are workers feeling the pressure from the top, and the outside world, to produce quick results. They ritualistically receive burdensome warnings about prospective problems. Eventually, warnings lose all meaning and workers ignore danger. Therefore, as sociologists argue, the normality of large-scale accidents persists. Reflecting recreancy, blame falls on people with minimal power who happen to be working in a labyrinth of processes and high-tech demands. Knowing there is more to the story, powerful entities continue to foster illusions of safety, sometimes in conjunction with uninformed politicians, to put us at ease and maintain the upper hand over the public. Consider the Launch Complex (LC) 373-4 disaster once more.

THE DISASTER: WHAT WE NOW KNOW

According to the government, the welder on Level 2 triggered a fire. However, others debate that account. What I would frame as "the darkside of organizational ritual" is unmistakable. Speculation continues that welding on Level 2 was not taking place, with official explanations being "muddled." Even if it was, workers at the site went through limited training. They may not have known much about the infrastructure in the facility. With little push from contractors to do so, they did not follow safety protocols. This happened for a variety of reasons. Laborers could not move up and down the ladder in the facility with certain safety equipment on due to limited space. Gas masks seemed impractical. They were older face coverings only providing minimal protection anyway. Recovered workers had contraband on their bodies, including cigarettes and flammable materials. Who would check that anyway? There was persistent confusion about the chain of command and reports of military personnel on site engaged in leisure activities rather than directly monitoring civilian workers. On the day of the disaster, security escorts with air warning sensors on their belts were not with civilians as required, but playing gin topside. Gary Lay, whose father was actually on one investigative committee, recently revealed an emergency power unit wire "shorted out." At the same time, a fuel line ruptured starting the blaze (for a recent discussion on this, see McCoy 2019).

Some say there was pressure to finish the Project Yard Fence updates quickly. At sites, warning sirens sounded frequently and it was hard to tell if something was truly an emergency. The design of the facility lent itself to "tight coupling." Failure in one area easily led to problems in others. You could not isolate Level 2, if that is where the fire occurred. To the detriment of the 53, the only option was shutting down the entire facility to contain flames and fumes, including the 758-ton door over the missile. Among other things, having so many people in the facility at once was not something the designers predicted. There was only one ladder to move up and down between levels if the elevator went out, poor lighting prevailed, heavy equipment blocked exits, there were poorly positioned escape routes, fire extinguishers had poor locations and performance, and ventilation was not optimal. Perhaps overlooked until now, consider the collimator room location. Sociologically, it is impossible for responsibility of the disaster to fall solely on one of the 53.

POST-DISASTER RITUAL AND SORROW:
WHAT WE NOW KNOW

Previous structural ritualization theory (SRT) research gives insight on disasters. The data in this book supports it and adds to existing disaster literature.

People dealing with the aftermath of technological disasters use old resources and find new ones to modify preexisting ritualized practices. They lean on traditional, formal rituals. They also depend on informal ones for comfort. Overall, rituals help people living post-disaster reconstruct their lives in meaningful ways. They allow survivors to create order where there is none and bridge the past to the future. Macro-level entities can aid this process. As SRT research on the 1934 earthquake in Lalitpur City, Nepal, shows, it is possible for the government to provide vulnerable citizens with adequate financial support and help build disaster-related memorials (Bhandari et al. 2011). For families of the 53, this unfortunately did not happen with LC 373-4.

In reaction to lifescape shifts, rituals of families, daughters, and sons of the 53 reflect a shared reverence for the sacred. Through the years, those left behind promoted positive affirmations of the dead. They placed value in their possessions and continued communicating, sometimes intrasubjectively, with men who suffered a cataclysmic fate. Engaging in funerals and cemetery rituals, they integrated personal artifacts and new forms of material symbolism into their being. This kept memories of their loved ones alive. Surviving families built chains of interaction, new social capital. Some of these relationships lasted for decades and helped families and individuals manage the breakdown of their lives. Surviving families attempted to work with powerful entities to establish memorials reflecting shared grief but experienced secondary trauma doing it. They also wanted to make the disaster meaningful to others by way of a civic ceremony acknowledging the 53. However, the Air Force and private contractors did not grasp the importance of their support or just did not care. Recreancy amplified when the government opposed rituals of remembrance, and at certain points, the distribution of possessions belonging to the dead. They gave in on some fronts, but still resisted the memorial, maintenance of its location, and its consistent placement.

Lawsuits provided uneducated and impoverished surviving families limited support, but they absolved contractor responsibility. They shifted accountability to the military. The Air Force was in a better position to quell complaints of vulnerable citizens. With ritualized stress already compounding, mothers experienced what Bourdieu (2020) called "hysteresis." They were disappointed and felt the pressure to take whatever the government offered. They gladly moved themselves away from legal fields of interaction for relief. This ritualistically upheld the maintenance of power in the hands of attorneys and the government. Those entities had the advantage in legitimizing their socially constructed definitions of reality, including what some might interpret as fantasy documents. Children's disenfranchised grief, shifting roles, negative mental health factors, and distrust of adult spending after the settlements created a microcosm of recreancy within families.

Immediately after the disaster, lacking a mature concept of death, children sometimes had persistent thoughts that their loss was not real. Perhaps following unwritten rules of grief, family members of the 53 followed socially prescribed gender norms on bereavement. Women had emotive responses, which I believe supported maximalist positions on the disaster. Some men, stoic, seemed more likely to take minimalist ones. Men were more likely to tell others, whether true or not, that they put the death of their father and the accident behind them to "move on." With that in mind, I do not see it as a surprise that key players in the memorial effort were daughters. A sign of times through their lives, hardly anyone discussed receiving professional psychological help, partly due to stigma. It really was not an option for many of them when they were young anyway. A sign of the times 50 years later, some adult children turned to social media to have their voices heard and seek continued support from others. Adding to the chronic sorrow experienced by families, multiple daughters and sons ritualistically constructed their identities around the disaster. Some still do, and offspring have followed suit. Though little analysis of lifelong disaster effects exists, some scholars have speculated that the effects of disasters "may be quite enduring" (Norris et al. 2002:241). Possibly creating "contaminated families," this project shows the ripple effects of sorrow related to technological disaster are not only long-term but also intergenerational.

RECOMMENDATIONS AND FUTURE RESEARCH

Multiple interviewees took solace in post-disaster interaction involving people with connections to the silo. Powerful entities often pride themselves in secrecy, sometimes necessary due to the nature of their practices. However, with future technological disasters, they should do their best to give survivors agency. Bring them together to help with post-disaster planning and advice on recovery (see Birkmann 2013; Gibson and Wisner 2016). Create forums for surviving families and people with elevated knowledge surrounding deaths, even if it is years later. Those entities should also do all they can to support surviving families as they transition through life without their loved ones. This includes developing appropriate financial responses, financial management skills if necessary, and working with families to establish memorials. This will not be an easy task, especially with people on both sides of the political spectrum continuously questioning motives. Powerful entities should also work to return private possessions to families and allow them access to disaster locations if it is safe and only if surviving family members want it.

Historical and cultural variation exists with aspects of grief. Regardless of how we manage sorrow, there is little doubt we do in fact manage it.

Traditional thanatology gives us a variety of sequential models that argue we move through linear steps on the way to healing. Recent theories imply multiple phases of grief exist, and we oscillate between them. Using data from this exploratory study of a disaster, I believe SRT's focus on disruption, deritualization, and reritualization (DDR) deserves more analysis since it enhances both perspectives and adds to existing disaster research. However, as with "closure" associated with grief, note disaster "recovery" may be a myth. Different people manage themselves in different ways post-disaster (for more information, see Norris et al. 2002). Recovery, like closure, is probably more of an open-ended, never resolving process. In my opinion, like grief, it unquestionably takes much longer than a few weeks to confront properly. Future analysts should push back against pharmaceutical and other medical-based initiatives while acknowledging this.

SRT underscores the role and value of social and personal rituals after loss. It helps us to understand taken-for-granted rituals that provide us with cognitive stability while at the same time holding the potential to transform our lives. Having specific ways to measure rituals of sorrow, such as salience, repetitiveness, homologousness, and resources, can be of benefit for scholars looking to pinpoint and rank specific post-loss behaviors. A link between fantasy documents and SRT analysis of fantasy imagery supporting organizational deviance is worth investigating too (Knottnerus et al. 2006). Notwithstanding, a call for the expansion of studies related to DDR has merit.

With this project, theoretical dynamics of disruption allowed me to better define the event, factors contributing to the type of people lost, and how those people prepared others for their possible demise. Many of the 53 men had limited resources and were willing to engage in risky work, especially due to the pay. Pre-disaster rituals show that some foresaw their deaths and consciously or subconsciously prepared their family members with discussions of dangerous work. Some took action to ensure extra financial security just in case. Do such anticipatory rituals create reaction variation in technological disasters? Do these kinds of rituals influence whether surviving family take maximalist or minimalist positions? This study shows surviving family members of technological disasters are more comfortable discussing post-disaster deritualization among family rather than personal disturbances. I wonder why. Regardless, there is more to explore at the intersection of family and personal dynamics, specifically within the household after technological disaster, whether applicable to ritualized strain or some familial-level of structurally reproduced recreancy (for related issues, see Edelstein 2002, 2004). This work thoroughly reviews specific behaviors associated with lifescape changes and adjustments, short- and long-term, post-disaster. How would the themes in this project compare to other disaster studies if using an SRT lens? Is it possible to move beyond case studies to answer such a question?

I do not believe DDR happen sequentially, but they do undoubtedly happen. People experience sorrow differently, but the crystallization of a DDR model of grief and/or disaster "recovery" is possible. It should focus on better defining disruption. Knottnerus's (2016; forthcoming) efforts provide a loose understanding of disruption. New research could blend it with the work of other scholars (see Garfinkel 1967; Vollmer 2013) to give clearer parameters. We could know more about the magnitude of disruptions on disaster and sorrow by concentrating on factors such as the origin and nature of the event, coercive participant involvement, incident duration, levels of anticipation, and the number of people affected. As Knottnerus (2016:158) states, "Research on disasters suggests that more attention should be given to assisting victims to reconstruct RSPs." Further conceptualization of disruption and the development of a DDR model could help open that door.

Besides what I have already mentioned, more research on the LC 373-4 disaster is possible. Future studies could focus on litigation (see Picou, Marshall, and Gill 2004; Gill and Picou 2008). Like Straub's (2021) recent analysis, it could review the role of the print media in shaping rural people's perceptions of risk and institutional dependence. Note that older articles I reviewed largely supported government interpretations of the event. As time moved forward, levels of skepticism appeared to increase. Is it possible to analyze this trend with LC 373-4 in comparison to other disasters? A deeper dive into government documents might provide more information on organizational characteristics surrounding the event. Moreover, not all families, daughters, and sons processed their losses the same. Other data might tell us specifically why. Perhaps some children had horrible fathers, and they believe their lives were better off without them. Is it worth talking to them? Are they the ones who did not want me to interview them? Some respondents had highly successful careers, ventured into political leadership positions, and owned their own businesses. How did that happen? Why did that happen?

With my connection to the disaster, this piece uses aspects of autoethnography. This benefited my ability to extract information from respondents that otherwise would have remained in the shadows, but it also took an extra toll on me. I believe the experience of doing autoethnography when focusing on a disaster is worthy of its own study. Using autoethnographical methods to supplement interviews and content analysis also created additional subjectivity. I would like to see others revisit the qualitative, exploratory themes of this research with a more objective position, perhaps utilizing quantitative methods to crosscheck reliability and validity.

BURYING THE TITAN II

Jockeying for military dominance continued after Ronald Reagan won the 1980 presidential election. He launched hard-nosed Cold War plans, such as The Strategic Defense Initiative, also known as the "Star Wars program." Figureheads wanted to abandon deterrence via mutual assured destruction. They wanted laser beams that could destroy nuclear missiles before impact. They believed the future of war was vehicles that could penetrate anti-aircraft defenses and small, precise intercontinental ballistic missiles (ICBMs). The stealth bomber soon came into being, along with the MX missile—the Peacemaker. Still, there were people who wanted to keep the old standard in place, even with more civilians living near Titan II locations. With a supreme fantasy documentation move, the Air Force awarded the 308th a trophy in 1982 for being the best Strategic Air Command wing and soon after gave it a humanitarian trophy for its work reaching out to local communities. This impression management was too little too late. LC 373-4 and the more recent LC 374-7 accident near Damascus, Arkansas, tainted the public's perception of the Titan II. Moreover, lawmakers argued that eliminating the Titans would produce significant government savings over just a few years. The overwhelming perception was that Titan IIs had to go (Conine 2015; The Military Standard 2021).

The deactivation order came on April 30, 1982. Project Rivet Cap would cost about $1 million per site. One location closed every six weeks. This involved the removal of the warhead, a crane pulling the missile out of the silo, civilian contractors salvaging still usable equipment, and finally demolition. Crews would remove the door over the silo, jackhammer the support structure to 25 feet below the surface, and then detonate 2,800 pounds of explosives in the gun barrel. Treaties required crews to stop at that point. The Soviets needed time to identify locations by air and confirm facilities inactive. Later, workers dug up the cableway between the launch bay and control center. Bulldozing rubble and dirt into the ground followed. Then, demolition crews put a concrete cap over the silo opening (Penson 2019; Stumpf 2000).

Local governments bought some site locations, using dirt for road construction. Citizens purchased and refurbished others as homes. I recently found two silos on the market at just under $500,000 not too far from the Titan Missile Museum (LC 571-7) in Arizona, where you can see the only Titan II left (Roberts 2015; Penson 2019; Zap 2020). Last year, officials put LC 373-9 near Vilonia, Arkansas, on the National Register of Historic Places. It joined 373-5, 374-5, and 374-7 (Dillard 2019; Bowden 2020). An interviewee said a man purchased the site next to my hometown to turn three levels into "living quarters." He is supposedly using YouTube to document the process. Regardless, in mid-1987 near Judsonia, 3 miles from Wilbur D.

Mills' hometown, the Air Force took LC 373-8 off alert. It was the last Titan II site in operation (Schlosser 2013). After nearly 25 years of intimidating the enemy and close to 20 years after families buried the 53, the government buried America's most destructive missile (Conine 2015). Nevertheless, it is apparent demolition in the lives of 53 families continued for years.

TAKING A DRIVE

Wrapping up this book, I decided to look at the Johns Hopkins Coronavirus Dashboard one last time. I could not find the original map I used when the pandemic started. I suppose it would not make sense anyway. I remember it represented clusters of the virus with red dots. If the old map existed, I suppose the entire United States would be under a crimson blanket. Tired of seeking COVID-19 information, I decided to put on Delphard's old felt hat and take a drive. Reflecting on what it means to be a father, I cut through communities familiar to the 53, such as Conway, Greenbrier, Enola, and Vilonia on my way to the Blasingame Cemetery in El Paso, Arkansas. I listened to news radio and heard that Kentucky's governor just held a ceremony to acknowledge everyone in the state who died of COVID-19. They placed a flag in the ground for each person lost to the virus (Schreiner 2021). I saw billboards with FBI announcements urging people to turn in information on those who broke into the U.S. Capitol. While driving, I tried to locate as many of the old missile sites in Arkansas I could along my path. There was not much to see, typically just remnants of old gates blocking trespassers from what is now farmland. At the crossroads of El Paso, I lingered while surveying the area. Memories and memories of memories rushed into my mind. Someone once told me that my mother and father met at a small store at this intersection. I can envision them talking for the first time. It is certainly not the case now, but they had to be smitten with each other then. I see playful flirting and smiling faces, with neither knowing that their fathers suffered the same horrific fate not far away in LC 373-4.

Driving down the road to the cemetery, I noticed changes. Pavement replaced gravel. I passed the houses of old friends that were hard to recognize and clear land where old oak trees used to stand guard over the hills. One thing that looked the same was the cemetery. Deep into winter, the wind chilled my bones after stepping outside of my vehicle. As I walked up, I noticed the cemetery association sign. It read, "Please contact an officer of the board before marking off plot or burying in this cemetery." With a fresh mound of dirt close to my family's plots not falling into the pattern of graves, I could tell people did not follow that rule. As with the silos, under a veil of secrecy, someone dug a hole and put something inside of it they believed to be important. Once there, I soon stood motionless in front of my grandfather's headstone. My Aunt Linda's marker glared at me from a few feet away.

After El Paso, I headed through Beebe on my way to Ward. I visited with Lucille where her body lays in Old Austin. She had secrets too. Just like the Air Force, she did not have much to say about them. While there, I thought about missile programs. It is amazing how something so important on a geopolitical level can influence the lives of communities, families, and people. I recalled Titans in the development of nuclear technology, its delivery, and the use of missiles. Names like Albert Einstein, Leo Szilard, Wernher von Braun, Robert Oppenheimer, Curtis LeMay, and Gus Grissom flooded my brain. I reflected on political Titans connected to silos in Arkansas. Names such as Sid McMath, Wilbur D. Mills, Dale Bumpers, and David Pryor jumped out to me. I headed to the Jacksonville Museum of Military History to see the memorial. It seemed smaller than I remembered, but the size of its meaning in my heart had grown so much since I last stood in front of it as a young man. Placing my right trembling hand on it, I once again visualized the gruesome imagery from *The Fall of the Titans* painting on the cover of this book. I thought of the men who died on August 9, 1965, and how they died. Already implied, they are Titans in their own right. Shedding a tear, I remembered another group of Titans too. All the daughters and sons of the men lost. Their fathers' lives had meaning, and their lives do too. I had one place left to go—LC 373-4. As *Arkansas Democrat-Gazette* reporter Jeannie Roberts (2015) said a few years ago, "Directions to the site of the worst nuclear weapon accident in the history of the U.S. are hard to come by." I was going to do my best to find it. I stopped to fill up my car with gas at a crowded station. My mask is firmly hugging my face while others, skeptical of government guidelines, stare me down with what seems like years of distrust in their eyes. Like the families of the 53, I was still looking for answers. This project let me know part of managing lifelong sorrow after a disaster is never finding them all. It reminds me of a letter a daughter wrote to me after her interview. Commenting on loss, she said, "We find ways to reprogram our gray cells, to reroute around broken brain activity. We think we're going to accomplish a satisfying conclusion, but . . . It still hurts."

References

Abrams, Courtney B, Karen Albright, and Aaron Panofsky. 2004. "Contesting the New York Community: From Liminality to the "New Normal" in the Wake of September 11." *City and Community* 3(3):189–220.

Adams, Tony E., Stacy Holman Jones, and Carolyn Ellis. 2015. *Autoethnography: Understanding Qualitative Research*. New York: Oxford University Press.

Alderman, Derek, Jordan Brasher, and Owen Dwyer. 2020. "Memorials and Monuments." Pp. 39–47 in *International Encyclopedia of Human Geography*, 2nd ed., edited by Audrey Kobayashi. Amsterdam: Elsevier.

Aldrich, Richard. 2012. *Building Resilience: Social Capital in Post-Disaster Recovery*. Chicago, IL: University of Chicago Press.

Allen, Arthur. 2020. "The Down Side of Getting Two COVID Vaccines Too Fast." *The Daily Beast*. Retrieved December 30, 2020 (https://www.thedailybeast.com/the-downside-to-getting-out-two-covid-vaccines-so-fast).

Allison, David. 2018, ed. *Controversial Monuments and Memorials: A Guide for Community Leaders*. Lanham, MA: Rowman and Littlefield.

Alperovitz, Gar. 2010. *The Decision to Use the Atomic Bomb*. New York: Knopf Doubleday Publishing Group.

American Psychiatric Association (APA). 2013. *Diagnostic and Statistical Manual of Mental Disorders*, 5th ed. Washington DC: APA.

Anderson, Michael. 2001. "'You Have to Get Inside the Person' or Making Grief Private: Image and Metaphor in the Therapeutic Reconstruction of Bereavement." Pp. 135–143 in *Grief, Mourning, and Death Ritual*, edited by Jenny Hockey, Jeanne Katz, and Neil Small. Philadelphia, PA: Open University Press.

Anthony, Michael Johnson. 2018. "The Sleeping Giant: The Effects of Housing Titan II Missiles in Arkansas and Kansas from 1962 to 1987." Thesis, Department of History, University of Arkansas.

Arkansas Gazette. 1965a. "Modifications Are Suspended at All Sites." August 11, p. 1A.

———. 1965b. "Flags to Fly at Half-Staff for Dead in Silo Disaster." August 11, p. 9A.

———. 1965c. "Eyewitness at Entrance to Silo Tunnel Felt Rush of Wind 'Like a Hurricane.'" August 11, p. 1A.

———. 1965d. "Blaze in Titan Silo Killed Most Persons of Any State Fire." August 11, p. 9A.

Armstrong, David. 1993. "Public Health Spaces and the Fabric of Identity." *Sociology* 27(3):493–410.

Atomic Heritage Foundation. 2019. "Leo Szilard." Retrieved February 1, 2020 (https://www.atomicheritage.org/profile/leo-szilard).

Baker, Nicholson. 2021. "The Lab Leak Hypothesis: For Decades Scientists Have Been Hot Wiring Viruses to Prevent a Pandemic, not Cause One... But What If?" *New York (Intelligencer).* Retrieved January 25, 2021 (https://nymag.com/intelligencer/article/coronavirus-lab-escape-theory.html).

Barlow, Aaron. 2020. *The Manhattan Project and the Dropping of the Atomic Bomb: The Essential Reference Guide.* Santa Barbara, CA: ABC-CLIO.

Bart, Catherine. 2020. "Summer Camps Adjust to COVID-19 Precautions." *Portland Press Herald.* Retrieved August 9, 2020 (https://www.pressherald.com/2020/08/07 /summer-camps-adjust-to-covid-19-precautions/).

Bartholomew, Darrell E., and Marlys J. Mason. 2020. "Facebook Rituals: Identifying Rituals of Social Networking Sites Using Structural Ritualization Theory." *Journal of Consumer Behaviour* 19(2):142–150.

Baudrillard, Jean. 1994. *Simulacra and Simulation.* Ann Arbor, MI: University of Michigan Press.

Beck, Ulrich. 1992. *Risk Society: Towards a New Modernity.* London: Sage.

Bell, Catherine. 1992. *Ritual Theory, Ritual Practice.* New York: Oxford University Press.

Bellentani, Federico, and Mario Panico. 2016. "The Meanings of Monuments and Memorials: Toward a Semiotic Approach." *International Journal of Semiotics* 2(1):28–46.

Berg, Bruce, and Howard Lune. 2018. *Qualitative Research Methods for the Social Sciences.* Boston, MA: Pearson.

Berger, Peter, and Thomas Luckmann. 1966. *The Social Construction of Reality: A Treatise in the Sociology of Knowledge.* New York: Anchor Books.

Bhandari, Roshan Bhakta, Norio Okada, and J. David Knottnerus. 2011. "Urban Ritual Events and Coping with Disaster Risk: A Case Study of Lalitpur, Nepal." *Journal of Applied Social Science* 5:13–32.

Birkmann, Joern. 2013. *Measuring Vulnerability to Natural Hazards: Toward Disaster Resilient Societies.* Tokyo: United Nations University Press.

Blaikie, Piers M., and Harold C. Brookfield. 1987. *Land Degradation and Society.* New York: Methuen.

Blum, Steven. 2020. "Urine Luck: Products to Help You Pee on the Go Are Proliferating During the Pandemic." *Los Angeles Magazine.* Retrieved June 11, 2021 https://www.lamag.com/lalifeandstyle/pee-during-the-pandemic/).

Bogue, Mike. 2017. *Apocalypse Then: American and Japanese Atomic Cinema, 1951-1967.* Jefferson, NC: McFarland and Co.

Bolin, Robert, and Liza Kurtz. 2018. "Race, Class, Ethnicity, and Disaster Vulnerability." Pp. 181–203 in *Handbook of Disaster Research*, 2nd ed., edited by Havidán Rodriguez, William Bonner, and Joseph E. Trainor. New York: Springer

Bolin, Robert, and Lois Stanford. 1998. *The Northridge Earthquake*. London: Routledge.

Bonder, Julian. 2009. "On Memory, Trauma, Public Space, Monuments, and Memorials." *Places* 21(1):62–69.

Bostdorff, Denise. 2017. "Obama, Trump, and Reflections on the Rhetoric of Political Chance." *Rhetoric and Public Affairs* 24:695–706.

Bourdieu, Pierre. 1977. Outline of a Theory of Practice, translated by R. Nice. Cambridge, MA: Cambridge University Press.

———. 1993. *The Field of Cultural Production: Essays on Art and Leisure*. New York: Columbia University Press.

———. 2020. *Habitus and Field: General Sociology Volume 2* (1982-1983). Oxford: Polity Press.

Bowden, Bill. 2020. "Missile Silo, Caboose Added to Historic List." *Northwest Arkansas Democrat-Gazette*. Retrieved January 2, 2021 (https://www.nwaonline.com/news/2020/nov/11/missile-silo-caboose-added-to-historic-list/).

Bowlby, John. 1977. *The Making and Breaking of Affectional Bonds*. London. Tavistock.

Bradfield, Robert. 2020. "'We Should Find a Way:' First Coast Families Waiting for Eldercare Facilities to Relax Visitation Rules." First Coast News. Retrieved August 29, 2020 (https://www.firstcoastnews.com/article/news/local/families-wait-for-elder-care-facilities-to-relax-visitation-rules-task-force-sends-reopening-recommendations-to-gov-desantis/77-332ea1c1-c9c9-4352-ba75-7cf3045dd57d).

Brennan, Michael, ed. 2016. *The A-Z of Death and Dying*. Santa Barbara, CA: ABC-CLIO.

Brym, Robert J. 2009. *Sociology as a Life or Death Issue*. Belmont: Wadsworth.

Buggs, Shantel Gabrieal. 2017. "Your Momma is Day-Glow White: Questioning the Politics of Racial Identity, Loyalty, and Obligation." *Identities* 24(4):379–397.

Burnett, Abby. 2015. *Gone to the Grave: Burial Customs of the Arkansas Ozarks, 1850-1950*. Jackson, MS: Oxford University Press.

Burns, Scott Z. 2011. *Contagion*. Los Angeles, CA: Warner Bros.

Carlin, Aiden, and Mark Lokanan. 2018. "Ritualisation and Money Laundering in the Swiss Banking Sector." *Journal of Money Laundering Control* 21(1):89–103.

Castree, Noel, William M. Adams, John Barry, Daniel Brockington, Bram Buscher, Esteve Corbera, David Demeritt, Roseleen Duffy, Ulrike Felt, Katja Neves, Peter Newell, Luigi Pellizzoni, Kate Rigby, Paul Robbins, Libby Robin, Deborah Rose, Andrew Ross, David Schlosberg, Sverker Sorlin, Paige West, Mark Whitehead, and Brian Wynne. 2014. "Changing the Intellectual Climate." *Nature Climate Change* 4:763–768.

Centers for Disease Control. 2020. "Considerations for Preventing the Spread of COVID-19 in Assisted Living Facilities." Centers for Disease Control and Prevention. Retrieved August 29, 2020 (https://www.cdc.gov/coronavirus/2019-ncov/hcp/assisted-living.html).

Chan, Adrienne, and Donald Fisher. 2014. *The Exchange University: Corporatization of Academic Culture*. Vancouver: UBC Press.

Chappell, Carl. 1968. *Seven Minus One: The Story of Gus Grissom*. Mitchell, IN: New Frontier Publishing.

Chew, Sing. 2007. *The Recurring Dark Ages: Ecological Stress, Climate Changes and System Transformation*. Lanham, MD: Altamira Press.

Chicago Tribune. 1965. "Seek Cause of Blast in Missile Silo – 53 Killed, 4 from Chicagoland." August 11, p. 1.

Christ, Mark K. 2016. "Titan II Missile Accident (1965)." *Encyclopedia of Arkansas*. Retrieved January 14, 2019 (https://encyclopediaofarkansas.net/entries/titan-ii-missile-accident-9001/).

Church, Scott. 2013. "Digital Gravescapes: Digital Memorializing on Facebook." *The Information Society* 29:184–189.

Clarke, Lee B. 1999. *Mission Improbable: Using Fantasy Documents to Tame Disaster*. Chicago, IL. University of Chicago Press.

Clarke, Lee B, and Rick Phillips. 2020. "What if Covid-19 is Here to Stay?" *Star-Ledger*. Retrieved September 3, 2020 (https://www.nj.com/opinion/2020/08/what-if-covid-19-is-here-to-stay-opinion.html).

Collins, Randall. 1975. *Conflict Sociology: Toward and Explanatory Science*. New York: Academic Press.

———. 1981. "On the Mircrofoundations of Macrosociology." *American Journal of Sociology* 86:984–1014.

———. 1987. "Interaction Ritual Chains, Power and Property: The Micro-Macro Connection as an Empirically Based Theoretical Problem." Pp. 193–206 in *The Micro-Macro Link*, edited by J. C. Alexander, B. Giesen, R. Munch, and N. J. Smelser. Berkely: University of California Press.

———. 2014. "Interaction Ritual Chains and Collective Effervescence" Pp. 295–311 in *Collective Emotions: Perspectives from Psychology, Philosophy, and Sociology*, edited by Christian Von Scheve and Mikko Salmela. Oxford: Oxford University Press.

Concha-Holmes, Amanda D., and Anthony Oliver-Smith, eds. 2019. *Disasters in Paradise: Natural Hazards, Social Vulnerability, and Development Decisions*. Lanham, MD: Lexington Books.

Conine, Gary B. 2015. *Not For Ourselves Alone: The Evolution and Role of the Titan II Missile in the Cold War*. North Charleston, SC: CreateSpace.

Couch Stephen R., and Steve Kroll-Smith 1985. "The Chronic Technical Disaster: Toward a Social Scientific Perspective." *Social Science Quarterly* 66(3):564–575.

———. 1992. "Controllability, Social Breakdown, and Technological Disasters: The Case of the Centralia Coal Mine Fire." Pp. 337–349 in *Natural and Technological Disasters: Causes, Effects, and Preventative Measures*, edited by Shyamal Majumdar, Gregory Forbes, E. W. Miller, and Robert Schmalz. Pennsylvania: Pennsylvania Academy of Sciences.

Cox, Brian. 2020. "Worries Grow Over a K-shaped Economic Recovery that Favors the Wealthy." *CNBC*. Retrieved September 10, 2020 (https://www.cnbc.com/2020/09/04/worries-grow-over-a-k-shaped-economic-recovery-that-favors-the-wealthy.html).

Crim, Brian E. 2018. *Our Germans, Project Paperclip, and the National Security State*. Baltimore, MD: Johns Hopkins University Press.

Cross, John. 2020. "Emergency Managers' Attitudes about Communication of Hazard Vulnerability by Monuments and Historical Markers." *International Journal of Mass Emergencies and Disasters* 38(2):201–215.

Cuny, Frederick C. 1994. *Disasters and Development*. Dallas, TX: Intertect Press.

Davies, Douglas J. 2005. *A Brief History of Death*. Malden, MA: Blackwell Publishing.

———. 2017. *Death, Ritual, and Belief*. London: Bloomsbury Publishing.

Delano, Daisha Lee, and J. David Knottnerus. 2018. "The Khmer Rouge, Ritual and Control." *Asian Journal of Social Science* 46(1–2):79–110.

DeSpelder, Lynne Ann, and Albert Lee Strickland. 2020. *The Last Dance: Encountering Death and Dying*. New York: McGraw-Hill Education.

Devine, Megan. 2017. *It's OK that You're Not OK: Meeting Grief and Loss in a Culture that Doesn't Understand*. Boulder, CO: Sounds True.

Dickinson, Tim. 2020. "The Four Men Responsible for America's COVID-19 Test Disaster." *Rolling Stone*. Retrieved September 3, 2020 (https://www.rollingstone.com/politics/politics-features/covid-19-test-trump-admin-failed-disaster-995930/).

Dillard, Tom. 2019. "The Titan Missile Silo Disasters." *Arkansas Democrat-Gazette*. Retrieved January 24, 2021 (https://www.arkansasonline.com/news/2019/may/19/the-titan-missile-silo-disasters-201905/).

D-maps.com. 2007-2021. *Map of Arkansas: Outline-Counties*. Retrieved June 1, 2021 (https://d-maps.com/carte.php?num_car=19687&lang=en).

Doka, Kenneth J. 1999. "Disenfranchised Grief." *Bereavement Care* 18(3):37–39.

Dorrien, Gary. 2020. *In a Post-Hegelian Spirit: Philosophical Ideology as Idealistic Discontent*. Waco, TX: Baylor University Press.

Douglas, Mary. 1970. *Natural Symbols*. New York: Vintage.

Drabek, Thomas E. 1986. *Human System Responses to Disaster: An Inventory of Sociological Findings*. New York: Springer-Verlag.

———. 2013. *The Human Side of Disaster*, 2nd ed. Boca Raton, FL: CRC Press.

Du Bois, W. E. B. 1953. *The Souls of Black Folk: Essays and Sketches*. New York: Blue Heron Press.

Duggar, DannaKay. 2014. "Jacksonville Museum of Military History." *Encyclopedia of Arkansas*. Retrieved January 2, 2021 (https://encyclopediaofarkansas.net/entries/jacksonville-museum-of-military-history-2867/).

Durkheim, Emile. [1893] 1965a. *The Division of Labor in Society*. New York: Free Press.

———. [1915] 1965b. *The Elementary Forms of Religious Life*. New York: Free Press.

———. [1897] 1966. *Suicide: A Study in Sociology*. New York: Free Press.

Dynes, Russell R. 1970. *Organized Behavior in Disaster*. Lexington, MA: Heath Lexington Books.

Easthope, Lucy. 2018. *The Recovery Myth: The Plans and Situated Realities of Post-Disaster Response*. London: Palgrave Macmillan.

Edelstein, Michael R. 2002. "Contamination: The Invisible Built Environment." Pp. 559–588 in *Handbook of Environmental Psychology*, edited by Robert Bechtel and Arza Churchman. Hoboken, NJ: John Wiley.

———. 2004. *Contaminated Communities: The Social and Psychological Impacts of Residential Toxic Exposure*, 2nd ed. Boulder, CO: Westview Press.

Edgley, Charles. 2013. *The Drama of Social Life: A Dramaturgical Handbook*. Farnham, Surrey, Ashgate Publishing Limited.

Egan, Matt. 2020. "Walmart Is Using Drones to Deliver COVID-19 Tests in Vegas." CNN. Retrieved September 27, 2020 (https://www.msn.com/en-us/money/companies/walmart-is-using-drones-to-deliver-covid-19-tests-in-vegas/ar-BB19lNLn).

Eidenbach, Peter L. 2010. *Alamogordo*. Charleston, SC: Arcadia Pub.

Ellis, Carolyn, Tony Adams, and Arthur Bochner. 2011. "Autoethnography: An Overview." *Forum: Qualitative Social Research* 12(1). Retrieved January 8, 2019 (http://www.qualitative-research.net/index.php/fqs/article/view/1589/3095).

Enarson, Elaine, and Betty H. Morrow, eds. 1998. *The Gendered Terrain of Disaster*. New York: Praeger.

Endter-Wada, Joanna, Jon Hofmeister, Rachel Mason, Steven McNabb, Eric Morrison, Stephanie Reynolds, Edward Robbins, Lynn Robbins, and Curtiss Brooks. 1993. *Social Indicators Study of Alaskan Coastal Villages*. Anchorage, AK: Minerals Management Service.

Engel, George L. 1961. "'Is Grief a Disease?' - A Challenge for Medical Research." *Psychosomatic Medicine* 23(1):18–22.

Erikson, Kai T. 1976. Everything in Its Path: Destruction of Community in the Buffalo Creek Flood. New York: Simon and Schuster.

———. 1994. *A New Species of Trouble: Explorations in Disasters, Trauma, and Community*. New York: W.W. Norton.

Etzioni, Amitai. 2000. "Toward a Theory of Public Ritual." *Sociological Theory* 18:1.

Eyre, Anne. 2001. "Post-disaster Rituals." Pp. 256–266 in *Grief, Mourning, and Death Ritual*, edited by Jenny Hockey, Jeanne Katz, and Neil Small. Philadelphia, PA: Open University Press.

Ferris, Sarah, Olivia Beavers, Melanie Zanona, Burgess Everett, and Marianne Levine. 2021. "Hill Chaos Turns Deadly After Rioters Storm Capitol." *Politico*. Retrieved January 8, 2021 (https://www.politico.com/news/2021/01/06/electoral-college-certification-halted-amid-massive-pro-trump-demonstration-455495).

Fischer, Henry W. 1998. *Response to Disaster: Fact Versus Fiction and Its Perpetuation: The Sociology of Disaster*, 2nd ed. Lanham, MD: University Press of America.

Fothergill, Alice, Enrique Maestas, and JoAnne DeRouen Darlington. 1999. "Race, Ethnicity, and Disasters in the United States: A Review of Literature." *Disasters* 23:156–173.

Fothergill, Alice, and Lori A. Peek. 2004. "Poverty and Disasters in the United States: A Review of Recent Sociological Findings. *Natural Hazards* 32:89–110.

Foxe, Fanne. 1975. *Fanne Foxe: The Stripper and Congressman*. New York: Pinnacle Books.

Frances, Allen. 2013. *Normal: An Insider's Revolt against Out-of-Control Psychiatric Diagnosis*. New York: William Morrow.

Francis, Doris, Leonie Kellaher, and Georgiana Neophytou. 2001. "The Cemetery: The Evidence of Continuing Bonds." Pp. 226–236 in *Grief, Mourning, and Death Ritual*, edited by Jenny Hockey, Jeanne Katz, and Neil Small. Philadelphia, PA: Open University Press.

Frank, Jerome. 1936. *Law and the Modern Mind*. New York: Tudor.

Freud, Sigmund. [1917] 1957. "Mourning and Melancholia." Pp. 237–258 in *the Standard Edition of the Complete Psychological Works of Sigmund Freud* edited by James Strachey. London: Hogarth Press.

Freudenburg, William R., Robert Grambling, Shirley Laska, and Kai T. Erikson. 2009. *Catastrophe in the Making: The Engineering of Katrina and the Disasters of Tomorrow*. Washington, DC: Island Press.

Fritz, Charles E. 1961. "Disasters." Pp. 651–694 in *Contemporary Social Problems*, edited by R. K. Merton and R. A. Nisbet. New York: Harcourt.

Fuchs, Thomas. 2017. "Presence in Absence: The Ambiguous Phenomenology of Grief." *Phenomenology and the Cognitive Sciences* 17:43–63.

Furniss, Tim. 1989. *One Small Step: The Apollo Missions, the Astronauts, the Aftermath*. Sparkford, UK: Haynes.

Gaillard, Jean-Christophe, and Pauline Texier. 2010. "Religion, Natural Hazards, and Disasters: An Introduction." *Religion* 40:81–84.

Gainor, Chris. 2018. *The Bomb and the Beginnings of America's Missile Age*. Baltimore, MD: Johns Hopkins University Press.

Garfinkel, Harold. 1956. "Conditions of Successful Degradation Ceremonies." *American Journal of Sociology* 61:420–424.

———. 1967. *Studies in Ethnomethodology*. Englewoods Cliffs, NJ: Prentice-Hall.

Gergen, Kenneth. 2010. *The Saturated Self: Dilemmas of Identity in Contemporary Life*. New York: Basic Books.

Gibson, Terry, and Ben Wisner. 2016. "Let's Talk about You... Opening Space for Local Experience, Action, and Learning in Disaster Risk Reduction." *Disaster Prevention and Management* 25(5):664–684.

Giddens, Anthony. 1984. *The Constitution of Society: Outline of the Theory of Structuration*. Berkeley and Los Angeles: University of California Press.

———. 1989. "A Reply to My Critics." Pp. 249–301 in Social Theory of Modern Societies: Anthony Giddens and His Critics, edited by D. Held and J. B. Thompson. Cambridge, UK: Cambridge University Press.

———. 1990. *The Consequences of Modernity*. Cambridge, UK: Polity Press.

———. 1991. Modernity and Self Identity. Cambridge, UK: Polity Press.

———. 1999. *Runaway World*. London: Profile.

Gill, Duane A. 1994. "Environmental Disaster and Fishery Co-Management in a Natural Resource Community: Impacts of the Exxon Valdez Oil Spill." Pp. 207–235 in *Folk Management in the World's Fisheries*, edited by Christopher Dyer and James McGoodwin. Boulder, CO: University of Colorado Press.

Gill, Duane A., and J. Steven Picou. 2008. "Technological Disaster and Chronic Community Stress." *Society and Natural Resources* 11(8):795–815.

Gill, Duane A., and Liesel A. Ritchie. 2018. "Contributions of Technological and Natech Disaster Research to the Social Science Disaster Paradigm." Pp. 39–60 in *Handbook of Disaster Research*, 2nd ed., edited by Havidán Rodriguez, William Donner, and Joseph E. Trainor. New York: Springer

Gill, Duane A., Liesel A. Ritchie, and J. Steven Picou. 2016. "Sociocultural and Psychosocial Impacts of the Exxon Valdez Oil Spill: Twenty-Four Years of Research in Cordova, Alaska." *The Extractive Industries and Society.* Retrieved September 12, 2020 (http://stevenpicou.com/pdfs/sociocultural-and-psychosocial -impacts-of-the-exxon-valdez-oil-spill.pdf).

Glennon, Lorraine, ed. 1999. *The 20th Century: An Illustrated History of Our Lives and Times*. North Dighton, MA: JG Press.

Goanta, Catalina, and Sofia Ranchordàs. 2020. *The Regulation of Social Media Influencers*. Northampton, MA: Edward Elgar Publishing.

Goffman, Erving. 1959. *The Presentation of Self in Everyday Life*. New York: Doubleday.

———. 1961. *Asylums*. Chicago, IL: Aldine Publishing Company.

———. 1963. *Stigma: Notes on the Management of Spoiled Identity*. Chicago, IL: Aldine Publishing Company.

———. 1967. *Interaction Ritual*. New York: Pantheon Books.

Gowdy, ShaCamree. 2020. "COVID-19 is Now the Third Leading Cause of Death in the U.S., Former CDC Director Says." *Houston Chronicle*. Retrieved September 6, 2020 (https://www.chron.com/coronavirus/article/COVID-19-is-now-the-third -leading-cause-of-death-15499712.php).

Granek, Leeat. 2010. "Grief as Pathology: The Evolution of Grief Theory in Psychology from Freud to the Present." *History of Psychology* 13(1):46–73.

Green, Bonnie, Jacob Lindy, Mary Grace, Goldine Glesser, Anthony Leonard, Mindy Korol, and Caroline Winget. 1990. "Buffalo Creek Survivors in the Second Decade: Stability of Stress Symptoms. *American Journal of Orthopsychiatrics* 60(1):43–54.

Greenberg, Gary. 2013. *The Book of Woe: The DSM and the Unmaking of Psychiatry*. New York: Blue Rider Press.

Group Report. 1965. "Launch Operations and Witness Group." Report for the President of the USAF Aerospace Missile Accident Investigations Board, Number 62-006.

Gruver, Mead. 2009. "Pollution an Enduring Legacy at Old Missiles Sites." *The Associated Press*. Retrieved September 7, 2020 (http://www.nbcnews.com /id/33255484/ns/us_news-environment/t/pollution-enduring-legacy-old-missile -sites/).

Guan, Jian, and J. David Knottnerus. 1999. "A Structural Ritualization Analysis of the Process of Acculturation and Marginalization of Chinese Americans." *Humboldt Journal of Social Relations* 25:43–95.

———. 2006. "Chinatown under Siege: Community Protest and Structural Ritualization Theory." *Humboldt Journal of Social Relations* 30:5–52.

Guerrieri, Vince. 2020. "40 Years Ago We Almost Blew Up Arkansas." *Popular Mechanics* Retrieved October 6, 2020 (https://www.popularmechanics.com/

military/weapons/a34061418/titan-ii-missile-explosion-damascus-arkansas-40-year-anniversary/).

Guiberson, Brenda. 2010. *Disasters: Natural and Man-Made Catastrophes through the Centuries.* New York: Henry Holt and Company.

Gusfield, Joseph, and Jerzy Michalowicz. 1984. "Secular Symbolism: Studies of Ritual, Ceremony, and the Symbolic Order in Modern Life." *Annual Review of Sociology* 10:417–435.

Guttmann, Allen. 2004. *From Ritual to Record: The Nature of Modern Sports.* New York: Columbia University Press.

Hancock, Dawson, and Bob Algozzine. 2006. *Doing Case Study Research.* New York: Teachers College Press.

Hancock, Stephen D., Ayana Allen, and Chance W. Lewis. 2015. *Autoethnography as a Lighthouse: Illuminating Race, Research, and the Politics of Schooling.* Charlotte, NC: Information Age Publishing.

Handberg, Roger. 2002. *Ballistic Missile Defense and the Future of American Security: Agendas, Perceptions, Technology, and Policy.* Westport, CT: Greenwood Press.

Hatter, Beverly. 1996. "Children and the Death of a Parent or Grandparent." Pp. 131–148 in *Handbook of Childhood Death and Bereavement*, edited by Charles Corr and Donna Corr. New York: Springer.

Hazel, Jean. 1999. "Blasingame Cemetery." White County Historical Society. Retrieved March 18, 2019 (http://www.argenweb.net/white/cems/Blasingame_Cemetery_files/blasingame_cemetery.htm).

Heefner, Gretchen. 2012. *The Missile Next Door: The Minuteman in the American Heartland.* Cambridge, MA: Harvard University Press.

Henger, Sue. 2015. *Beyond the Dark Veil: Post-Mortem and Mourning Photography from the Thanatos Archive*, 2nd ed. San Francisco, CA: Grand Central Press.

Henslin, James M. 2019. *Essential of Sociology: A Down-To-Earth Approach.* 13th ed. New York: Pearson.

Hicks, L. 2000. "Silo Fire Survivor Tells His Story." Daily Citizen, May 7. Retrieved January 14, 2020 (http://www.themilitarystandard.com/missile/titan2/silo_fire_survivor.php).

Higgs, Heath. 2020. "Governor Hutchinson Issues Mask Mandate in Arkansas." Retrieved July 20, 2020 (https://www.nwahomepage.com/lifestyle/health/coronavirus/gov-hutchinson-issues-mask-mandate-in-arkansas/).

Hijiya, James. 2000. "The Gita of Robert Oppenheimer." *Proceedings of the American Philosophical Society* 144(2):123–167.

Ho, Bach, and Kunio Shirahada. 2019. "Barriers to Elder Consumers' Use of Support Services: Community Support in Japan's Super-Aged Society." *Journal of Nonprofit and Public Sector Marketing.* Retrieved March 18, 2020 (https://www.tandfonline.com/doi/abs/10.1080/10495142.2019.1589625).

Hockey, Jenny. 1992. "The Acceptable Face of Human Grieving: The Clergy's Role in Managing Emotional Expression During Funerals." *The Sociological Review* 40(1):129–148.

————. 2001. "Changing Death Rituals." Pp. 185–211 in *Grief, Mourning and Death Ritual*, edited by Jenny Hockey, Jeanne Katz, and Neil Small. Philadelphia, PA: Open University Press.

Hodges, Stan H., and Jason S. Ulsperger. 2005. "Presentations of the Paranormal: Impression Management Strategies and Professionalization Tactics of Psychics and Spirit Mediums." *Free Inquiry in Creative Sociology* 33(1):35–50.

Holinger, Dorothy P. 2020. *The Anatomy of Grief*. New Haven, CT: Yale University Press.

Horwitz, Allan V. 2020. "The Medicalization of Grief." Pp. 171–187 in *Exploring Grief: Towards a Sociology of Sorrow*, edited by Michael Hviid Jacobsen and Anders Petersen. New York: Routledge.

Hughes, Sherick A., and Julie L. Pennington. 2017. *Autoethnography: Process, Product, and Possibility for Critical Social Research*. Thousand Oaks: Sage.

Hurd, Ellis, ed. 2019. *The Reflexivity of Pain and Privilege: Autoethnographic Collections of Mixed Identity*. Boston, MA: Brill Sense.

Impact Assessment, Inc. 1990. *Economic, Social, and Psychological Impact Assessment of the Exxon Valdez Oil Spill*. Anchorage, AK: Oiled Mayors Subcommittee.

————. 1998. *Exxon Valdez Oil Spill, Cleanup, and Litigation*. LaJolla, CA: Minerals Management Service.

Jacobsen, Michael Hviid, and Anders Petersen, eds. 2020a. *Exploring Grief: Towards a Sociology of Sorrow*. New York: Routledge.

————. 2020b. "Introduction." Pp. 1–18 in *Exploring Grief: Towards a Sociology of Sorrow*, edited by Michael Hviid Jacobsen and Anders Petersen. New York: Routledge.

————. 2020c. "Grief in an Individualized Society: A Critical Corrective to the Advancement of Diagnostic Culture." Pp. 205–224 in *Exploring Grief: Towards a Sociology of Sorrow*, edited by Michael Hviid Jacobsen and Anders Petersen. New York: Routledge.

Jakoby, Nina R. 2012. "Grief as a Social Emotion: Theoretical Perspectives." *Death Studies* 36(8):679–711.

Jakoby, Nina R., and Riona A. Anderau. 2020. "A Story of Loss: Self-Narration of Grief and Public Feeling Rules." Pp. 84–103 in *Exploring Grief: Towards a Sociology of Sorrow*, edited by Michael Hviid Jacobsen and Anders Petersen. New York: Routledge.

Janis, Irving. 1972. *Victims of Groupthink*. Boston, MA: Houghton Mifflin.

Jerolleman, Alessandra. 2019. *Disaster Recovery through the Lens of Justice*. London: Palgrave-Pivot.

Johnson, Kevin, J. David Knottnerus, and Duane A. Gill. In Progress. *Disasters and the Power of Ritual: A Theoretical Perspective*. Stillwater, OK: Oklahoma State University.

Joiner, Thomas. 2007. *Why People Die by Suicide*. Cambridge, Mass: Harvard University Press.

Karlsson, Håkan, and Tomás Diez Acosta. 2020. *The Last Year of President Kennedy and the "Multiple Path" Policy toward Cuba*. New York: Routledge.

Kastenbaum, Robert. 2016. *Death, Society, and Human Experience*, 11th ed. New York: Routledge.

Kaufman, Gil. 2016. "Miranda Lambert Gets Emotional Performing Song She Co-Wrote with Ex Blake Shelton." *Billboard*. Retrieved September 22, 2020 (https://www.billboard.com/articles/columns/country/7454402/miranda-lambert -gets-emotional-performing-over- you).

Kearl, Michael. 1989. *Endings: A Sociology of Death and Dying*. New York: Oxford University Press.

Kelly, Cynthia C. 2007. *The Manhattan Project: The Birth of the Atomic Bomb in the Words of Its Creators, Eyewitnesses, and Historians*. New York: Black Dog and Leventhal.

Kerrigan, Michael. 2017. *The History of Death*. London: Amber Books.

Kertzer, David. 1988. *Ritual, Politics, and Power*. New Haven: Yale University Press.

Knottnerus, J. David. 1997. "The Theory of Structural Ritualization." Pp. 257–279 in *Advances in Group Processes*, edited by B. Markovsky, M. J. Lovaglia and L. Troyer. Greenwich, CT: JAI Press.

———. 1999. "Status Structures and Ritualized Relations in the Slave Plantation System." Pp. 139–147 in *Plantation Society and Race Relations*, edited by Thomas J. Durant, Jr. and J. David Knottnerus. Westport, CT: Praeger.

———. 2002. "Agency, Structure and Deritualization: A Comparative Investigation of Extreme Disruptions of Social Order." Pp. 85–106 in *Structure, Culture and History: Recent Issues in Social Theory*, edited by Sing C. Chew and J. David Knottnerus. Lanham, MD: Rowman & Littlefield.

———. 2005. "The Need for Theory and the Value of Cooperation: Disruption and Deritualization." *Sociological Spectrum* 1:5–9.

———. 2010. "Collective Events, Rituals, and Emotions." Pp. 39–61 in *Advances in Group Processes*, Volume 27, edited by S. R. Thye and E. J. Lawler. Bingley, United Kingdom: Emerald Group Publishing Limited.

———. 2014. "Religion, Ritual, and Collective Emotion." Pp. 312–325 in *Collective Emotions: Perspectives from Psychology, Philosophy, and Sociology*, edited by C. Von Scheve and M. Salmela. Oxford: Oxford University Press.

———. 2016. *Ritual as a Missing Link: Sociology, Structural Ritualization Theory, and Research*. London: Routledge.

———. Forthcoming. *Polar Expeditions: Rituals, Crews, and Hazardous Ventures*. New York: Routledge.

Knottnerus, J. David, and Phyllis E. Berry. 2002. "Spartan Society: Structural Ritualization in an Ancient Social System." *Humboldt Journal of Social Relations* 27:1–42.

Knottnerus, J. David, and David G. LoConto. 2003. "Strategic Ritualization and Ethnicity: A Typology and Analysis of Ritual Enactments in an Italian American Community." *Sociological Spectrum* 23:425–461.

Knottnerus, J. David, David L. Monk, and Edward Jones. 1999. "The Slave Plantation System from a Total Institution Perspective." Pp. 17–27 in *Plantation Society and Race Relations*, edited by T. J. Durant, Jr. and J. D. Knottnerus. Westport, CT: Praeger.

Knottnerus, J. David, Jason S. Ulsperger, Summer Cummins, and Elaina Osteen. 2006. "Exposing Enron: Media Representations of Ritualized Deviance in Corporate Culture." *Crime, Media, Culture* 2:177–195.

Knottnerus, J. David, Jean L. Van Delinder, and Jennifer Edwards. 2011. "Strategic Ritualization and Power: Nazi Germany, The Orange Order, and Native Americans" Pp. 73–105 in *Ritual as a Missing Link: Sociology, Structural Ritualization Theory and Research*, J. David Knottnerus. Boulder, CO: Paradigm Publishers.

Knottnerus, J. David, and Frédérique Van de Poel-Knottnerus. 1999. *The Social Worlds of Male and Female Children in the Nineteenth Century French Educational System: Youth, Rituals and Elites*. Lewiston, NY: Edwin Mellen Press.

Kourlis, Rebecca Love, Melinda Taylor, Andre Schepard, and Marsha Kline Pruett. 2013. "IAALS' Honoring Families Initiative: Courts and Communities Helping Families in Transition Arising from Separation or Divorce." *Family Court Review* 51(3):351–376.

Kroll-Smith, Steve. 2018. *Recovering Inequality: Hurricane Katrina, the San Francisco Earthquake of 1906, and the Aftermath of Disaster*. Austin, TX: University of Texas Press.

Kroll-Smith, Steve, Vern Baxter, and Pam Jenkins. 2015. *Left to Chance: Hurricane Katrina and the Story of Two New Orleans' Neighborhoods*. Austin, TX: University of Texas Press.

Kroll-Smith, Steve, and Stephen Couch. 1990. *The Real Disaster is Above Ground: A Mine Fire and Social Conflict*. Lexington, KY: University Press of Kentucky.

———. 1993. "Technological Hazards: Social Responses as Traumatic Stressors." Pp. 79–91 in *International Handbook of Traumatic Stress Syndromes*, edited by John P. Wilson and Beverley Raphael. New York: Plenum Press.

Krüger, Fred, Greg Bankoff, Terry Cannon, Benedikt Orlowski, and Lisa Schipper. 2015. *Cultures and Disasters: Understanding Cultural Framings in Disaster Risk Reduction*. London: Routledge.

Kübler-Ross, Elisabeth. 1969. *On Death and Dying: What the Dying Have to Teach Doctors, Nurses, Clergy, and Their Own Families*. New York: Macmillan.

LaGrossa, Alyson. 1980. "Explosion at Searcy Silo Ranks as Worst." *Arkansas Democrat*, September 20, p. 1B.

Lake, Rebecca. 2015. "Television Statistics: 23 Mind Numbing Facts to Watch." Retrieved September 18, 2020 (https://www.creditdonkey.com/television-statistics.html).

Lanier, Christina, and Kristen DeVall. 2017. "How'd You Do It? Applying Structural Ritualization Theory to Drug Courts." *Journal of Drug Issues*. Retrieved February 26, 2018 (https://journals.sagepub.com/doi/abs/10.1177/0022042616687119#).

Lazarus, Richard S., and Susan Folkman. 1984. *Stress, Appraisal, and Coping*. New York: Springer Publishing.

Leander, Anna. 2010. "Habitus and Field." Pp. 3255–3259 in *The International Studies Encyclopedia*, edited by R. Denemark. Malden, MA: Wiley-Blackwell.

Lester, James. 1976. *A Man for Arkansas*. Little Rock, AR: Rose Publishing.

Levine, Adeline. 1982. *Love Canal: Science, Politics, and People*. Lexington, MA: Lexington Books.

Lewis, Matthew. 2018. "Social Identity in Religious Rituals: An Observational Study about Rituals and Symbolic Influence on Social Identity." Thesis, Uppsala University.

Liang, Bin, J. David Knottnerus, and Michael Long. 2016. "What Do Clients Achieve in Drug/DUI Court: Examining Intended and Unintended Outcomes." *The Justice System Journal*. Retrieved March 24, 2016 (https://www.tandfonline.com/doi/full/10.1080/0098261X.2016.1151841).

Lim, David, Joanne Kenen, and Lauren Morello. 2020. "What We Know - And Still Don't Know - About Trump's Fight with Coronavirus." *Politico*. Retrieved October 4, 2020 (https://www.politico.com/news/2020/10/04/what-we-know-trump-coronavirus-426130).

Lin, Xiaohua, Jian Guan, and J. David Knottnerus. 2011. "Organizational and Leadership Practice of Micro Ethnic Entrepreneurship in Multicultural Context: A Structural Reproduction Analysis." *International Journal of Business Anthropology* 2:48–65.

Lindemann, Erich. 1944. "Symptomatology and Management of Acute Grief." *American Journal of Psychiatry* 151(6):155–160.

———. 1979. *Beyond Grief: Studies in Crisis Intervention*. New York: Jason Aronson Inc.

Lockbaum, Dave. 2018. "Fatal Accident at Arkansas Nuclear One." *Union of Concerned Scientists*. Retrieved September 3, 2020 (https://allthingsnuclear.org/dlochbaum/fatal accident-at-arkansas-one).

Lofland, John. 1985. "The Social Shaping of Emotion: The Case of Grief." *Symbolic Interaction* 8(2):171–190.

Lowe, Lindsey. 2020. "Grocery Stores to Offer Elderly Only Shopping Hours Amid Corona Concerns." Retrieved March 18, 2020 (https://www.msn.com/en-us/foodanddrink/other/grocery-stores-offer-elderly-only-shopping-hours-amid-coronavirus-concerns/ar-BB11gAER).

Lubit, Roy, and Spencer Eth. 2003. "Children, Disasters, and the 9/11 World Trade Center Attack." Pp. 63–96 in *Trauma and Disaster, Responses and Management*, edited by Robert J. Ursano and Ann E. Norwood. Washington, DC: American Psychiatric Publishing.

Luvaas, Brent. 2017. "Unbecoming: The Aftereffects of Autoethnography." *Ethnography* 20(2):245–262.

Maddox, Robert James. 2004. *Weapons for Victory: The Hiroshima Decision*. Columbia, MO: University of Missouri Press.

Mahaffey, James A. 2014. *Atomic Accidents: A History of Nuclear Meltdowns and Disasters: from the Ozark Mountains to Fukushima*. New York: Pegasus Books.

Mamun, Mohammed A., Nafisa Huq, Zinat Fatima Papia, Sadia Tasfina, and David Gosal. 2019. "Prevalence of Depression among Bangladeshi Village Women Subsequent to a Natural Disaster: A Pilot Study." *Psychiatry Research* 276:124–128.

Mansoor, Sanya. 2020. "Gender Reveal Event Sparks California Wildfire That Burns Through More Than 7,000 Acres." *Time*. Retrieved September 14, 2020 (https://time.com/5886598/gender-reveal-california-wildfire/).

Marcuse, Harold. 2010. "Holocaust Memorials: The Emergence of a Genre." *The American Historical Review* 115(1):53–89.

Matthews, David. 2020. "Black Lives Matter Protesters Beaten at Pro-Police Rally in Colorado." Retrieved August 11, 2020 (https://www.nydailynews.com/news /national/ny-black-lives matter-protesters-beaten-pro-police-rally-colorado-2020 0809 dxkhldw5vrbuljvovxaly5wgou-story.html).

Matthews, Melvin. 2011. *Duck and Cover: Civilian Defense Images in Film and Television from the Cold War to 9/11*. Jefferson, NC: McFarland and Company.

Mazewski, Joanna. 2020. "Chrissy Teigen Shares HEARTBREAKING Photos of Deadly Miscarriage, but Fans Divided Over Public Grief on Instagram." *Daily Soap Dish*. Retrieved October 4, 2020 (https://dailysoapdish.com/2020/10/chrissy -teigen-shares-heartbreaking-photos-of-deadly-miscarriage-but-fans-divided-over -public-grief-on-instagram/).

McCabe, Pamela. 2020. "Lee's Private and Charter Schools Balance First Day Excitement with New COVID-19 Policies." *Fort-Meyers News Press*. Retrieved August 15, 2020 (https://www.news-press.com/story/news/education /2020/08/14/lees-private-charter-schools-balance-first-day-joy-covid-polices /5571250002/).

McCarthy, John D., and Mayer N. Zald. 2002. "The Enduring Vitality of the Resource Mobilization Theory of Social Movements." Pp. 533–565 in *Handbook of Sociological Theory*, edited by J. H. Turner. New York: Plenum Publishers.

McClellan (John) Papers. 1965. Records Pertaining to the Department of Defense. Series 134, Box 470, Folders 3-4. Special Collections. Riley-Hickingbotham Library, Ouachita Baptist University.

McCoy, Kerry. 2019. "Gary Lay of GWL Advertising on Surviving the 1965 Titan II Missile Disaster in Searcy, AR." *Up in Your Business with Kerry McCoy*. Retrieved July 6, 2021 (https://www.youtube.com/watch?v=z_WE7fAN9NU).

McManus, Ruth, Tony Walter, and Leon Claridge. 2017. "Restoration and Loss after Disaster: Applying the Dual Process Model of Coping in Bereavement." *Death Studies* 42(7):405–414.

McMath, Sid. 2003. *Promises Kept*. Fayetteville, AR: University of Arkansas Press.

Meij, Jan-Martijn, Meghan D. Probstfield, Joseph M. Simpson, and J. David Knottnerus. 2013. "Moving Past Violence and Vulgarity: Structural Ritualization and Constructed Meaning in the Heavy Metal Subculture." Pp. 60–69 in *Music Sociology: Examining the Role of Music in Social Life*, edited by S. T. Horsfall, J. Meij, and M. D. Probstfield. Boulder, CO: Paradigm Publishers.

Méndez, Mariza. 2013. "Autoethnography as a Research Method: Advantages, Limitations, and Criticisms." *Columbian Applied Linguistics Journal* 15:279–287.

Mietkiewicz, Nathan, Jennifer Balch, Tania Schoennagel, Stefan Leyk, Lise A. St. Denis, and Bethany A. Bradley. 2020. "In the Line of Fire: Consequences of Human-Ignited Wildfires to Homes in the U.S. (1992-2015)." *Fire* 3(3):1–20.

Mills, C. Wright. 1940. "Situated Actions and Vocabularies of Motive." *American Sociological Review* 5(6):904–913.

Minton, Carol, and J. David Knottnerus. 2008. "Ritualized Duties: The Social Construction of Gender Inequality in Malawi." *International Review of Modern Sociology* 34:181–210.

Mitchell, J. Sage, and Ilhem Allagui. 2019. "The Gulf Information War: Car Decals, Civic Rituals, and Changing Conceptions of Nationalism." *International Journal of Communication* 12:1368–1388.

Mitford, Jessica. 1963. *The American Way of Death*. Greenwich, CT: Fawcett.

Mitra, Aditi, and J. David Knottnerus. 2004. "Royal Women in Ancient India: The Ritualization of Inequality in a Patriarchal Social Order." *International Journal of Contemporary Sociology* 41:215–231.

_____. 2008. "Sacrificing Women: A Study of Ritualized Practices among Women Volunteers in India." *Voluntas: International Journal of Voluntary and Nonprofit Organizations* 19:242–267.

Monk, Ray. 2014. *Robert Oppenheimer: A Life inside the Center*. New York: Anchor Books.

Morris, Yvonne. 2020. Correspondence with Director, Titan Missile Museum, March 4.

Morse, Tal. 2017. *The Mourning News: Reporting Violent Death in the Global Age*. New York: Peter Lang.

Neimeyer, Robert. 2011. *Grief and Bereavement in Contemporary Society: Bridging Research and Practice*. New York: Routledge.

Neimeyer, Robert, and Nancy Hogan. 2001. "Quantitative or Qualitative? Measurement Issues in the Study of Grief." Pp. 89–118 in *Handbook of Bereavement Research: Consequences, Coping, and Care*, edited by M. Stroebe, R. O. Hansson, W. Stroebe, and H. Schut. Washington, DC: American Psychological Association.

Norris, Fran H., Matthew J. Friedman, and Patricia J. Watson. 2002. "60,000 Disaster Victims Speak: Part II. Summary and Implications of the Disaster Mental Health Research." *Psychiatry* 65(3):240–260.

Ojo, Sanya, and Sonny Nwankwo. 2020. "God in the Marketplace: Pentecostalism and Marketing Ritualization among Black Africans in the U.K." *Journal of Enterprising Communities: People and Places in the Global Economy*. Retrieved August 29, 2020 (https://www.emerald.com/insight/content/doi/10.1108/JEC-12-2019-0126/full/html).

Ortlipp, Michelle. 2008. "Keeping and Using Reflective Journals in the Qualitative Research Process." *The Qualitative Report* 13(4):695–705.

Orum, Anthony M., Joe R. Feagin, and Gideon Sjoberg. 1991. "The Case Study Approach in Social Research." Pp. 1–26 in *A Case for the Case Study*, edited by J. R. Feagin, A. M. Orum, and G. Sjoberg. New York: Teachers College Press.

Orval Eugene Faubus Papers. 1965. Records Pertaining to Non-Government and Inter-Government Organizations. Series 12, Box 444, Folder 2. Special Collections. Fayetteville, AR: University of Arkansas Libraries.

_____. 1966. Records Pertaining to Non-Government and Inter-Government Organizations. Series 12, Box 444, Folder 3. Special Collections. Fayetteville, AR: University of Arkansas Libraries.

Pardee, Jessica. 2014. *Surviving Katrina: The Experiences of Low Income African American Women*. First Forum Press. Boulder, CO.

Parkes, Collin M. [1972] 2001. *Bereavement: Studies of Grief in Adult Life*. 3rd ed. London: Routledge.

Penson, Chuck. 2019. *The Titan II Handbook: A Civilian's Guide to the Most Powerful ICBM America Ever Built.* 3rd ed. Tucson, AZ: Penson.

———. 2020. "Another Diagram," Email. September 28.

Perrow, Charles. 1984. *Normal Accidents: Living with High-Risk Technologies.* New York: Basic Books.

Peterson, Eva. 2020. "The Fall of the Titans, 1588-1590." The Statens Museum for Kunst, National Gallery of Denmark. Retrieved February 7, 2020 (https://www.smk.dk/en/highlight/the-fall-of-the-titans-1588-1590/).

Pickering, David. 1995. *Dictionary of Superstitions.* London: Cassell.

Picou, Steven, Marshall, Brent, and Duane A. Gill. 2004. "Disaster, Litigation, and the Corrosive Community." *Social Forces* 82:1497–1526.

Picou, Steven, and Cecelia Martin. 2007. "Long-term Community Impacts of the Exxon Valdez Oil Spill: Patterns of Social Disruption and Psychological Stress Seventeen Years after the Disaster." Retrieved September 12, 2020 (htps://www.researchgate.net/publicaiton/228893156_Long-Term_Community_Impacts_of_the_Exxon_Valdez_Oil_Spil_Patterns_of_Social_Disruption_and_Psychological_Stress_Seventeen_Years_after_the_Disaster.

Post, Paul, Ronald Grimes, Albertina Nugteren, Per Pettersson, and Hessel Zondag. 2003. *Disaster Ritual: Explorations of an Emerging Ritual Repertoire.* Leuvun, Belgium: Peeters Publishers.

Pryor, David. 2003. "Foreword" Pp. xvii–xxii in *Promises Kept,* edited by Sid McMath. Fayetteville, AR: University of Arkansas Press.

Quarantelli, Enrico L. 1954. "The Nature and Conditions of Panic." *American Journal of Sociology* 60:267–275.

———. 1960. "Images of Withdrawal Behavior in Disasters: Some Basic Misconceptions." *Social Problems* 8:68–79.

Raab, Diane. 2013. "Transpersonal Approaches to Autoethnographic Research and Writing." *The Qualitative Report* 18(42):1–19.

Rabin, Roni Caryn. 2020. "Coronavirus Threatens Americans with Underlying Conditions." *New York Times.* Retrieved March 18, 2020 (https://www.nytimes.com/2020/03/12/health/coronavirus-midlife-conditions.html).

Rambo, Carol, and John C. Pruitt. 2019. "At Play in the Fields of Qualitative Research and Autoethnography." *International Review of Qualitative Research* 12(3):219–242.

Rando, Therese. 1984. *Grief, Dying, and Death: Clinical Interventions for Caregivers.* Champaign, IL: Research Press.

Raphelson, Samantha. 2018. "She Will Not Be Missed: Children Deliver Harsh Send-off in Mother's Death Notice." NPR. Retrieved October 2, 2020 (https://www.npr.org/2018/06/07/617948070/she-will-not-be-missed-children-deliver-harsh-send-off-in-mother-s-obituary).

Rappaport, Roy A. 1999. *Ritual and Religion in the Making of Humanity.* Cambridge, MA: Cambridge University Press.

Rawnsley, Adam. 2021. "Tennessee Health Workers Accused of Turning Away Elderly Vaccine Recipient Hopefuls to Give Doses to Friends." *The Daily Beast.* Retrieved January 2, 2021 (https://www.thedailybeast.com/tennessee-health

-workers-accused-of-turning-away-elderly-vaccine-recipient-hopefuls-to-give
-doses-to-friends).

Raymond, Adam K. 2020. "The Johns Hopkins Coronavirus Dashboard Gets 1.2
Billion Interactions a Day." *New York (Intelligencer)*. Retrieved April 16, 2020
(https://nymag.com/intelligencer/2020/04/jhus-coronavirus-site-gets-1-2-billion
-interactions-a-day.html).

Ricciardelli, Rose, and Pegah Memarpour. 2016. "I Was Trying to Make My Stay
There More Positive: Rituals and Routines in Canadian Prisons." *Criminal Justice
Studies* 29(3):179–198.

Ritchie, Liesel A. 2012. "Individual Stress, Collective Trauma, and Social Capital
in the Wake of the Exxon Valdez Oil Spill. *Sociological Inquiry* 82(2):187–211.

Ritchie, Liesel A., and Duane A. Gill. 2007. "Social Capital Theory as an
Integrating Framework for Technological Disaster Research." *Sociological Inquiry*
82(2):187–211.

Ritchie, Liesel A., Duane A. Gill, and Courtney N. Farnham. 2013. "Recreancy
Revisited: Beliefs about Institutional Failure Following the Exxon Valdez Oil
Spill." *Society and Natural Resources* 26:655–671.

Ritzer, George. 2011. *The McDonaldization of Society*. 6th ed. Los Angeles, CA: Pine
Forge.

Roberts, Jeannie. 2015. "Slab, Rusty Pipes Mark the Spot: Missile Silo Fire Killed
53." Arkansas Democrat-Gazette, August 8, p. 1A.

Roberts, Karlene, and Robert Bea. 2001. "Must Accidents Happen? Lessons
from High-Reliability Organizations." *Academy of Management Perspectives*
15(3):70–78.

Robles, Edward G. 1962. "Combustion and Degradation Products of N2O4 and
UDMH-Hydrazine Mixtures." Paper presented at the *USAF Sanitary and
Industrial Hygiene Engineering Symposium*. Vandenberg Air Force Base, CA,
October 9–12.

Rodin, Mari, Michael Downs, John Petterson, and John Russell. 1992. "Community
Impacts Resulting from the Exxon Valdez Oil Spill." *Industrial Crisis Quarterly*
6:219–234.

Rose, Herbert. 2015. *A Handbook of Greek Mythology*. London: Routledge.

Rosenblatt, Paul C. 2005. "Grieving Families and the 9/11 Disaster." Pp. 85–104 in
Death, Bereavement, and Mourning, edited by Sam Heilman. New Brunswick, NJ:
Transaction Publishers.

Rubin, Simon. 1999. "The Two Track Model of Bereavement." *Death Studies*
23(8):681–714.

Running, Steven W. 2006. "Is Global Warming Causing More, Larger Wildfires?"
Science Express. Retrieved September 4, 2020 (https://science.sciencemag.org/
content/sci/early/2006/07/06/science.1130370.full.pdf).

Russell, Greg. 1987. "Missile Silo Construction Was A Boon to Economy." *Log
Cabin Democrat*. August 23, p. 12A.

Sanchez, Alfred. 2013. "Crane Collapse - Stator Drop." DRP Counterpart Meeting.
Retrieved September 3, 2020 (https://adamswebsearch2.nrc.gov/webSearch2/main
.jsp?AccessionNumber=ML14008A375).

Sarabia, Daniel, and J. David Knottnerus. 2009. "Ecological Stress and Deritualization in East Asia: Ritual Practices during Dark Age Phases." *International Journal of Sociology and Anthropology* 1(1):12–25.

Sax, Leonard. 2013. "A Critique of DSM-5: Is It a License to Diagnose Anyone with Anything?" *Psychology Today.* Retrieved October 1, 2020 (https://www.psychologytoday.com/us/blog/sax-sex/201306/critique-dsm-5).

Schlosser, Eric. 2013. *Command and Control: Nuclear Weapons, the Damascus Accident, and the Illusion of Safety.* New York: Penguin.

Schneider-Hector, Dietmar. 1993. *White Sands: The History of a National Monument.* Albuquerque, NM: University of New Mexico Press.

Schreiner, Bruce. 2021. "Kentucky Remembers COVID-19 Deaths with Statehouse Ceremony." *Commonwealth Journal.* Retrieved January 23, 2021 (https://www.somerset-kentucky.com/covid-19/kentucky-remembers-covid-19-deaths-with-statehouse-ceremony/article_1fd0322e-5dba-11eb-bdb0-2f6fe3094dd7.html).

Scott, Stuart. 2017. "A Voice from the Other Side?" *Skepticism* 78:83–89.

Searcy Daily Citizen. 1965a. "Rescue Teams Labor Through Night in Vain Search for Living." August 10, p. 1.

———. 1965b. "Red Cross Works Through Night at Missile Site." August 10, p. 1.

———. 1965c. "Here Is Complete List of the Dead." August 10, p. 1.

Sell, Jane, J. David Knottnerus, and Christina Adcock-Azbill. 2013. "Disruptions in Task Groups." *Social Science Quarterly* 94:715–731.

Sell, Jane, J. David Knottnerus, Christopher Ellison, and Heather Mundt. 2000. "Reproducing Social Structure in Task Groups: The Role of Structural Ritualization." *Social Forces* 79:453–475.

Sen, Basudhara, and J. David Knottnerus. 2016. "Ritualized Ethnic Identity: Asian Indian Immigrants in the Southern Plains. *Sociological Spectrum* 36:37–56.

Sheets, Megan, and Emily Crane. 2020. "U.S. Has Deadliest Day of Pandemic So Far." *Daily Mail.* Retrieved December 20, 2020 (https://www.dailymail.co.uk/news/article-9061919/US-breaks-record-coronavirus-deaths-3-400.html).

Sherwin, Martin J. 2003. *A World Destroyed: Hiroshima and Its Legacies.* Stanford, CA: Stanford University Press.

———. 2020. *Gambling with Armageddon: Nuclear Roulette from Hiroshima to the Cuban Missile Crisis, 1945-1962.* New York: Alfred A. Knopf.

Shilts, Randy. 1988. *And the Band Played On: Politics, People, and the AIDS Epidemic.* New York: Penguin Books.

Showalter, Pamela S., and Mary Meyers. 1994. "Natural Disasters in the United States as Release Agents of Oil, Chemical, or Radiological Materials between 1980-1989: Analysis and Recommendations." *Risk Analysis* 14(2):169–182.

Shrivastava, Paul. 1987. *Bhopal: Anatomy of a Crisis.* New York: Doubleday.

Silverman, Phyllis, Steven Nickman, and J. William Worden. 1995. "Detachment Revisited: The Child's Reconstruction of a Dead Parent." Pp. 260–270 in *The Path Ahead*, edited by Lynne Ann DeSpelder and Albert Lee Strickland. Mountain View, CA: Mayfield Publishing Company.

Simmel, Georg. 1906. "The Sociology of Secret Societies." *American Journal of Sociology* 11:441–498.

Simon, Naomi, M. Katherine Shear, Charles Reynolds, Stephen Cozza, Christine Mauro, Sidney Zisook, Natalia Skritskaya, Donald Robinaugh, Matteo Malgaroli, Julia Spandorfer, and Barry Lebowitz. 2020. "Commentary on Evidence in Support of a Grief-related Condition as a DSM Diagnosis." *Depression and Anxiety* 37(1):9–16.

Simpson, Joseph, J. David Knottnerus, and Michael J. Stern. 2018. "Virtual Rituals: Community, Emotion, and Ritual in Massive Multiplayer Online Role-playing Games - A Quantitative Test and Extension of Structural Ritualization Theory." *Socius* 4(4). Retrieved January 3, 2021 (https://journals.sagepub.com/doi/full/10 .1177/2378023118779839).

Smith Family Cares. 2020. "Raymond Wright." Retrieved November 1, 2020 (https:// www.smithfamilycares.com/obituary/Raymond-Wright).

Smith, Laura. 2017. "In 1974, A Stripper Known as the 'Tidal Basin Bombshell' Took Down the Most Powerful Man in Washington." *Timeline*. Retrieved March 28, 2020 (https://timeline.com/wilbur-mills-tidal-basin-3c29a8b47ad1).

Smith, Suzanne. 2005. "Laid Out in Big Mamma's Kitchen: African Americans and the Personalized Theme Funeral." Pp. 159–180 in *American Behavioral History: An Introduction*, edited by Peter Stearns. New York: New York University Press.

Soeffner, Hans-Georg. [1996] 2018. *The Order of Ritual: The Interpretation of Everyday Life*. New York: Routledge.

Spradley, James P. 1979. *The Ethnographic Interview*. New York: Holt, Rinehart, and Winston.

Stearns, Peter N. 2020. "Grief in Modern History: An Ongoing Evolution." Pp. 21–36 in *Exploring Grief: Towards a Sociology of Sorrow,* edited by Michael Hviid Jacobsen and Anders Petersen. New York: Routledge.

Stemen, Sara E. 2020. "They're in My Heart, Mind, and Cells: What Continuing Bonds Reveal about Social Networks." *The Gerontologist*. Retrieved January 20, 2020 (https://academic.oup.com/gerontologist/advance-article-abstract/doi/10 .1093/geront/gnz188/5697461?redirectedFrom=fulltext).

Stillion, Judith, and Thomas Attig, eds. 2015. *Death, Dying, and Bereavement: Contemporary Perspectives, Institutions, and Practices*. New York, Springer.

Strang, Charles F. 1967. *Titan II Launch Facility Accident Briefing, Little Rock Air Force Base*. Norton AFB, CA: Directorate of Aerospace Safety.

Straub, Adam M. 2021. "Natural Disaster's Don't Kill People, Governments Kill People." Hurricane Maria, Puerto Rico-recreancy, and 'Risk Society'." *Natural Hazards* 105:1603–1621.

Stroebe, Margaret S., and Henk Schut. 1999. "The Dual Process Model of Coping with Bereavement: Rationale and Description." *Death Studies* 23(3):197–224.

Stumpf, David K. 2000. *Titan II: A History of a Cold War Missile Program*. Fayetteville, AR: University of Arkansas Press.

Tampone, Kevin. 2020. "Coronavirus in New York: Total Deaths Pass 15,000, but 'We're in a Better Place,' Cuomo Says." Retrieved April 22, 2020 (https://www .syracuse.com/coronavirus/2020/04/coronavirus-in-ny-total-deaths-pass-15000 -but-new-deaths-below-500-again.html).

Tarde, Gabriel. 2013. *The Laws of Imitation*. Redditch: Read Books.

Tessler, Minda, and Katherine Nelson. 1994. "Making Memories: The Influence of Joint Encoding on Later Recall by Young Children." *Consciousness and Cognition* 3(3–4):307–326.

The Military Standard. 2021. "Titan II at LRAFB." *The Military Standard - Titan II*. Retrieved January 3, 2021 (http://themilitarystandard.com/missile/titan2/lr_afb.php).

Thornburg, P. Alex, J. David Knottnerus, and Gary R. Webb. 2007. "Disaster and Deritualization: A Re-interpretation of Findings from Early Disaster Research." *The Social Science Journal* 44:161–166.

———. 2008. "Ritual and Disruption: Insights from Early Disaster Research." *International Journal of Sociological Research* 1:91–109.

Tierney, Kathleen. 2019. *Disasters: A Sociological Approach*. Medford, MA: Polity.

Tiller, D. Elaine. 2002. "Rituals and Stories: Creative Approaches to Loss in Later Life." Pp. 337–350 in *Living with Grief: Loss in Later Life*, edited by Kenneth Doka. Washington, DC: Hospice Foundation of America.

Tsakanikos, Elias. 2004. "Latent Inhibition, Visual Pop-out and Schizotypy: Is Disruption of Latent Inhibition Due to Enhanced Stimulus Salience?" *Personality and Individual Differences* 37(7):1347–1358.

Turnnidge, Sarah. 2021. "China Denies Entry to WHO Experts Investigating COVID Origin." Huffington Post. Retrieved January 7, 2021 (https://www.huffingtonpost.co.uk/entry/china-denies-entry-who-experts-investigating-covid-origin).

Tyson-Rawson, Kirsten. 1996. "Adolescent Responses to the Death of a Parent." Pp. 155–172 in *Handbook of Adolescent Death and Bereavement*, edited by Charles Corr and David Balk. New York: Springer.

Ulsperger, Jason S. and J. David Knottnerus. 2007. "Long-term Care Workers and Bureaucracy: The Occupational Ritualization of Maltreatment in Nursing Homes and Recommended Policies." *Journal of Applied Social Science* 1:52–70.

———. 2008. "The Social Dynamics of Elder Care: Rituals of Bureaucracy and Physical Neglect in Nursing Homes." *Sociological Spectrum* 28:357–388.

———. 2009a. "Illusions of Affection: Bureaucracy and Emotional Neglect in Nursing Homes." *Humanity and Society* 33:238–259.

———. 2009b. "Institutionalized Elder Abuse: The Bureaucratic Ritualization and Transformation of Physical Neglect in Nursing Homes." Pp. 134–155 in *Bureaucratic Culture and Escalating World Problems*, edited by J. D. Knottnerus and B. Phillips. Boulder, CO: Paradigm Publishers.

———. 2010. "Enron: Organizational Rituals as Deviance." Pp. 291–294 in *Readings in Deviant Behavior*, 6th ed., edited by Alex Thio, Thomas C. Calhoun, and Addrain Conyers. New York: Allyn and Bacon.

———. 2016. *Elder Care Catastrophe: Rituals of Abuse in Nursing Homes--and What You Can Do About It*. London: Routledge.

———. 2020. "Care Giving Without the Care: The Deviant Treatment of Residents in Nursing Homes." In *Deviance Today*, 2nd ed., edited by A. Conyers and T. C. Calhoun, New York: Routledge.

Ulsperger, Jason S., J. David Knottnerus, and Kristen Ulsperger. 2014. "Bureaucratic Rituals in Nursing Homes: The "CARE Model" and Culture Change." *The International Journal of Aging and Society* 3(3):21–33.

_____. 2017. "The Importance of Rituals in Understanding Mass Homicide: A Structural Ritualization Analysis of the Ronald Gene Simmons Murders." Pp. 199–230 in *Rituals: Past, Present, and Future Perspectives*, edited by E. Bailey. New York: Nova Science Publishers.

Ulsperger, Jason S., Jericho McElroy, Haley Robertson, and Kristen Ulsperger. 2015. "Senior Companion Program Volunteers: Exploring Experiences, Transformative Rituals, and Recruitment/Retention Issues." *The Qualitative Report* 20(9):1458–1475.

Ulsperger, Jason S., and Kristen Ulsperger. 2017. "Community, Regional Identity, and Civic Agriculture: A Structural Ritualization Analysis of Rural Online Farmers' Market Sellers." *Journal of Rural Social Sciences* 32(2):98–124.

Ulsperger, Jason S., Kristen Ulsperger, and Jennifer Partin. 2015. "Seeing Stigma: An Autoethnographic Exploration of Parent-Child Reactions to Sight Disorder and Recommended Applications for Self-Adjustment." Presented at the annual meeting of the Mid-South Sociological Association, October 22, Mobile, AL.

USAF. 1965. *Searcy Accident Report Delivered to Congress - Air Force Research Agency*. Montgomery, AL: Maxwell Air Force Base.

Valentish, Jenny. 2020. "A Fertile Time for Death Disruptors: People are Finding Meaning in these New Rituals." *The Guardian*. Retrieved September 26, 2020 (https://www.theguardian.com/lifeandstyle/2020/sep/18/a-fertile-time-for-death-disruptors-people-are-finding-meaning-in-these-new-rituals).

Van de Poel-Knottnerus, Frédérique. 2005. "Waris Dirie and the Ritualization of FGM: When Rites Can Be Wrong." *Quarterly Journal of Ideology* 28(3–4):1–21.

Van de Poel-Knottnerus, Frédérique, and J. David Knottnerus. 2002. *Literary Narratives on the Nineteenth and Early Twentieth-Century French Elite Educational System*. Lewiston, NY: Edwin Mellen Press.

Van den Bogaard, Levi. 2017. "Leaving Quietly? A Quantitative Study of Rituals and How They Affect Life Satisfaction." *Working, Aging, and Retirement* 3(1):55–65.

Van Gennep, Arnold [1909] 1960. *The Rites of Passage*. Chicago: University of Chicago Press.

Varner, Monica K. and J. David Knottnerus. 2010. *American Golf and the Development of Civility: Rituals of Etiquette in the World of Golf*. Koln, Germany: LAP Lambert Academic Publishing.

Vaughan, Diane. 1992. "Regulating Risk: Implications of the Challenger Accident." Pp. 235–253 in *Organizations, Uncertainties, and Risk*, edited by J. F. Short, Jr. and L. Clarke. Boulder, CO: Westview Press.

_____. 2016. *The Challenger Launch Decision: Risky Technology, Culture, and Deviance at NASA*. Chicago, IL: University of Chicago Press.

Vollmer, Hendrik. 2013. *The Sociology of Disruption, Disaster, and Social Change*. New York: Cambridge University Press.

Wakefield, Jerome, and Mark Schmitz. 2013. "When Does Depression Become a Disorder? Using Recurrence Rates to Evaluate the Validity of Proposed Changes in Major Depression Diagnostic Thresholds." *World Psychiatry* 12:440–452.

Walter, Tony. 2008. "The New Public Mourning." Pp. 241–262 in *Handbook of Bereavement, Research, and Practice: Advances in Theory and Intervention*, edited by Margaret S. Stroebe and Emmy van den Blink. Washington, DC: American Psychological Association.

Ward, Bob. 2005. *Dr. Space: The Life of Wernher von Braun*. Annapolis, MD: Naval Institute Press.

Warner, W. Lloyd. 1959. *The Living and the Dead: A Study of the Symbolic Life of Americans* (Yankee City Series). New Haven: Yale University Press.

———. 1962. *American Life: Dream and Reality*. Revised ed. Chicago: University of Chicago Press.

Webb, Gary R. 2007. "The Sociology of Disaster." Pp. 278–285 in *21st Century Sociology: Reference Handbook*, edited by C. Brant and D. Peck. Thousand Oaks, CA: Sage.

———. 2018. "The Cultural Turn in Disaster Research: Understanding Resilience and Vulnerability through the Lens of Culture." Pp. 109–121 in *Handbook of Disaster Research*, edited by H. Rodriquez, W. Donner, and J. E. Trainor. Cham, Switzerland: Springer International Publishing.

Weber, Max. 1946. *From Max Weber: Essays in Sociology*. Translated by Hans Gerth and C. Wright Mills. New York: Oxford University Press.

Weisaeth, Lars. 1994. "Psychological and Psychiatric Aspects of Technological Disasters." Pp. 72–102 in *Individual and Community Responses to Trauma and Disaster: The Structure of Human Chaos*, edited by Robert Ursano, Brian McCaughey, and Carol Fullerton. New York: Cambridge University Press.

Weitez, Karen. 1999. *Cold War Infrastructure for Strategic Air Command: The Bomber Mission*. Washington, DC: U.S. Army Corps of Engineers.

Welky, Ali, and Mike Keckhaver. 2013. *Encyclopedia of Arkansas Music*. Butler Center Books: Little Rock, AR.

Wells, H. G. 1913. *The World Set Free: A Story of Mankind*. New York: E.P. Dutton and Company.

Wenger, Dennis, and Jack Weller. 1973. *Disaster Subculture: The Cultural Residue of Community Disasters*. Columbus, OH: Ohio State University Disaster Research Center.

Widmayer, Christine. 2018. "The Feminist Strikes Back: Performative Mourning in the Twitter Response to Carrie Fisher's Death." *New Directions in Folk Lore* 15(1/2):50–76.

Wilde, Oscar. 2016. *Decay of Lying*. Richmond, VA: Alma Classics.

Wisner, Ben. 2019. "Disaster Studies at 50: Time to Wear Bifocals." Pp. 47–68 in *Disaster Research and the Second Environmental Crisis: Assessing the Challenges Ahead*, edited by J. Kendra, Scott Knowles, and Tricia Wacthendorf. Cham, Switzerland: Springer Publishing International.

Womack, John. 1997. *Titan Tales: Diary of a Titan II Missile Crew Commander*. Franklin, NC: Soliloquy.

Worden, J. William. [1991] 2018. *Grief Counseling and Grief Therapy*. 5th ed. New York: Springer.

Wu, Yanhong, and J. David Knottnerus. 2005. "Ritualized Daily Practices: A Study of Chinese 'Educated Youth.'" *Shehui* 6:167–185.

———. 2007. "The Origins of Ritualized Daily Practices: From Lei Feng's Diary to Educated Youth's Diaries." *Shehui* 1:98–119.

———. 2008. "Ritualized Daily Practices: A Study of Chinese 'Educated Youth.'" Pp. 340–348 in *Research Methods in Social Science*, by Qiu Liping. Chongqing: Chongqing University Press.

Zachary, G. Pascal. 1997. *Endless Frontier: Vannevar Bush, Engineer of the American Century*. New York: The Free Press.

Zap, Claudine. 2020. "Two More Titan II Nuclear Missile Silos Blast onto the Market in Arizona." Realtor.com. Retrieved January 5, 2021 (https://www.realtor.com/news/unique-homes/two-more-titan-missile-silos-for-sale-in-arizona/).

Zaretsky, Robert. 2020. "Are Monument Protests Missing These Memorials' Contribution to Our Collective Memory?" *The Washington Post*. Retrieved October 2, 2020 (https://www.washingtonpost.com/opinions/2020/06/27/are-monument-protests-missing-these-memorials-contribution-our-collective-memory/).

Zaumseil, Manfred, and Silke Schwarz. 2013. "Understandings of Coping: A Critical Review of Coping Theories for Disaster Contexts." Pp. 45–83 in *Cultural Psychology of Coping with Disasters*, edited by Manfred Zaumseil, Silke Schwarz, Mechthild von Vacano, Gavin Brent Sullivan, and Johana Prawitasari-Hadiyono. New York: Springer.

Index

Note: Italic page numbers refer to figures and tables.

About the Author

As an H. L. Minton scholar, **Jason S. Ulsperger** obtained his BS from the University of Central Arkansas in 1997. He earned his MA in sociology from Arkansas State University in 1999. That same year, he received the Student Award of Excellence from the Southwest Society on Aging. He completed his PhD in sociology at Oklahoma State University in 2003, where he won the O. D. Duncan Award while studying social psychology and organizational deviance. He is currently professor of sociology at Arkansas Tech University, where he teaches psychosocial aspects of death and dying and social gerontology. He holds faculty excellence awards in both teaching and scholarship. In addition to coauthoring *Elder Care Catastrophe* (2016), he is the primary author of over 60 journal articles, book chapters, and encyclopedia entries. He recently finished a term as president of the Mid-South Sociological Association and is currently a regional representative for Alpha Kappa Delta, the international sociology honor society. Within the last year, his university recognized him with the Mentoring Award for Distinguished Advising, and an honor society he sponsors won the Alpha Phi Sigma national award for service.

www.ingramcontent.com/pod-product-compliance
Lightning Source LLC
Chambersburg PA
CBHW062026270326
41929CB00014B/2327